THE UNDERFOOT

into the sun

To Mom, who changed my life by bringing home a Dungeon Master's Guide, encouraged every creative outlet I ever wiggled into (some of which I'm still inside), and taught me that going a little bit crazy was the only sane way to live.

–Ben Fisher

For my mother, Sandra E. Whitten, the best English and creative writing teacher I ever had; and for all the educators in my family and in this great wide world who have dedicated their lives to helping others learn.

–Emily S. Whitten

For Mom: Thank you for embracing your weirdo kid's desire to go to anime conventions, video game tournaments, and comic shops. Without your unwavering love and support, these books would never have happened.

–Michelle Nguyen

THE UNDERFOOT

into the sun

BOOK 2

Written by Ben Fisher and Emily S. Whitten
Illustrated by Michelle Nguyen
Color Assistance by Adrian Ricker
Lettered by Thom Zahler
World Map by Eric Orchard
H.A.P. Burrow Map by Thom Zahler

ONI PRESS

AN ONI PRESS PUBLICATION

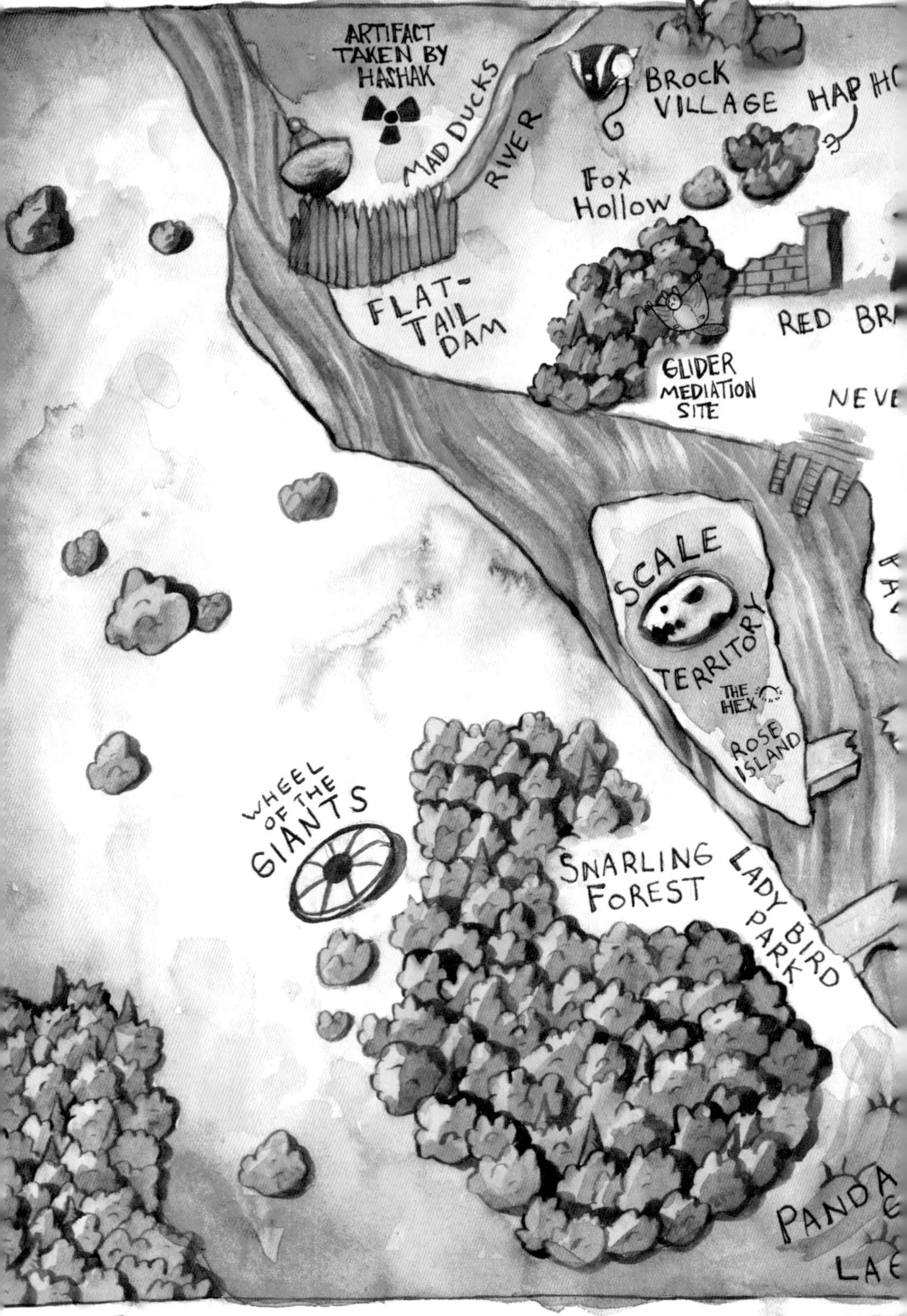
ARTIFACT TAKEN BY HASHAK
MAD DUCKS
RIVER
BROCK VILLAGE
FOX HOLLOW
FLAT-TAIL DAM
GLIDER MEDIATION SITE
SCALE TERRITORY
THE HEX
ROSE ISLAND
WHEEL OF THE GIANTS
SNARLING FOREST
LADY BIRD PARK

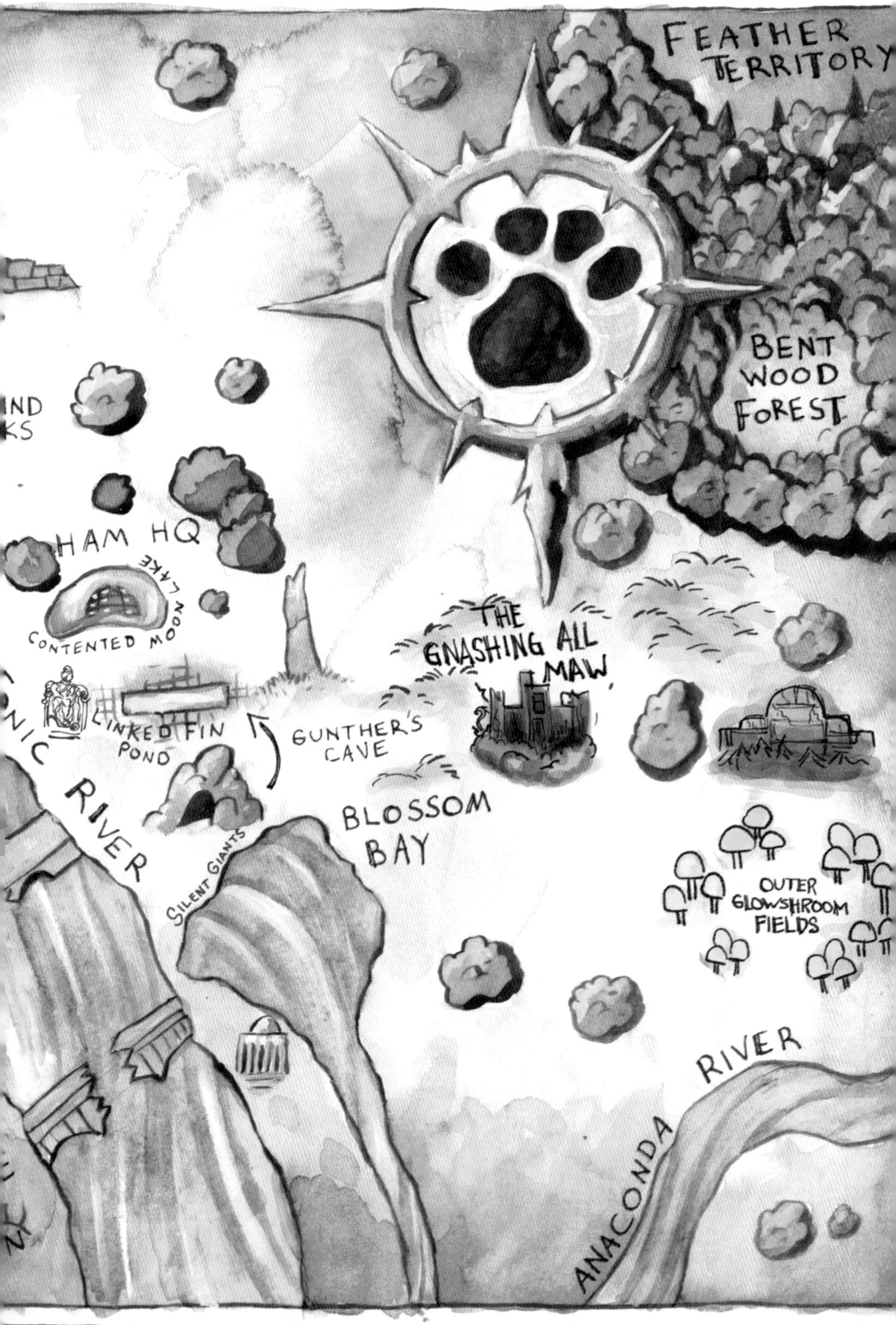
FEATHER TERRITORY
BENT WOOD FOREST
HAM HQ
CONTENTED MOON LAKE
LINKED FIN POND
GUNTHER'S CAVE
THE GNASHING ALL MAW
BLOSSOM BAY
SILENT GIANTS
RIVER
OUTER GLOWSHROOM FIELDS
ANACONDA RIVER

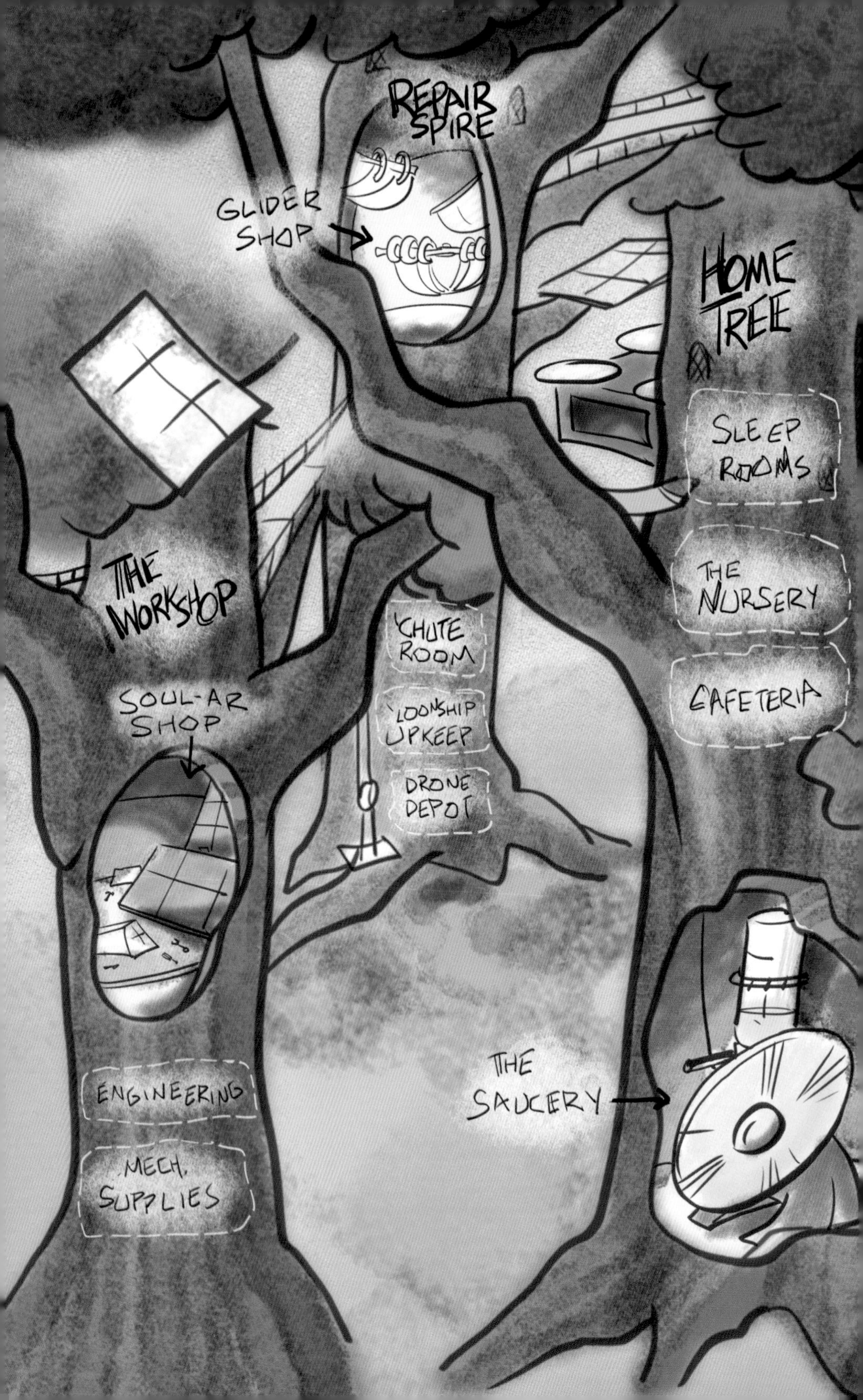

REPAIR SPIRE
GLIDER SHOP
HOME TREE
SLEEP ROOMS
THE NURSERY
CAFETERIA
THE WORKSHOP
CHUTE ROOM
LOONSHIP UPKEEP
DRONE DEPOT
SOUL-AR SHOP
ENGINEERING
MECH. SUPPLIES
THE SAUCERY

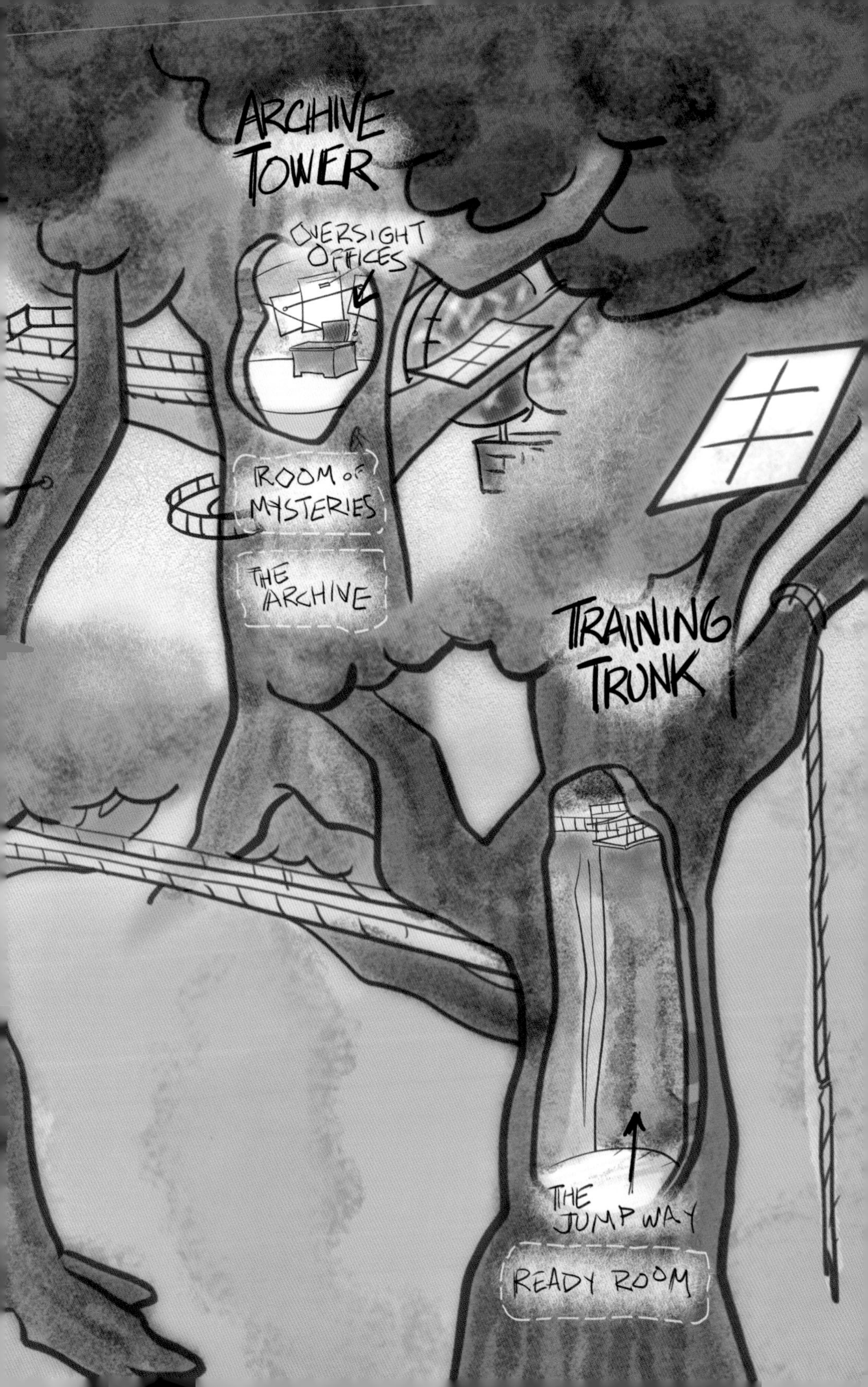
ARCHIVE TOWER
OVERSIGHT OFFICES
ROOM OF MYSTERIES
THE ARCHIVE
TRAINING TRUNK
THE JUMP WAY
READY ROOM

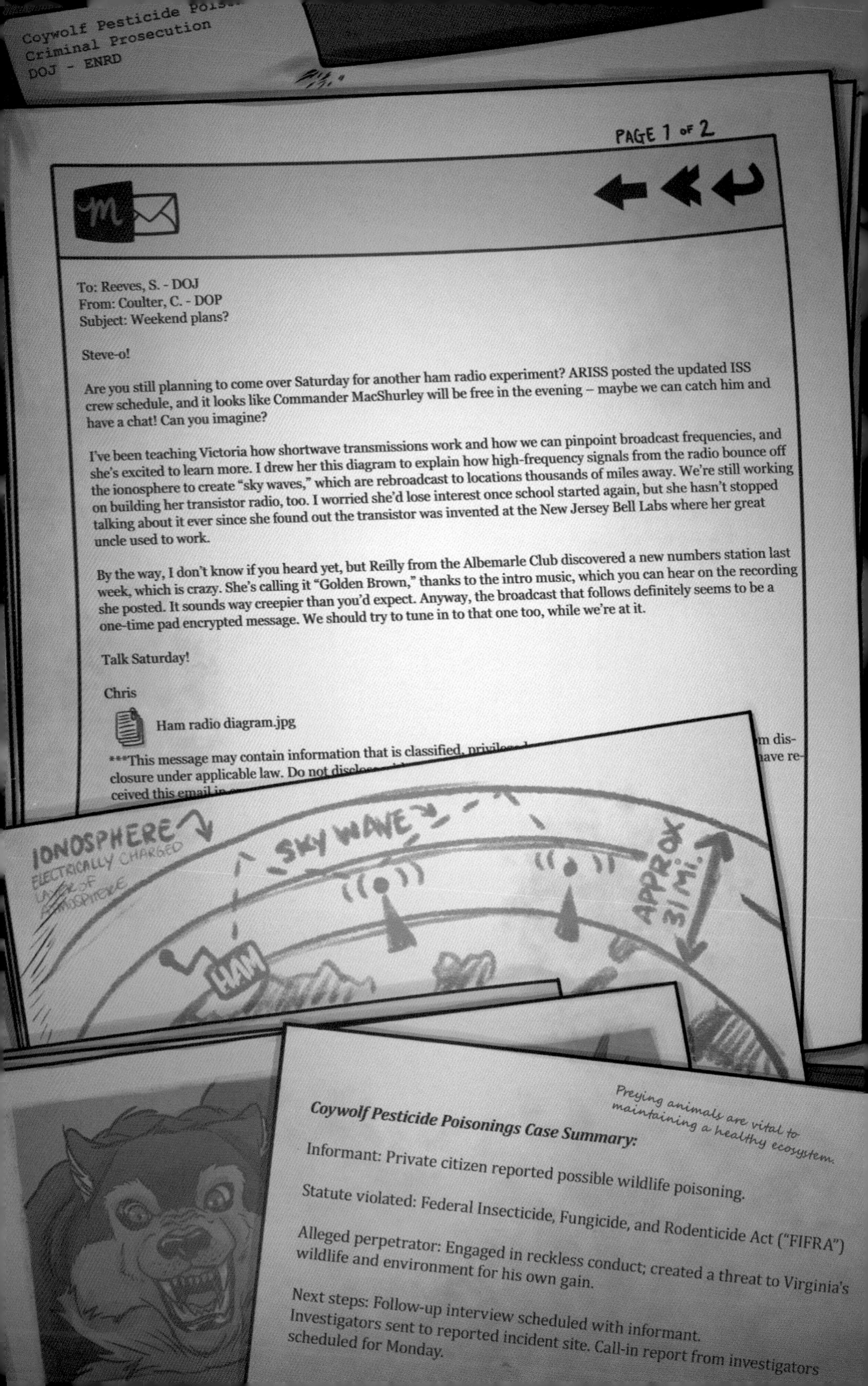
Coywolf Pesticide Poiso
Criminal Prosecution
DOJ - ENRD
PAGE 1 OF 2
To: Reeves, S. - DOJ
From: Coulter, C. - DOP
Subject: Weekend plans?
Steve-o!
Are you still planning to come over Saturday for another ham radio experiment? ARISS posted the updated ISS crew schedule, and it looks like Commander MacShurley will be free in the evening – maybe we can catch him and have a chat! Can you imagine?
I've been teaching Victoria how shortwave transmissions work and how we can pinpoint broadcast frequencies, and she's excited to learn more. I drew her this diagram to explain how high-frequency signals from the radio bounce off the ionosphere to create "sky waves," which are rebroadcast to locations thousands of miles away. We're still working on building her transistor radio, too. I worried she'd lose interest once school started again, but she hasn't stopped talking about it ever since she found out the transistor was invented at the New Jersey Bell Labs where her great uncle used to work.
By the way, I don't know if you heard yet, but Reilly from the Albemarle Club discovered a new numbers station last week, which is crazy. She's calling it "Golden Brown," thanks to the intro music, which you can hear on the recording she posted. It sounds way creepier than you'd expect. Anyway, the broadcast that follows definitely seems to be a one-time pad encrypted message. We should try to tune in to that one too, while we're at it.
Talk Saturday!
Chris
Ham radio diagram.jpg
***This message may contain information that is classified, privileg
closure under applicable law. Do not disclo
IONOSPHERE
ELECTRICALLY CHARGED
SKY WAVE
APPROX 31 MI.
HAM
Preying animals are vital to maintaining a healthy ecosystem.
Coywolf Pesticide Poisonings Case Summary:
Informant: Private citizen reported possible wildlife poisoning.
Statute violated: Federal Insecticide, Fungicide, and Rodenticide Act ("FIFRA")
Alleged perpetrator: Engaged in reckless conduct; created a threat to Virginia's wildlife and environment for his own gain.
Next steps: Follow-up interview scheduled with informant. Investigators sent to reported incident site. Call-in report from investigators scheduled for Monday.

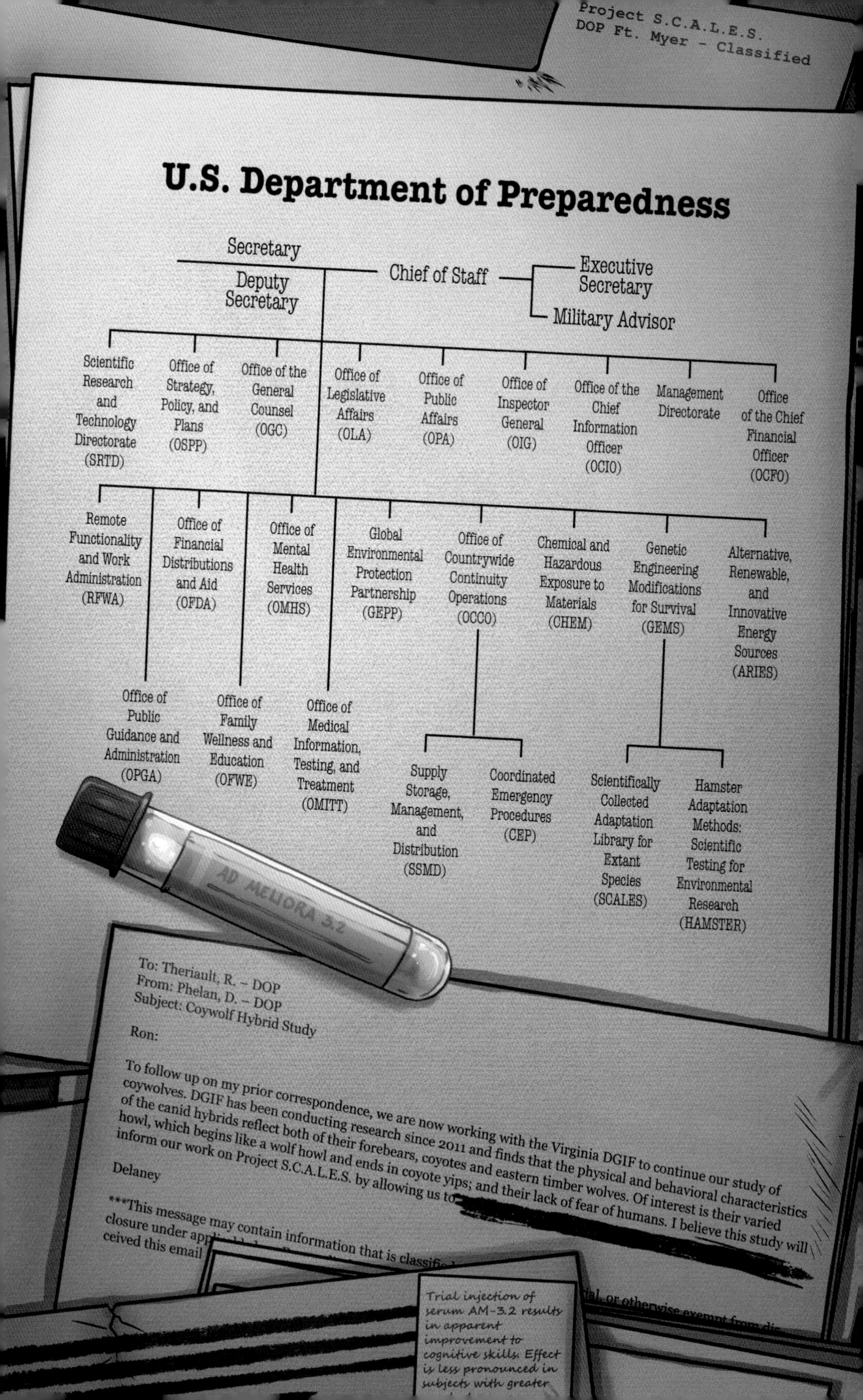
Project S.C.A.L.E.S.
DOP Ft. Myer - Classified
U.S. Department of Preparedness
Secretary
Deputy Secretary
Chief of Staff
Executive Secretary
Military Advisor
Scientific Research and Technology Directorate (SRTD)
Office of Strategy, Policy, and Plans (OSPP)
Office of the General Counsel (OGC)
Office of Legislative Affairs (OLA)
Office of Public Affairs (OPA)
Office of Inspector General (OIG)
Office of the Chief Information Officer (OCIO)
Management Directorate
Office of the Chief Financial Officer (OCFO)
Remote Functionality and Work Administration (RFWA)
Office of Financial Distributions and Aid (OFDA)
Office of Mental Health Services (OMHS)
Global Environmental Protection Partnership (GEPP)
Office of Countrywide Continuity Operations (OCCO)
Chemical and Hazardous Exposure to Materials (CHEM)
Genetic Engineering Modifications for Survival (GEMS)
Alternative, Renewable, and Innovative Energy Sources (ARIES)
Office of Public Guidance and Administration (OPGA)
Office of Family Wellness and Education (OFWE)
Office of Medical Information, Testing, and Treatment (OMITT)
Supply Storage, Management, and Distribution (SSMD)
Coordinated Emergency Procedures (CEP)
Scientifically Collected Adaptation Library for Extant Species (SCALES)
Hamster Adaptation Methods: Scientific Testing for Environmental Research (HAMSTER)
AD MELIORA 3.2
To: Theriault, R. – DOP
From: Phelan, D. – DOP
Subject: Coywolf Hybrid Study
Ron:
To follow up on my prior correspondence, we are now working with the Virginia DGIF to continue our study of coywolves. DGIF has been conducting research since 2011 and finds that the physical and behavioral characteristics of the canid hybrids reflect both of their forebears, coyotes and eastern timber wolves. Of interest is their varied howl, which begins like a wolf howl and ends in coyote yips; and their lack of fear of humans. I believe this study will inform our work on Project S.C.A.L.E.S. by allowing us to [redacted]
Delaney
***This message may contain information that is classifi
closure under app
ceived this email
ial, or otherwise exempt from di
Trial injection of serum AM-3.2 results in apparent improvement to cognitive skills. Effect is less pronounced in subjects with greater

CHAPTER ONE

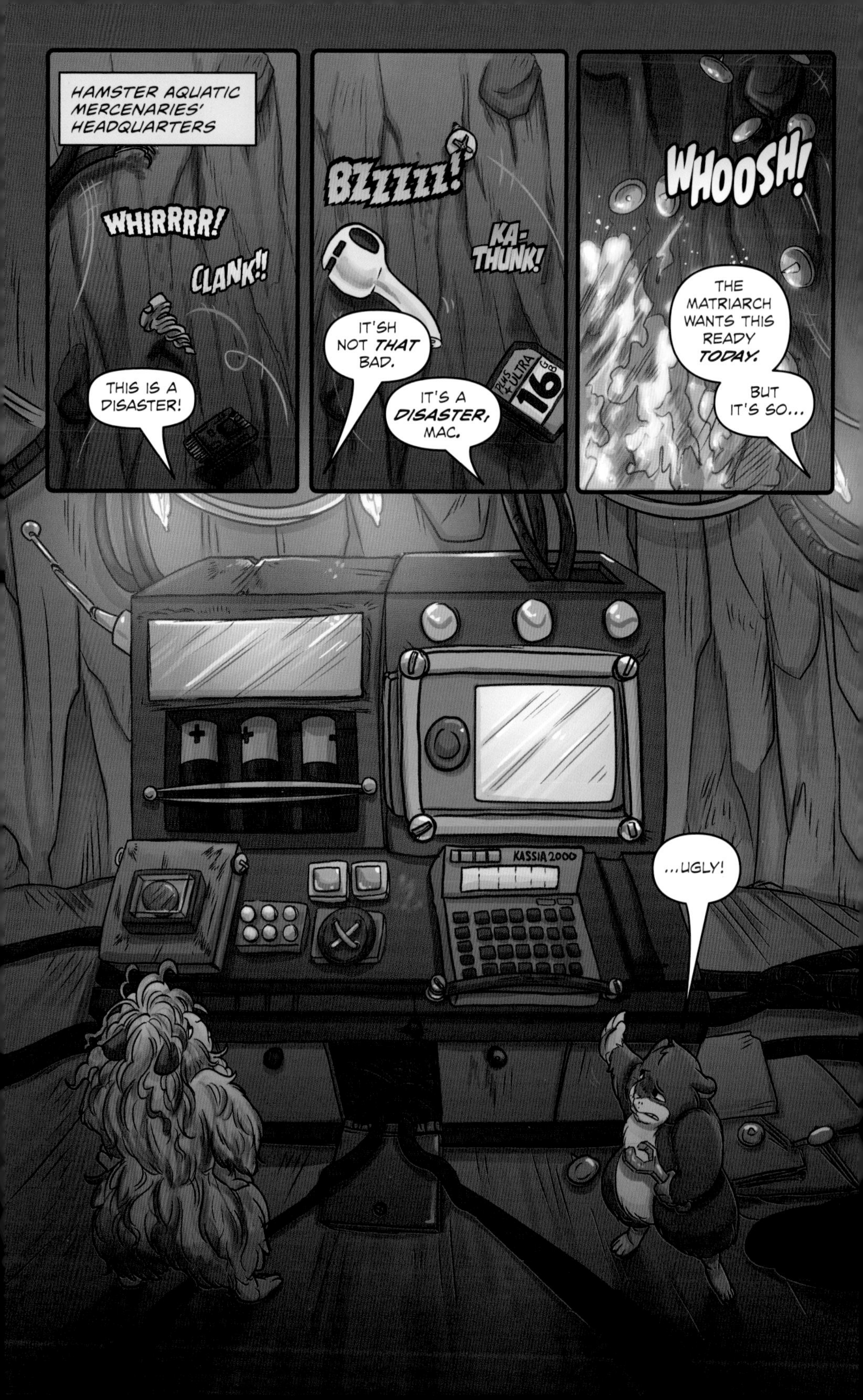

HAMSTER AQUATIC MERCENARIES' HEADQUARTERS
WHIRRRR!
CLANK!!
THIS IS A DISASTER!
BZZZZZ!
KA-THUNK!
IT'SH NOT THAT BAD.
IT'S A DISASTER, MAC.
WHOOSH!
THE MATRIARCH WANTS THIS READY TODAY.
BUT IT'S SO...
KASSIA 2000
...UGLY!

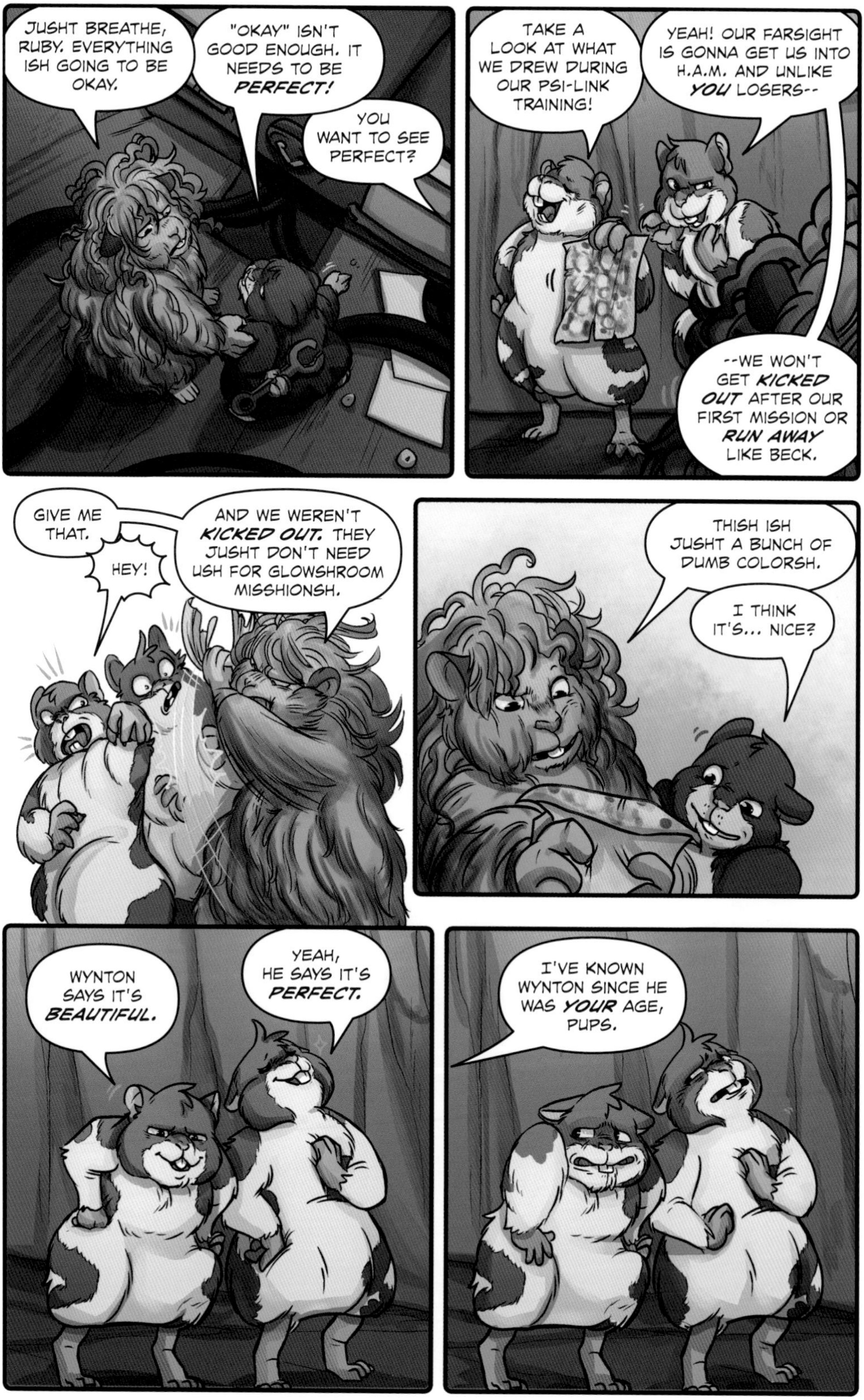
JUSHT BREATHE, RUBY. EVERYTHING ISH GOING TO BE OKAY.
"OKAY" ISN'T GOOD ENOUGH. IT NEEDS TO BE *PERFECT!*
YOU WANT TO SEE PERFECT?
TAKE A LOOK AT WHAT WE DREW DURING OUR PSI-LINK TRAINING!
YEAH! OUR FARSIGHT IS GONNA GET US INTO H.A.M. AND UNLIKE *YOU* LOSERS--
--WE WON'T GET *KICKED OUT* AFTER OUR FIRST MISSION OR *RUN AWAY* LIKE BECK.
GIVE ME THAT.
HEY!
AND WE WEREN'T *KICKED OUT.* THEY JUSHT DON'T NEED USH FOR GLOWSHROOM MISSHIONSH.
THISH ISH JUSHT A BUNCH OF DUMB COLORSH.
I THINK IT'S... NICE?
WYNTON SAYS IT'S *BEAUTIFUL.*
YEAH, HE SAYS IT'S *PERFECT.*
I'VE KNOWN WYNTON SINCE HE WAS *YOUR* AGE, PUPS.

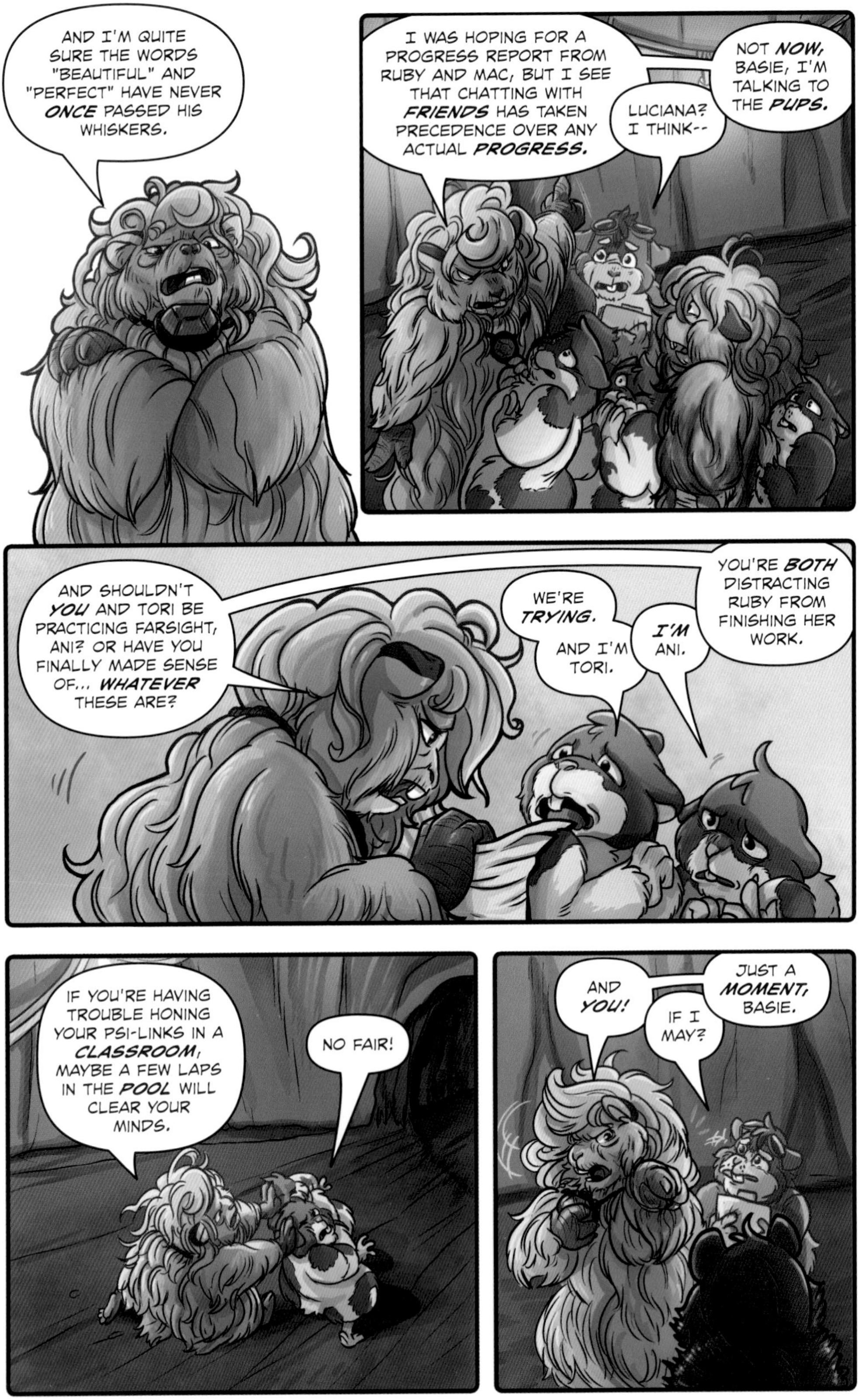
AND I'M QUITE SURE THE WORDS "BEAUTIFUL" AND "PERFECT" HAVE NEVER *ONCE* PASSED HIS WHISKERS.
I WAS HOPING FOR A PROGRESS REPORT FROM RUBY AND MAC, BUT I SEE THAT CHATTING WITH *FRIENDS* HAS TAKEN PRECEDENCE OVER ANY ACTUAL *PROGRESS.*
LUCIANA? I THINK--
NOT *NOW,* BASIE, I'M TALKING TO THE *PUPS.*
AND SHOULDN'T *YOU* AND TORI BE PRACTICING FARSIGHT, ANI? OR HAVE YOU FINALLY MADE SENSE OF... *WHATEVER* THESE ARE?
WE'RE *TRYING.*
AND I'M TORI.
I'M ANI.
YOU'RE *BOTH* DISTRACTING RUBY FROM FINISHING HER WORK.
IF YOU'RE HAVING TROUBLE HONING YOUR PSI-LINKS IN A *CLASSROOM,* MAYBE A FEW LAPS IN THE *POOL* WILL CLEAR YOUR MINDS.
NO FAIR!
AND *YOU!*
IF I MAY?
JUST A *MOMENT,* BASIE.

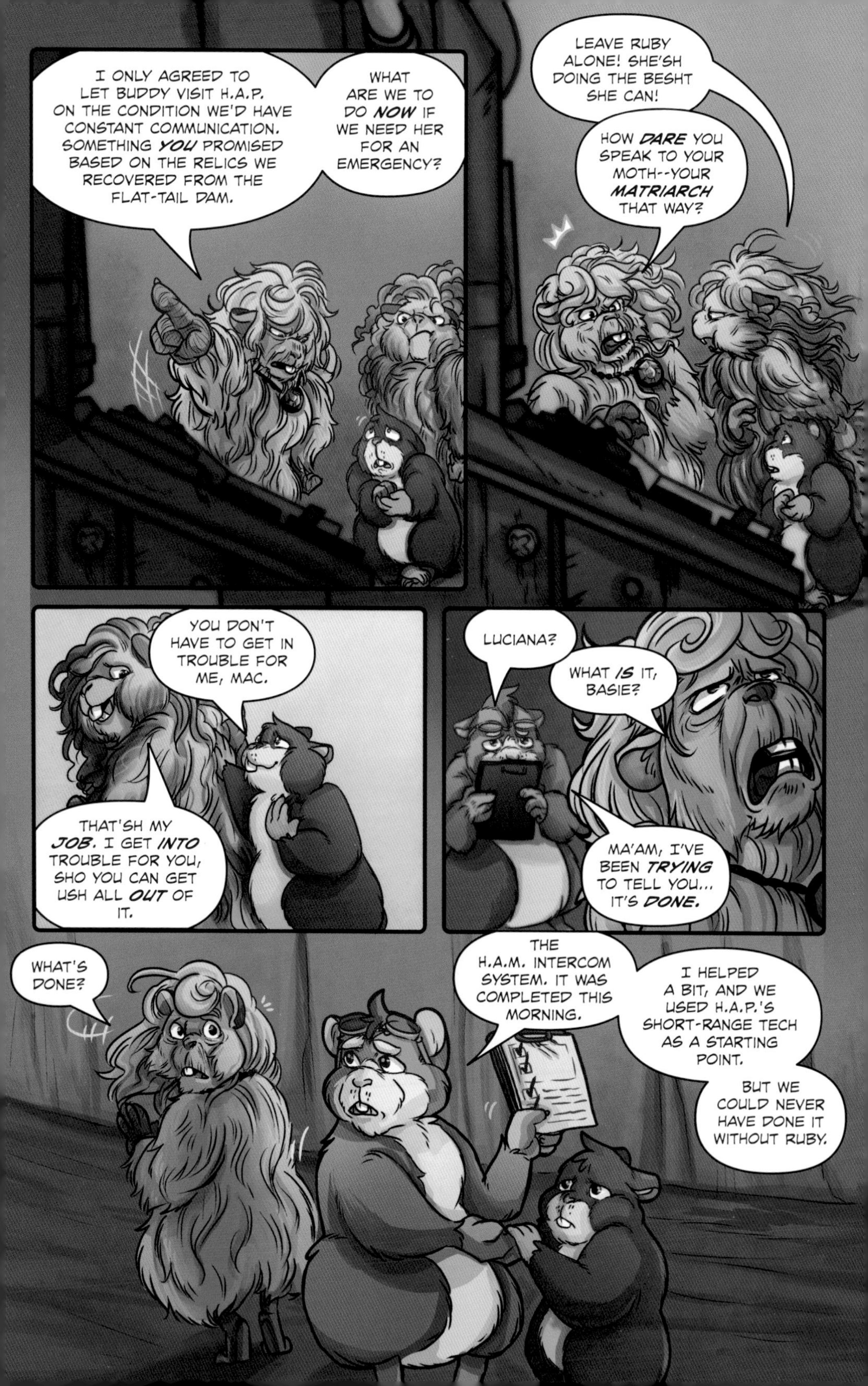
I ONLY AGREED TO LET BUDDY VISIT H.A.P. ON THE CONDITION WE'D HAVE CONSTANT COMMUNICATION. SOMETHING *YOU* PROMISED BASED ON THE RELICS WE RECOVERED FROM THE FLAT-TAIL DAM.
WHAT ARE WE TO DO *NOW* IF WE NEED HER FOR AN EMERGENCY?
LEAVE RUBY ALONE! SHE'SH DOING THE BESHT SHE CAN!
HOW *DARE* YOU SPEAK TO YOUR MOTH--YOUR *MATRIARCH* THAT WAY?
YOU DON'T HAVE TO GET IN TROUBLE FOR ME, MAC.
THAT'SH MY *JOB*. I GET *INTO* TROUBLE FOR YOU, SHO YOU CAN GET USH ALL *OUT* OF IT.
LUCIANA?
WHAT *IS* IT, BASIE?
MA'AM, I'VE BEEN *TRYING* TO TELL YOU... IT'S *DONE.*
WHAT'S DONE?
THE H.A.M. INTERCOM SYSTEM. IT WAS COMPLETED THIS MORNING.
I HELPED A BIT, AND WE USED H.A.P.'S SHORT-RANGE TECH AS A STARTING POINT.
BUT WE COULD NEVER HAVE DONE IT WITHOUT RUBY.

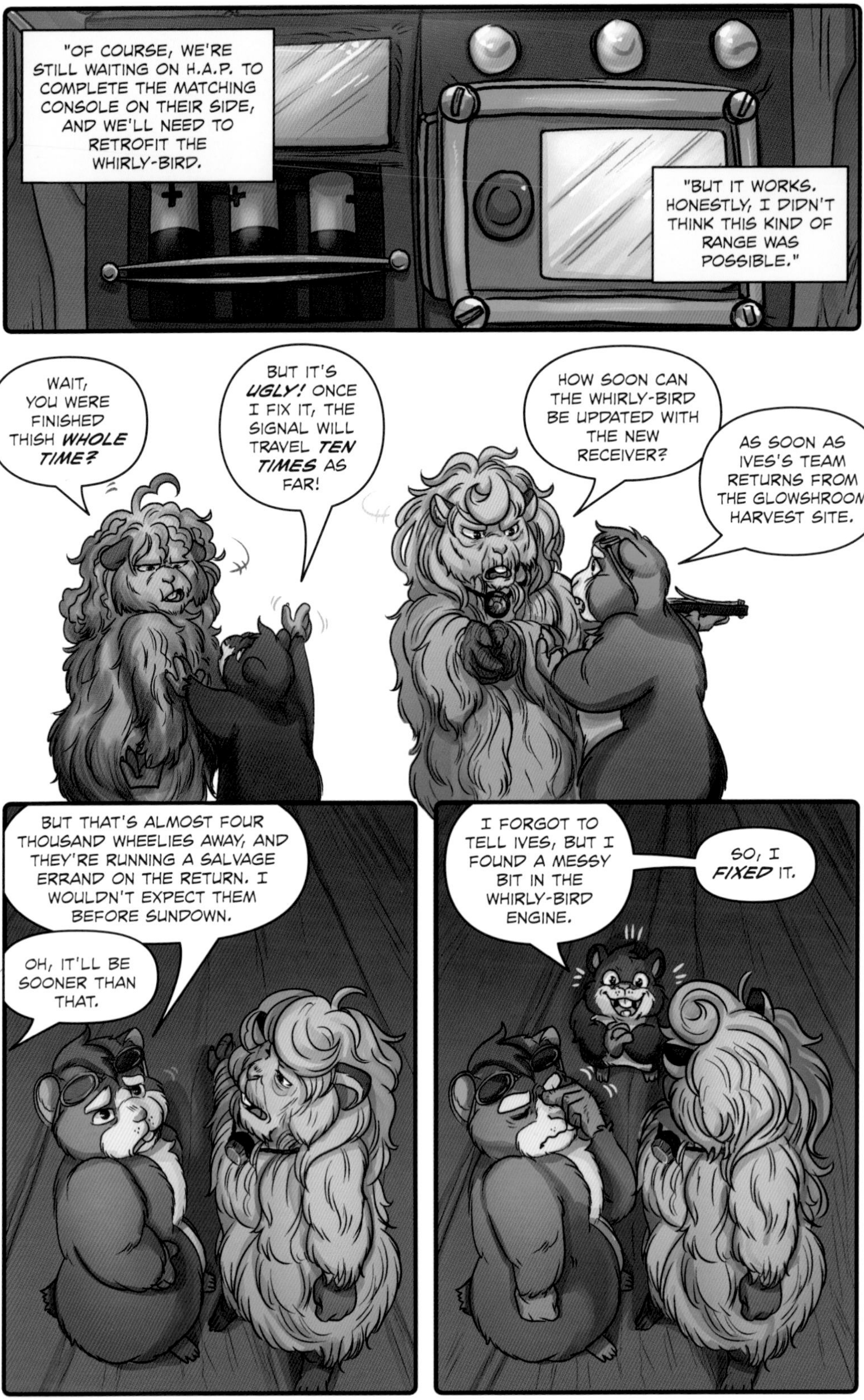
"OF COURSE, WE'RE STILL WAITING ON H.A.P. TO COMPLETE THE MATCHING CONSOLE ON THEIR SIDE, AND WE'LL NEED TO RETROFIT THE WHIRLY-BIRD.
"BUT IT WORKS. HONESTLY, I DIDN'T THINK THIS KIND OF RANGE WAS POSSIBLE."
WAIT, YOU WERE FINISHED THISH *WHOLE TIME?*
BUT IT'S *UGLY!* ONCE I FIX IT, THE SIGNAL WILL TRAVEL *TEN TIMES* AS FAR!
HOW SOON CAN THE WHIRLY-BIRD BE UPDATED WITH THE NEW RECEIVER?
AS SOON AS IVES'S TEAM RETURNS FROM THE GLOWSHROOM HARVEST SITE.
BUT THAT'S ALMOST FOUR THOUSAND WHEELIES AWAY, AND THEY'RE RUNNING A SALVAGE ERRAND ON THE RETURN. I WOULDN'T EXPECT THEM BEFORE SUNDOWN.
OH, IT'LL BE SOONER THAN THAT.
I FORGOT TO TELL IVES, BUT I FOUND A MESSY BIT IN THE WHIRLY-BIRD ENGINE.
SO, I *FIXED* IT.

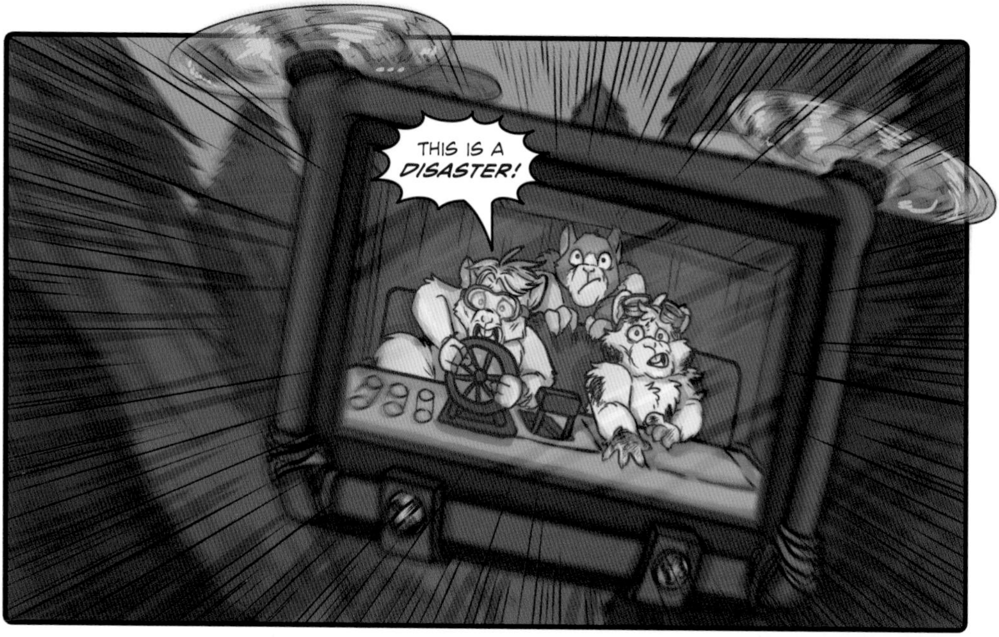
THIS IS A DISASTER!

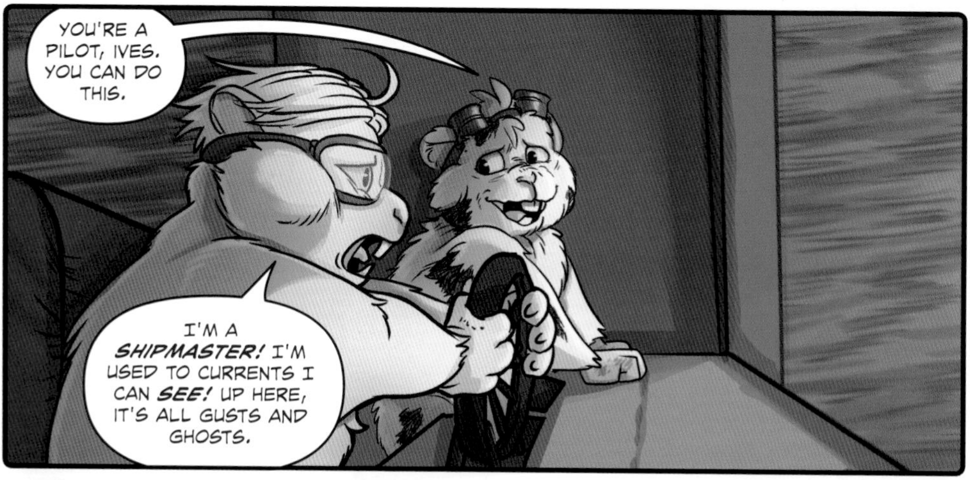
YOU'RE A PILOT, IVES. YOU CAN DO THIS.
I'M A SHIPMASTER! I'M USED TO CURRENTS I CAN SEE! UP HERE, IT'S ALL GUSTS AND GHOSTS.

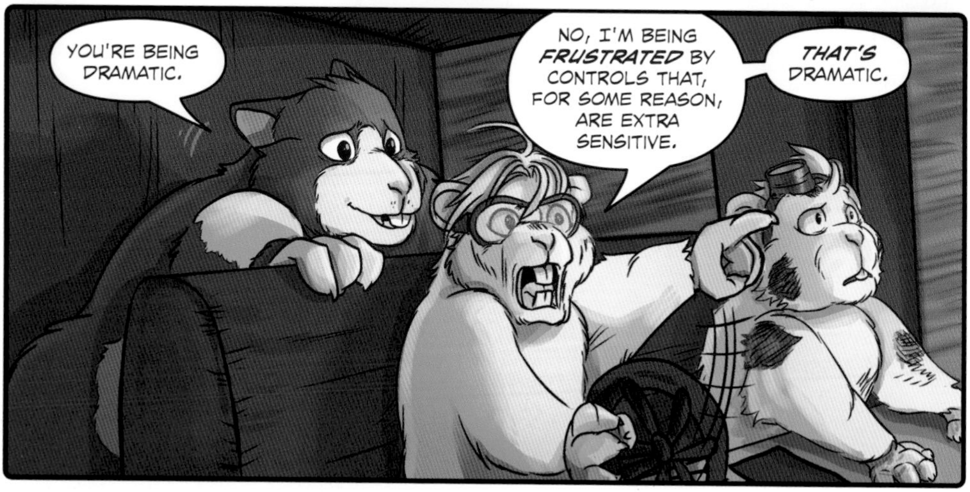
YOU'RE BEING DRAMATIC.
NO, I'M BEING FRUSTRATED BY CONTROLS THAT, FOR SOME REASON, ARE EXTRA SENSITIVE.
THAT'S DRAMATIC.

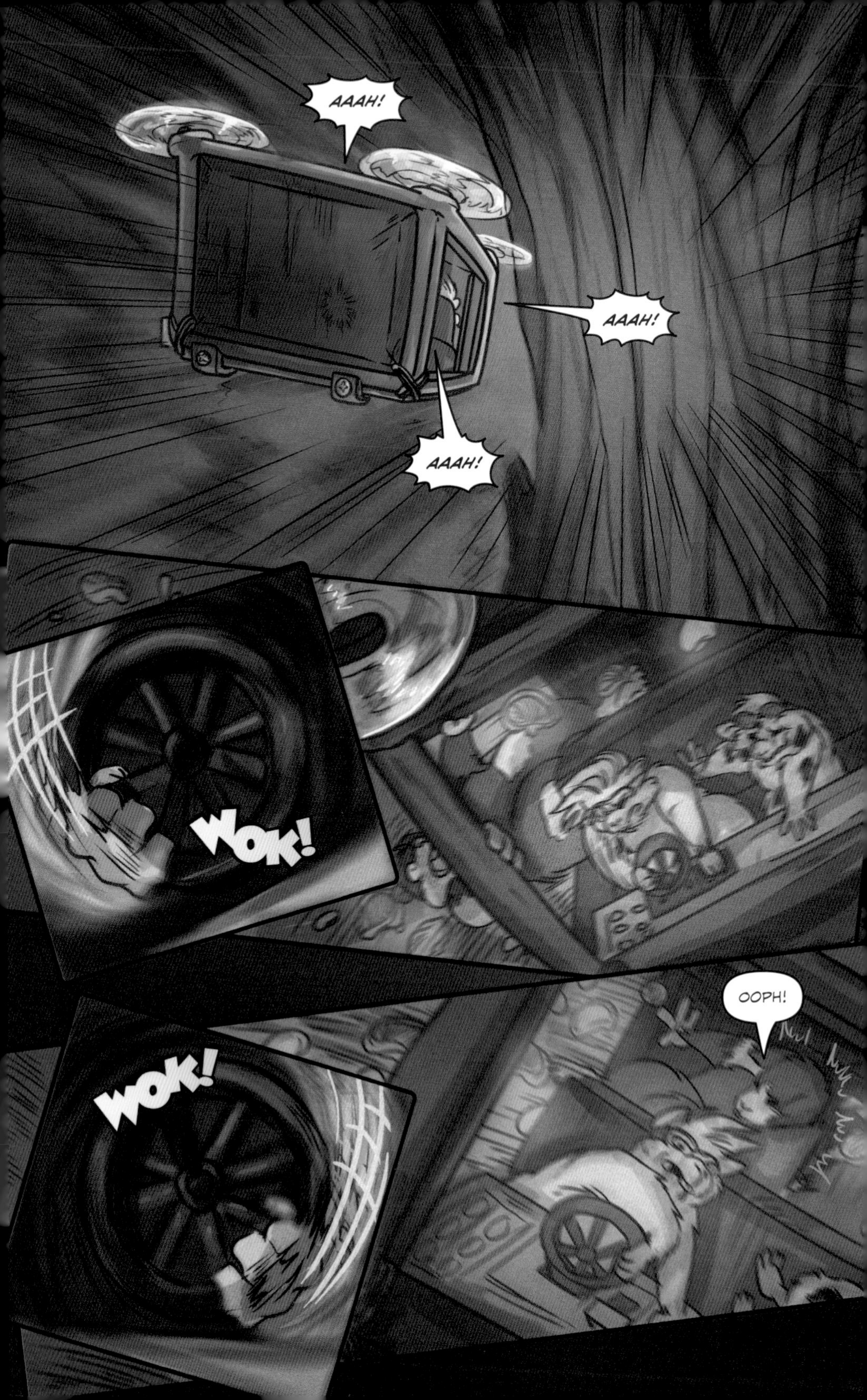
AAAH!
AAAH!
AAAH!
WOK!
WOK!
OOPH!

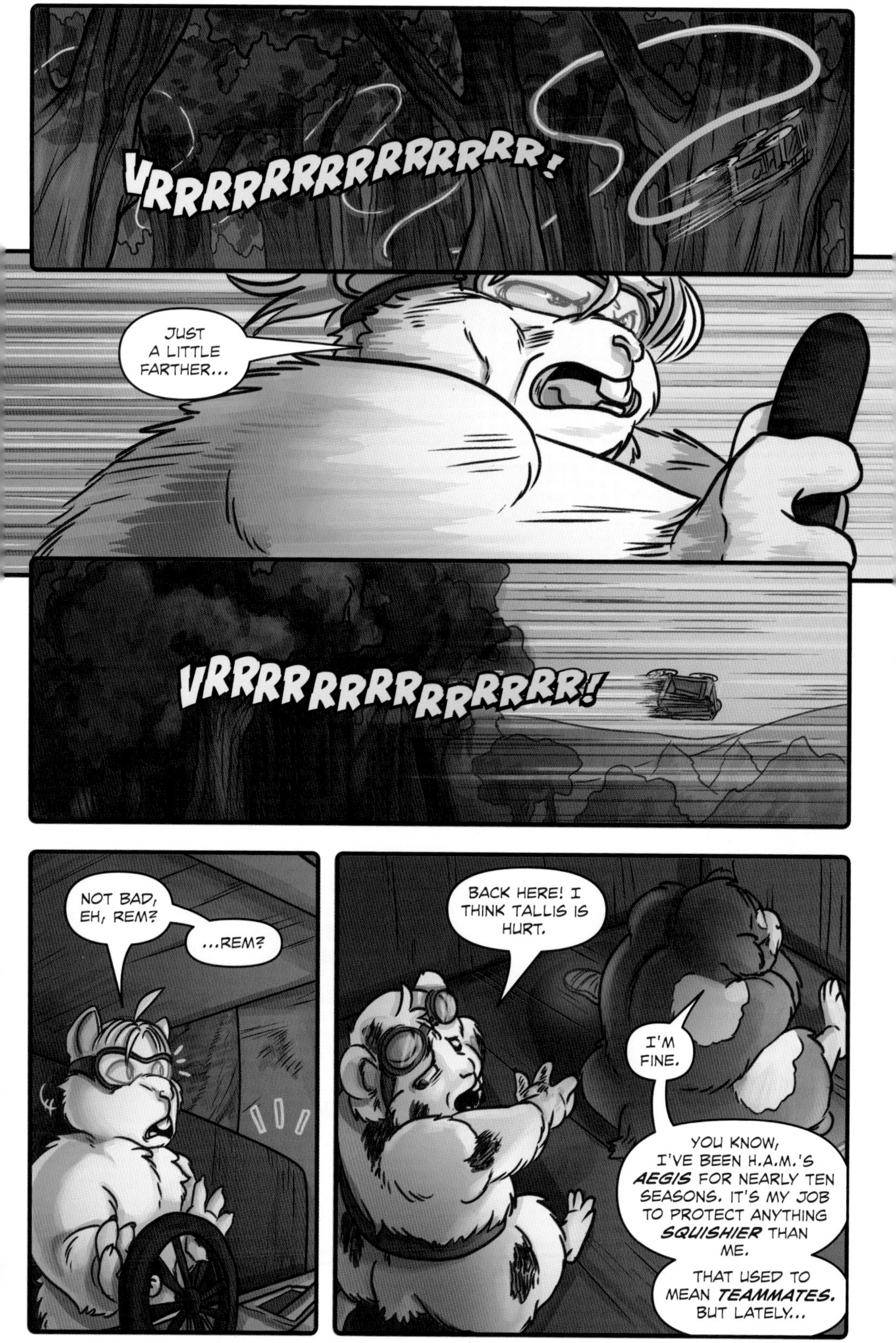
VRRRRRRRRRRRRR!
JUST A LITTLE FARTHER...
VRRRRRRRRRRRRRR!
NOT BAD, EH, REM?
...REM?
BACK HERE! I THINK TALLIS IS HURT.
I'M FINE.
YOU KNOW, I'VE BEEN H.A.M.'S AEGIS FOR NEARLY TEN SEASONS. IT'S MY JOB TO PROTECT ANYTHING SQUISHIER THAN ME.
THAT USED TO MEAN TEAMMATES. BUT LATELY...

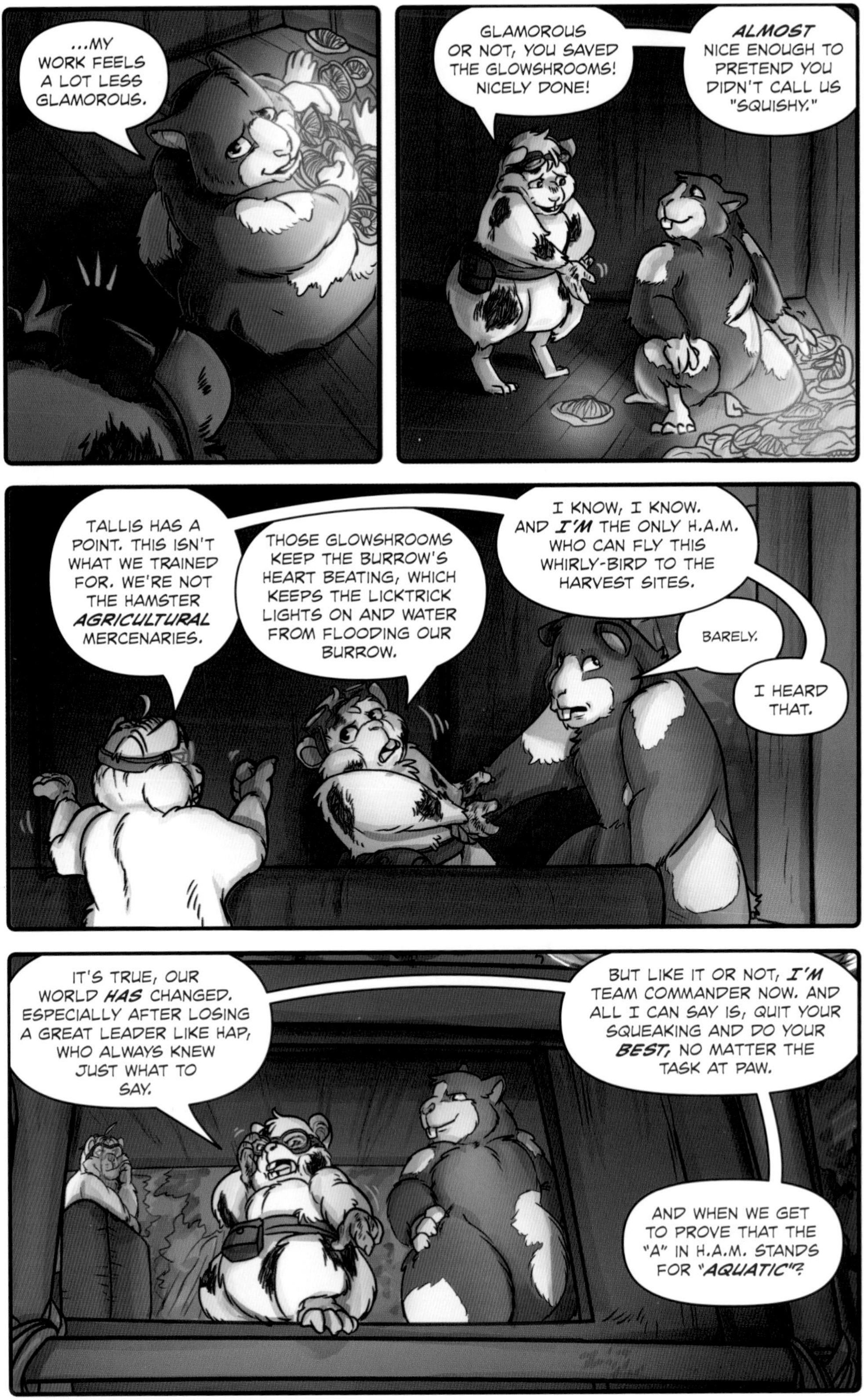
...MY WORK FEELS A LOT LESS GLAMOROUS.
GLAMOROUS OR NOT, YOU SAVED THE GLOWSHROOMS! NICELY DONE!
ALMOST NICE ENOUGH TO PRETEND YOU DIDN'T CALL US "SQUISHY."
TALLIS HAS A POINT. THIS ISN'T WHAT WE TRAINED FOR. WE'RE NOT THE HAMSTER AGRICULTURAL MERCENARIES.
THOSE GLOWSHROOMS KEEP THE BURROW'S HEART BEATING, WHICH KEEPS THE LICKTRICK LIGHTS ON AND WATER FROM FLOODING OUR BURROW.
I KNOW, I KNOW. AND I'M THE ONLY H.A.M. WHO CAN FLY THIS WHIRLY-BIRD TO THE HARVEST SITES.
BARELY.
I HEARD THAT.
IT'S TRUE, OUR WORLD HAS CHANGED. ESPECIALLY AFTER LOSING A GREAT LEADER LIKE HAP, WHO ALWAYS KNEW JUST WHAT TO SAY.
BUT LIKE IT OR NOT, I'M TEAM COMMANDER NOW. AND ALL I CAN SAY IS, QUIT YOUR SQUEAKING AND DO YOUR BEST, NO MATTER THE TASK AT PAW.
AND WHEN WE GET TO PROVE THAT THE "A" IN H.A.M. STANDS FOR "AQUATIC"?

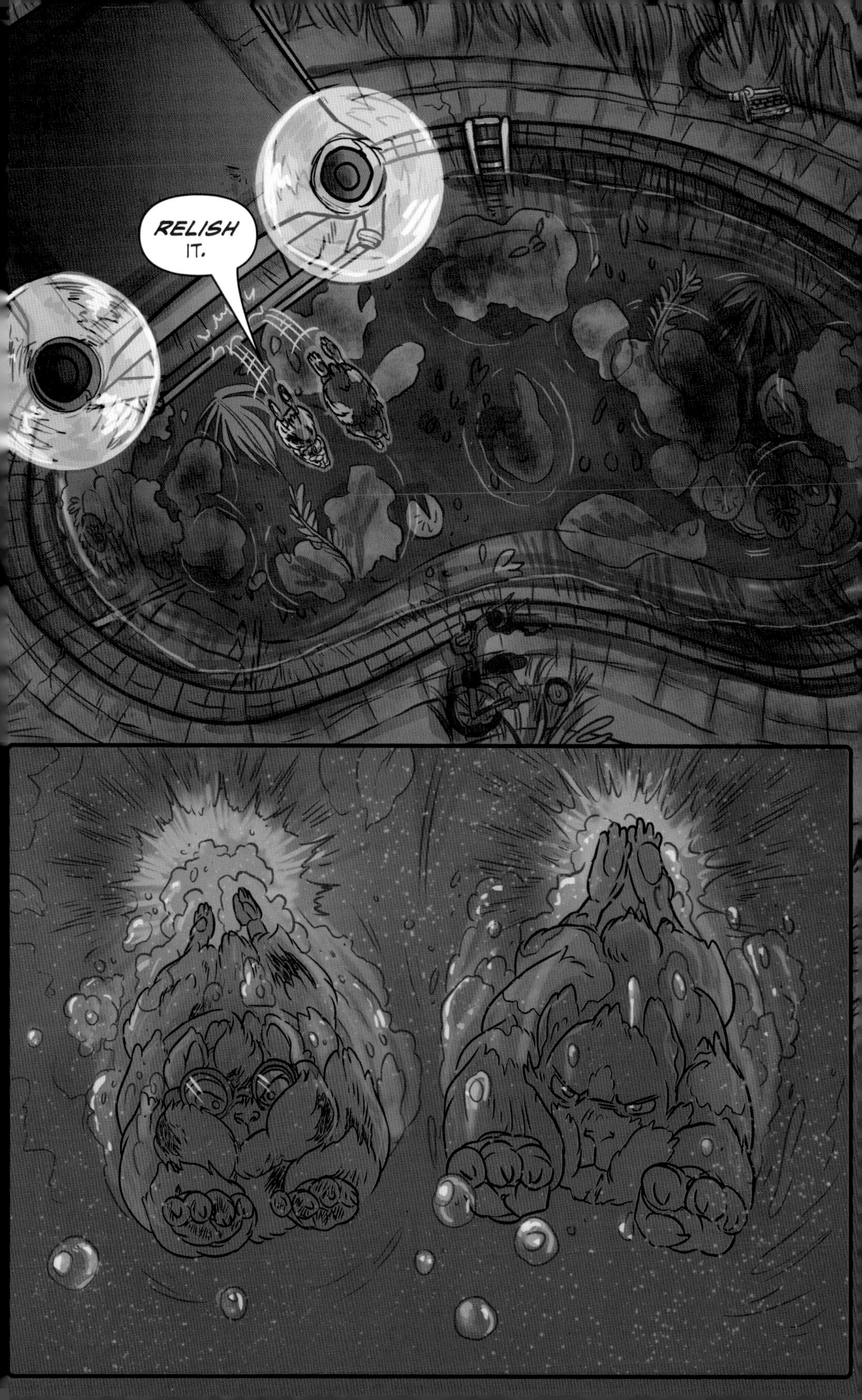
RELISH IT.

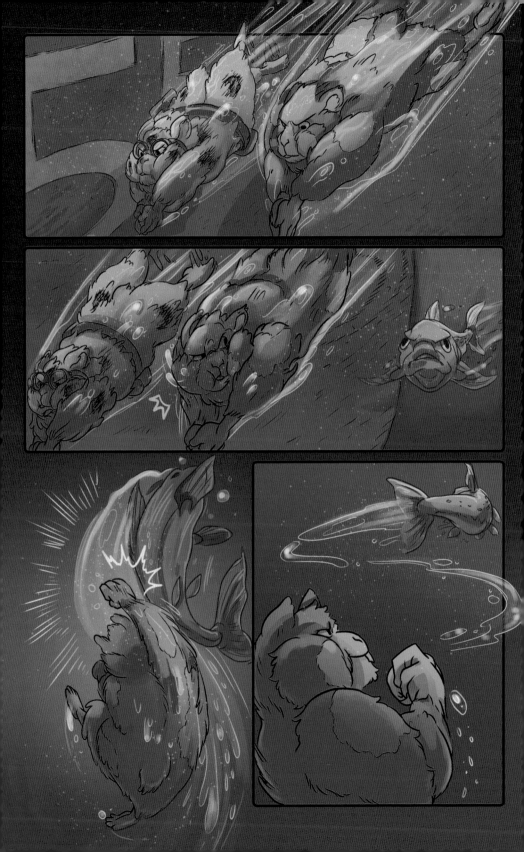

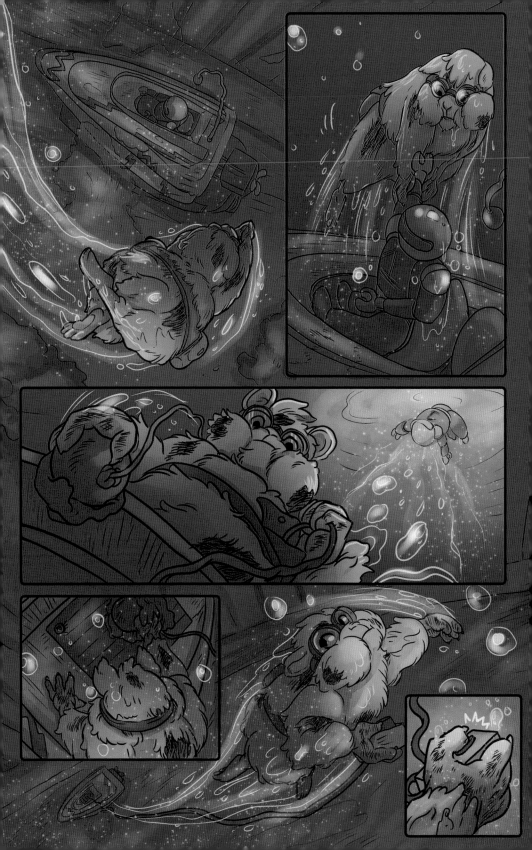

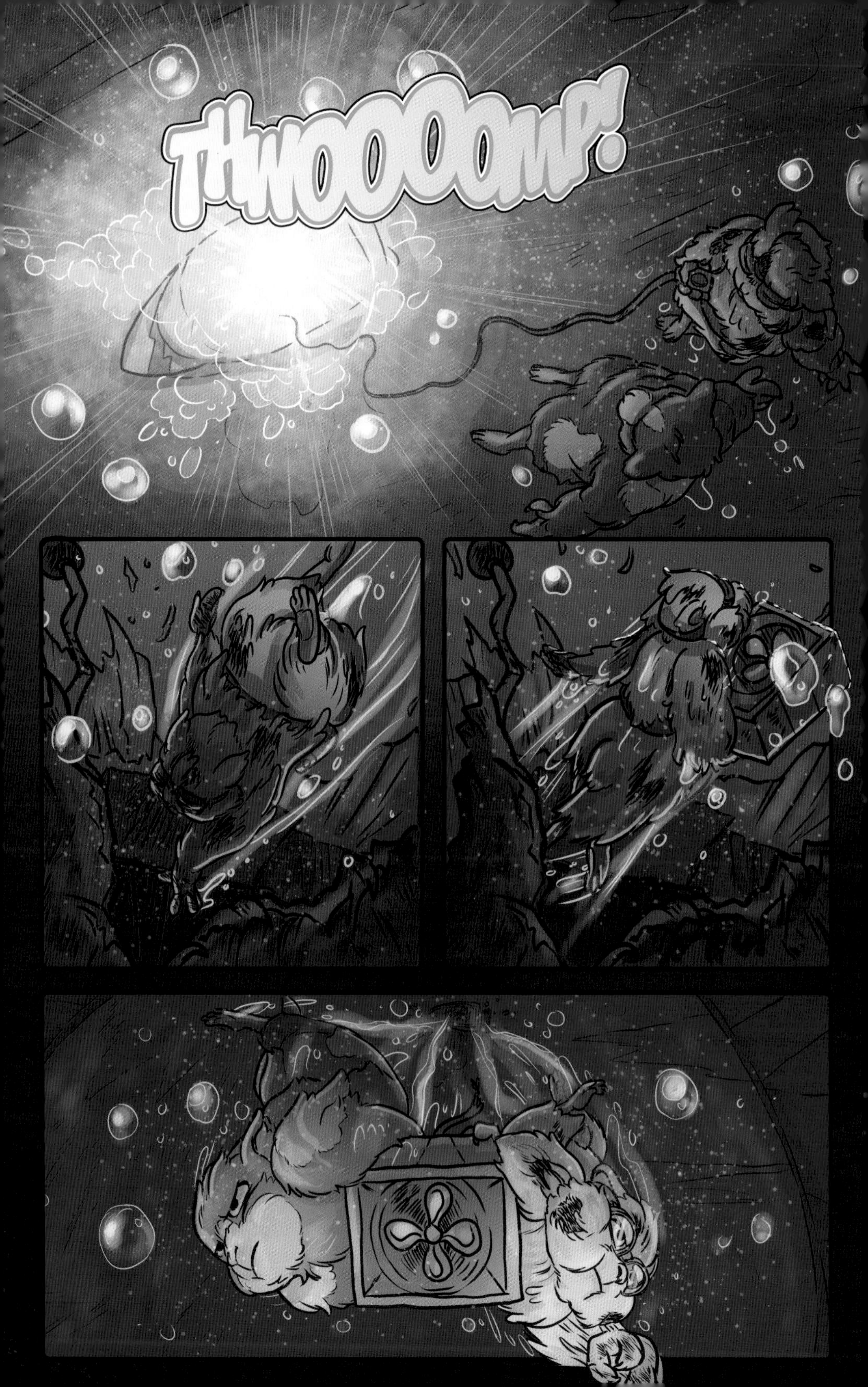
THWOOOOMP!

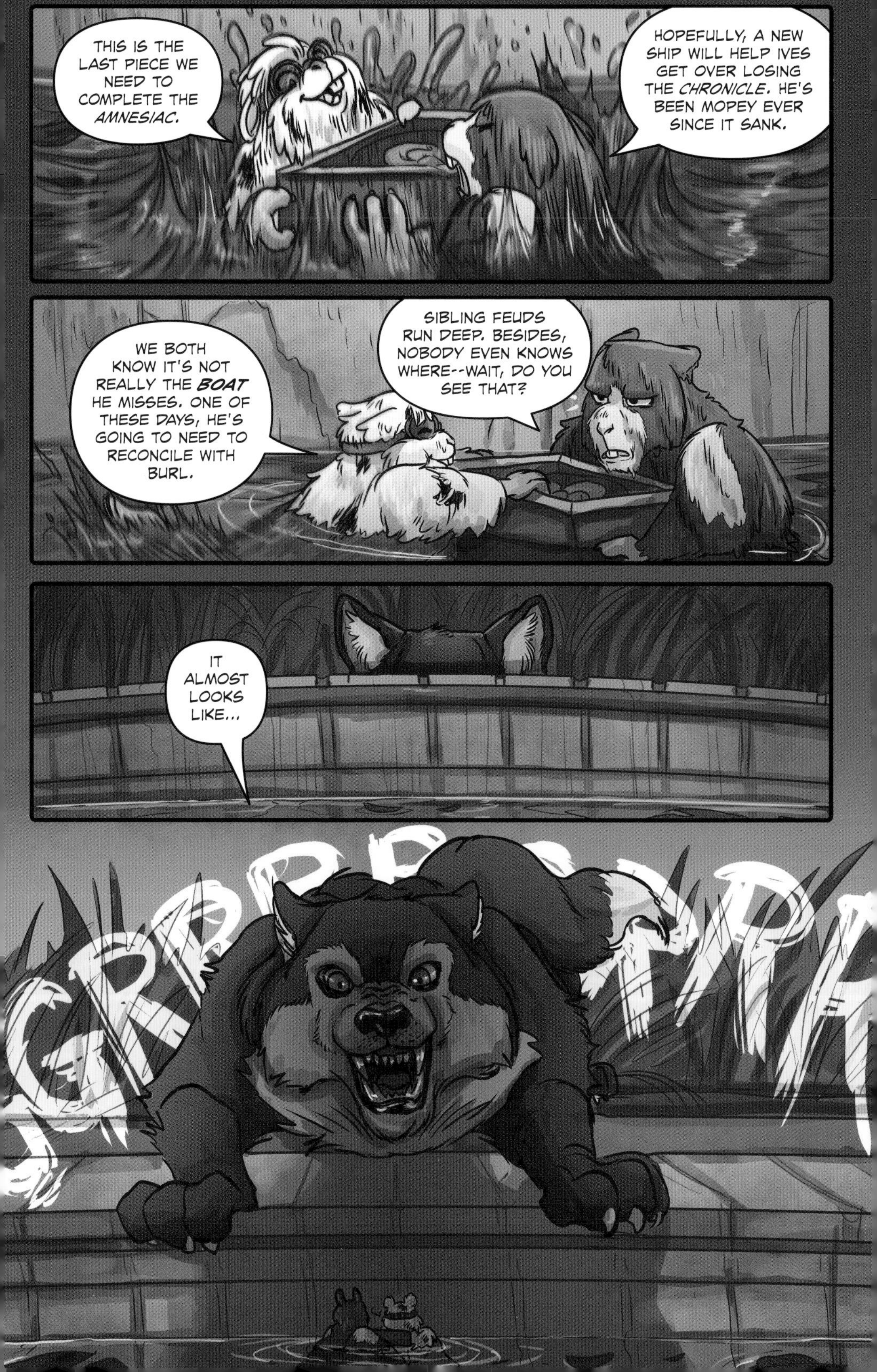
THIS IS THE LAST PIECE WE NEED TO COMPLETE THE *AMNESIAC*.
HOPEFULLY, A NEW SHIP WILL HELP IVES GET OVER LOSING THE *CHRONICLE*. HE'S BEEN MOPEY EVER SINCE IT SANK.
WE BOTH KNOW IT'S NOT REALLY THE ***BOAT*** HE MISSES. ONE OF THESE DAYS, HE'S GOING TO NEED TO RECONCILE WITH BURL.
SIBLING FEUDS RUN DEEP. BESIDES, NOBODY EVEN KNOWS WHERE--WAIT, DO YOU SEE THAT?
IT ALMOST LOOKS LIKE...
GRRRRRR

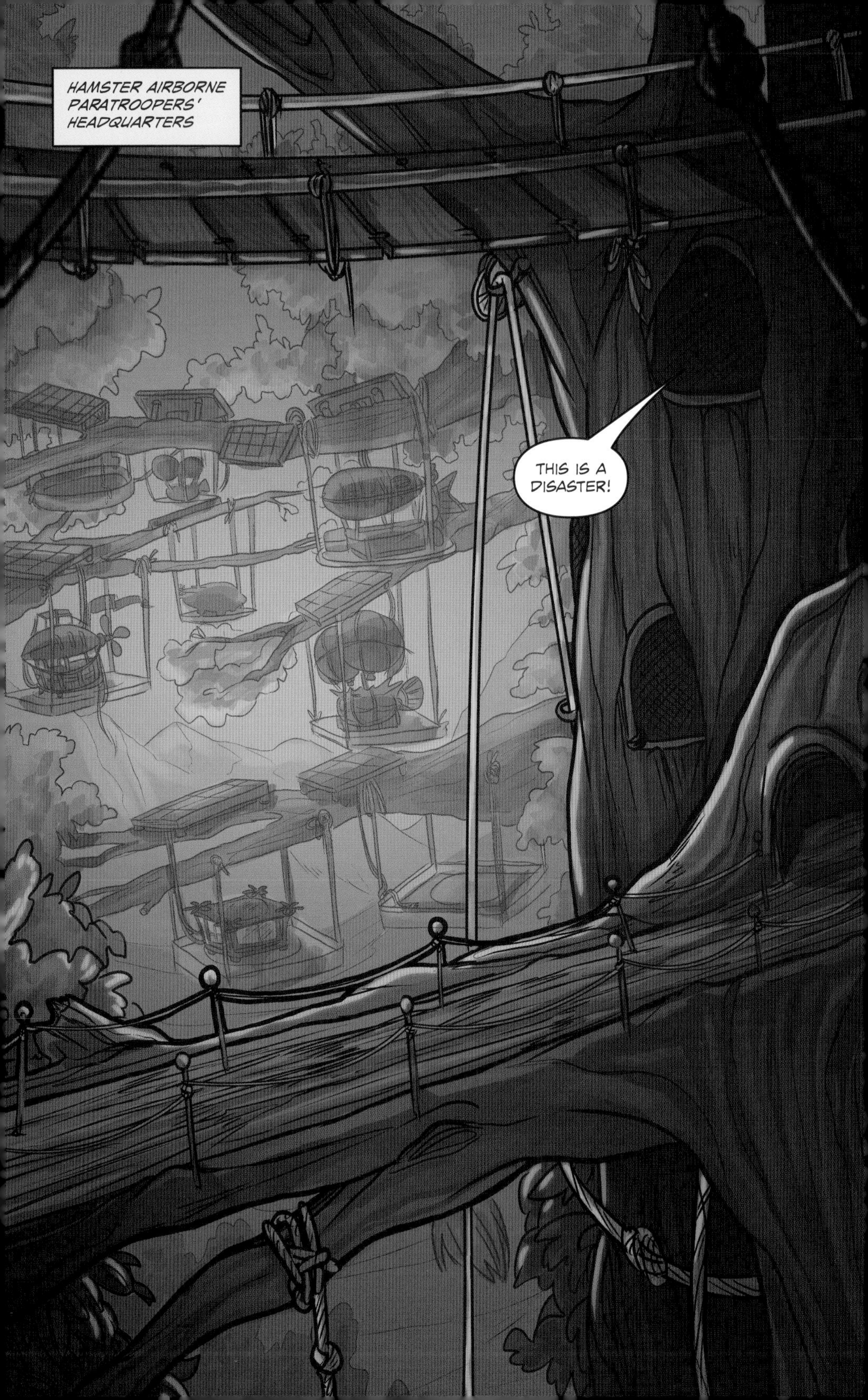
HAMSTER AIRBORNE PARATROOPERS' HEADQUARTERS
THIS IS A DISASTER!

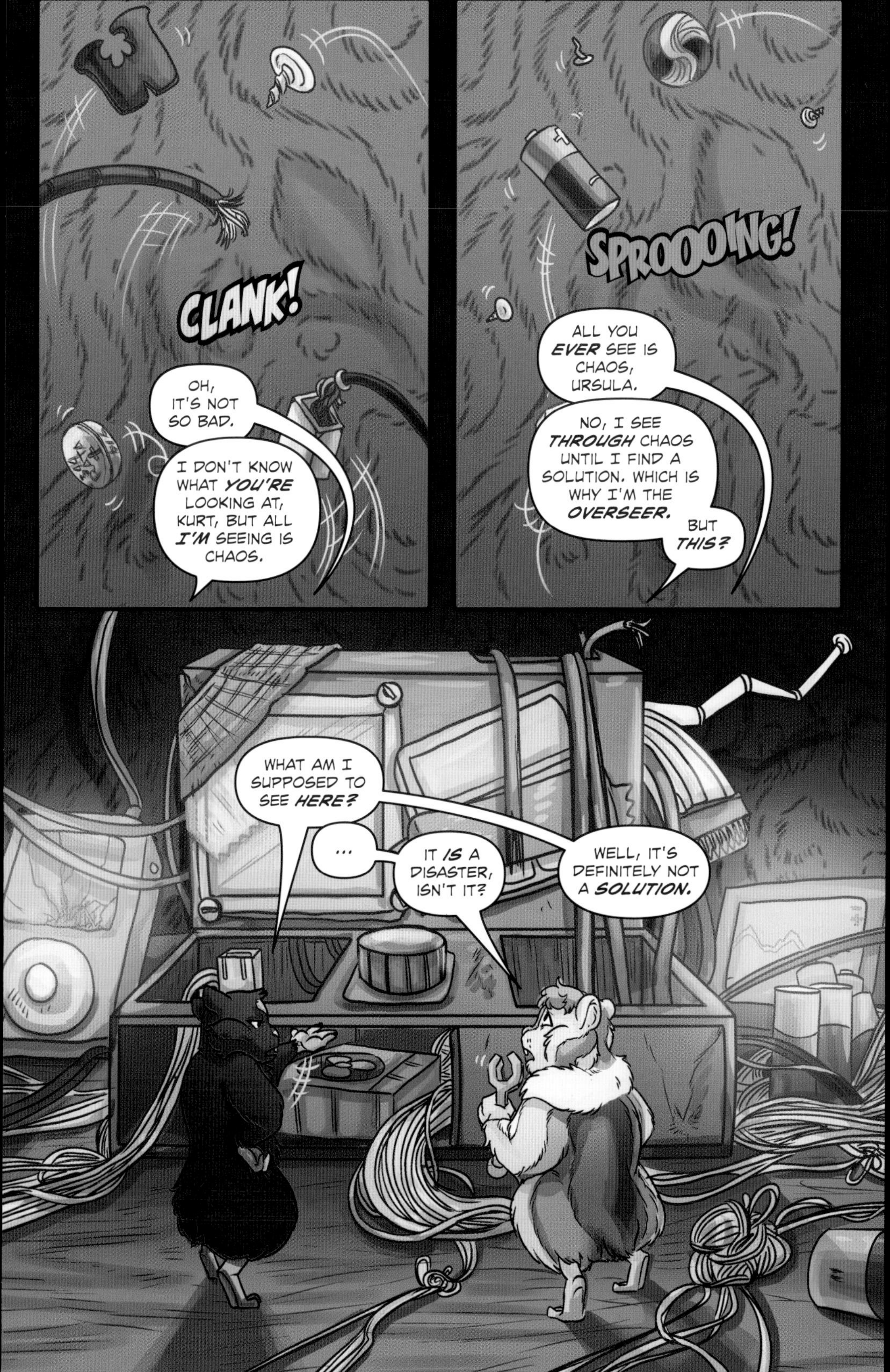
CLANK!
OH, IT'S NOT SO BAD.
I DON'T KNOW WHAT YOU'RE LOOKING AT, KURT, BUT ALL I'M SEEING IS CHAOS.
SPROOOING!
ALL YOU EVER SEE IS CHAOS, URSULA.
NO, I SEE THROUGH CHAOS UNTIL I FIND A SOLUTION. WHICH IS WHY I'M THE OVERSEER.
BUT THIS?
WHAT AM I SUPPOSED TO SEE HERE?
WELL, IT'S DEFINITELY NOT A SOLUTION.
...
IT IS A DISASTER, ISN'T IT?

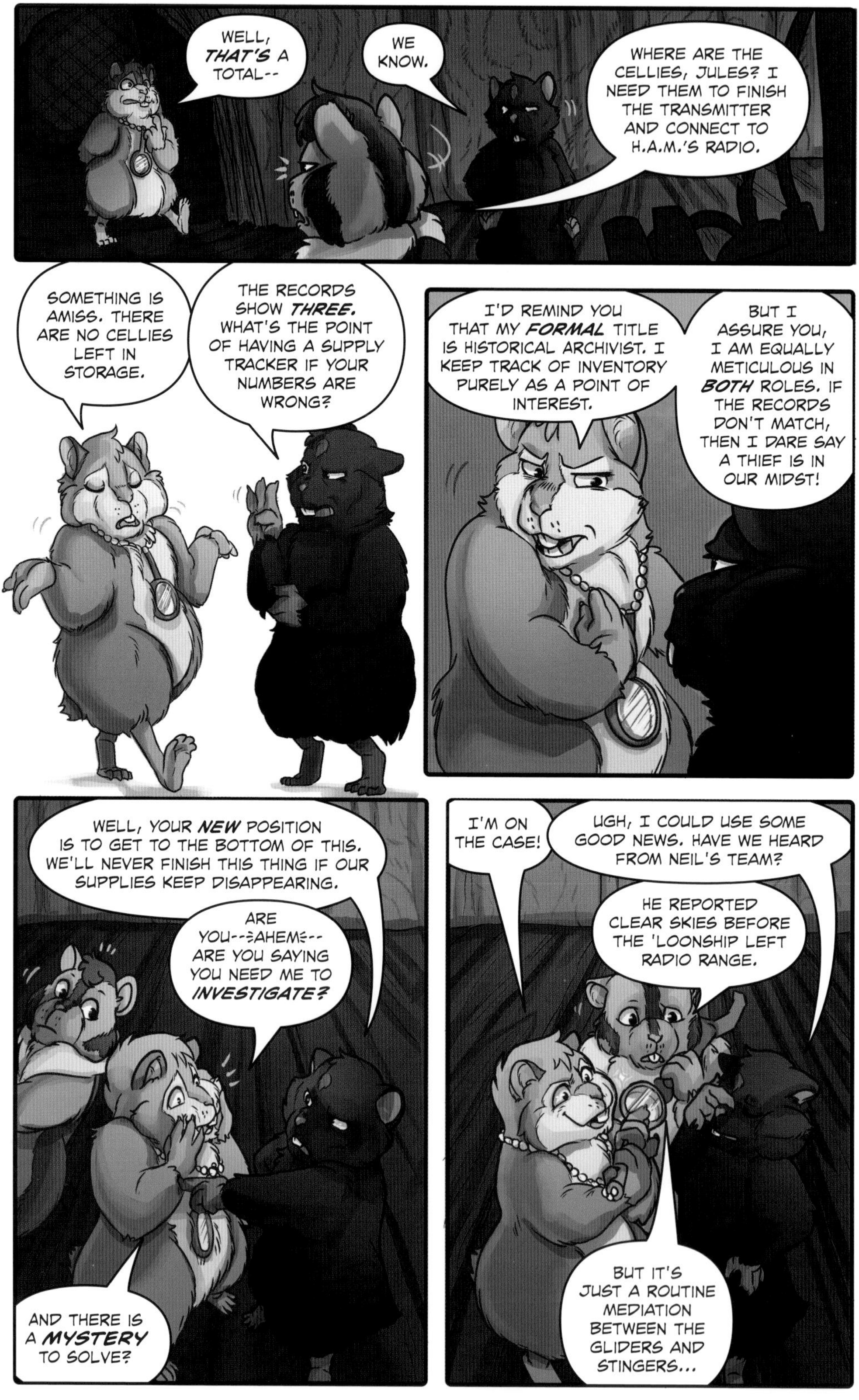
WELL, THAT'S A TOTAL--
WE KNOW.
WHERE ARE THE CELLIES, JULES? I NEED THEM TO FINISH THE TRANSMITTER AND CONNECT TO H.A.M.'S RADIO.
SOMETHING IS AMISS. THERE ARE NO CELLIES LEFT IN STORAGE.
THE RECORDS SHOW THREE. WHAT'S THE POINT OF HAVING A SUPPLY TRACKER IF YOUR NUMBERS ARE WRONG?
I'D REMIND YOU THAT MY FORMAL TITLE IS HISTORICAL ARCHIVIST. I KEEP TRACK OF INVENTORY PURELY AS A POINT OF INTEREST.
BUT I ASSURE YOU, I AM EQUALLY METICULOUS IN BOTH ROLES. IF THE RECORDS DON'T MATCH, THEN I DARE SAY A THIEF IS IN OUR MIDST!
WELL, YOUR NEW POSITION IS TO GET TO THE BOTTOM OF THIS. WE'LL NEVER FINISH THIS THING IF OUR SUPPLIES KEEP DISAPPEARING.
ARE YOU--AHEM--ARE YOU SAYING YOU NEED ME TO INVESTIGATE?
AND THERE IS A MYSTERY TO SOLVE?
I'M ON THE CASE!
UGH, I COULD USE SOME GOOD NEWS. HAVE WE HEARD FROM NEIL'S TEAM?
HE REPORTED CLEAR SKIES BEFORE THE 'LOONSHIP LEFT RADIO RANGE.
BUT IT'S JUST A ROUTINE MEDIATION BETWEEN THE GLIDERS AND STINGERS...

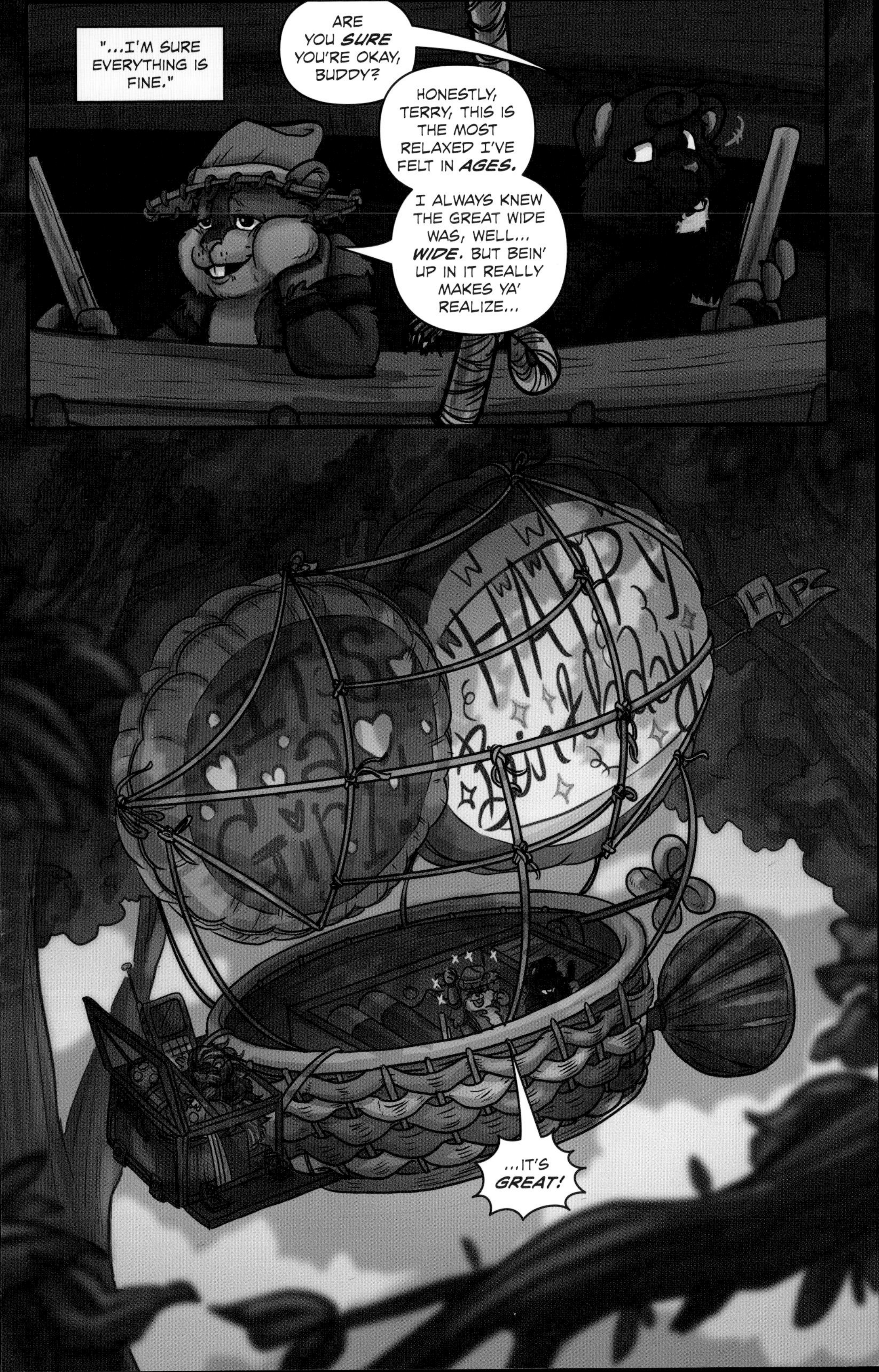
"...I'M SURE EVERYTHING IS FINE."
ARE YOU SURE YOU'RE OKAY, BUDDY?
HONESTLY, TERRY, THIS IS THE MOST RELAXED I'VE FELT IN AGES.
I ALWAYS KNEW THE GREAT WIDE WAS, WELL... WIDE. BUT BEIN' UP IN IT REALLY MAKES YA' REALIZE...
HAPPY Birthday
...IT'S GREAT!

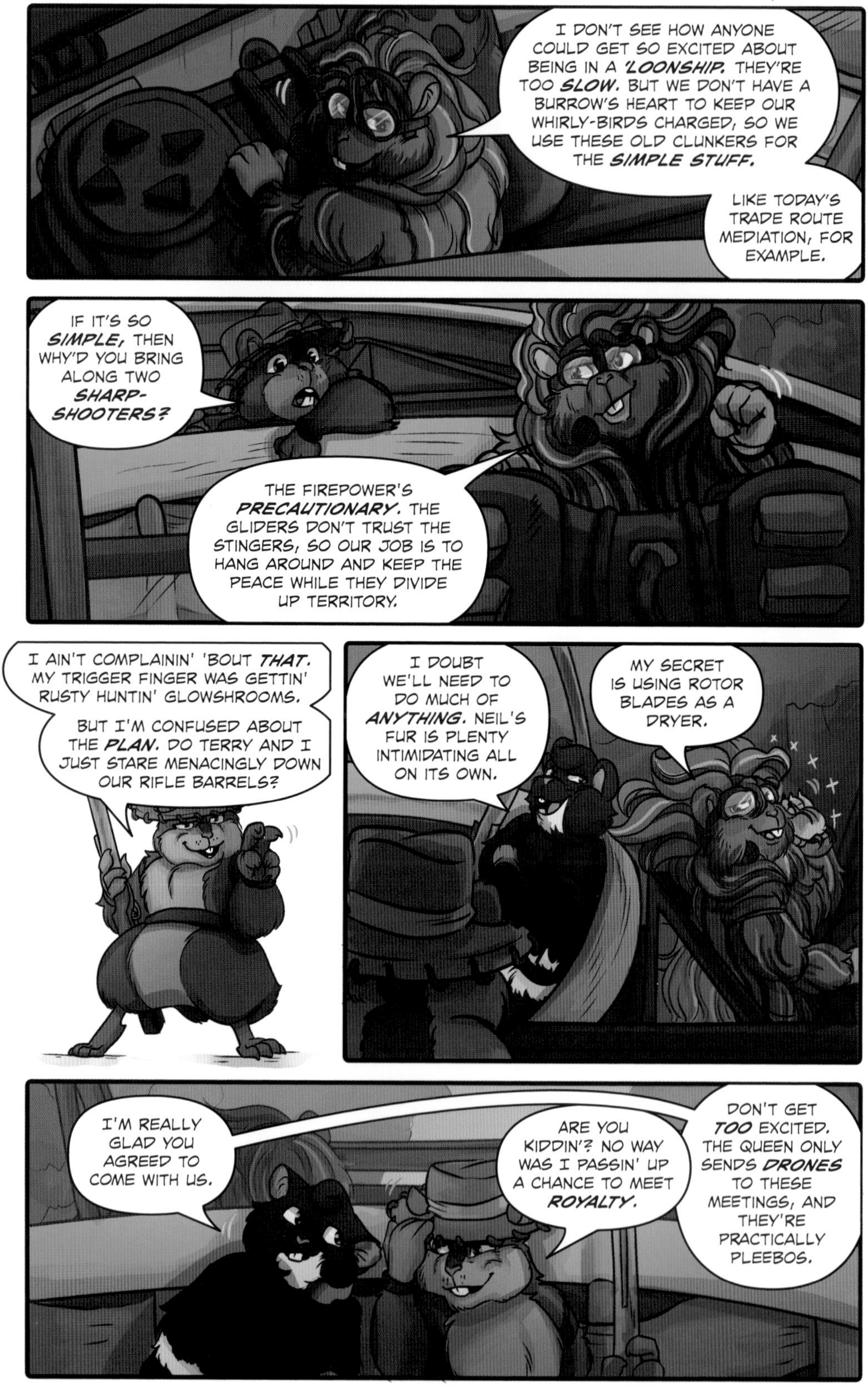

I DON'T SEE HOW ANYONE COULD GET SO EXCITED ABOUT BEING IN A 'LOONSHIP. THEY'RE TOO SLOW. BUT WE DON'T HAVE A BURROW'S HEART TO KEEP OUR WHIRLY-BIRDS CHARGED, SO WE USE THESE OLD CLUNKERS FOR THE SIMPLE STUFF.
LIKE TODAY'S TRADE ROUTE MEDIATION, FOR EXAMPLE.
IF IT'S SO SIMPLE, THEN WHY'D YOU BRING ALONG TWO SHARP-SHOOTERS?
THE FIREPOWER'S PRECAUTIONARY. THE GLIDERS DON'T TRUST THE STINGERS, SO OUR JOB IS TO HANG AROUND AND KEEP THE PEACE WHILE THEY DIVIDE UP TERRITORY.
I AIN'T COMPLAININ' 'BOUT THAT. MY TRIGGER FINGER WAS GETTIN' RUSTY HUNTIN' GLOWSHROOMS.
BUT I'M CONFUSED ABOUT THE PLAN. DO TERRY AND I JUST STARE MENACINGLY DOWN OUR RIFLE BARRELS?
I DOUBT WE'LL NEED TO DO MUCH OF ANYTHING. NEIL'S FUR IS PLENTY INTIMIDATING ALL ON ITS OWN.
MY SECRET IS USING ROTOR BLADES AS A DRYER.
I'M REALLY GLAD YOU AGREED TO COME WITH US.
ARE YOU KIDDIN'? NO WAY WAS I PASSIN' UP A CHANCE TO MEET ROYALTY.
DON'T GET TOO EXCITED. THE QUEEN ONLY SENDS DRONES TO THESE MEETINGS, AND THEY'RE PRACTICALLY PLEEBOS.

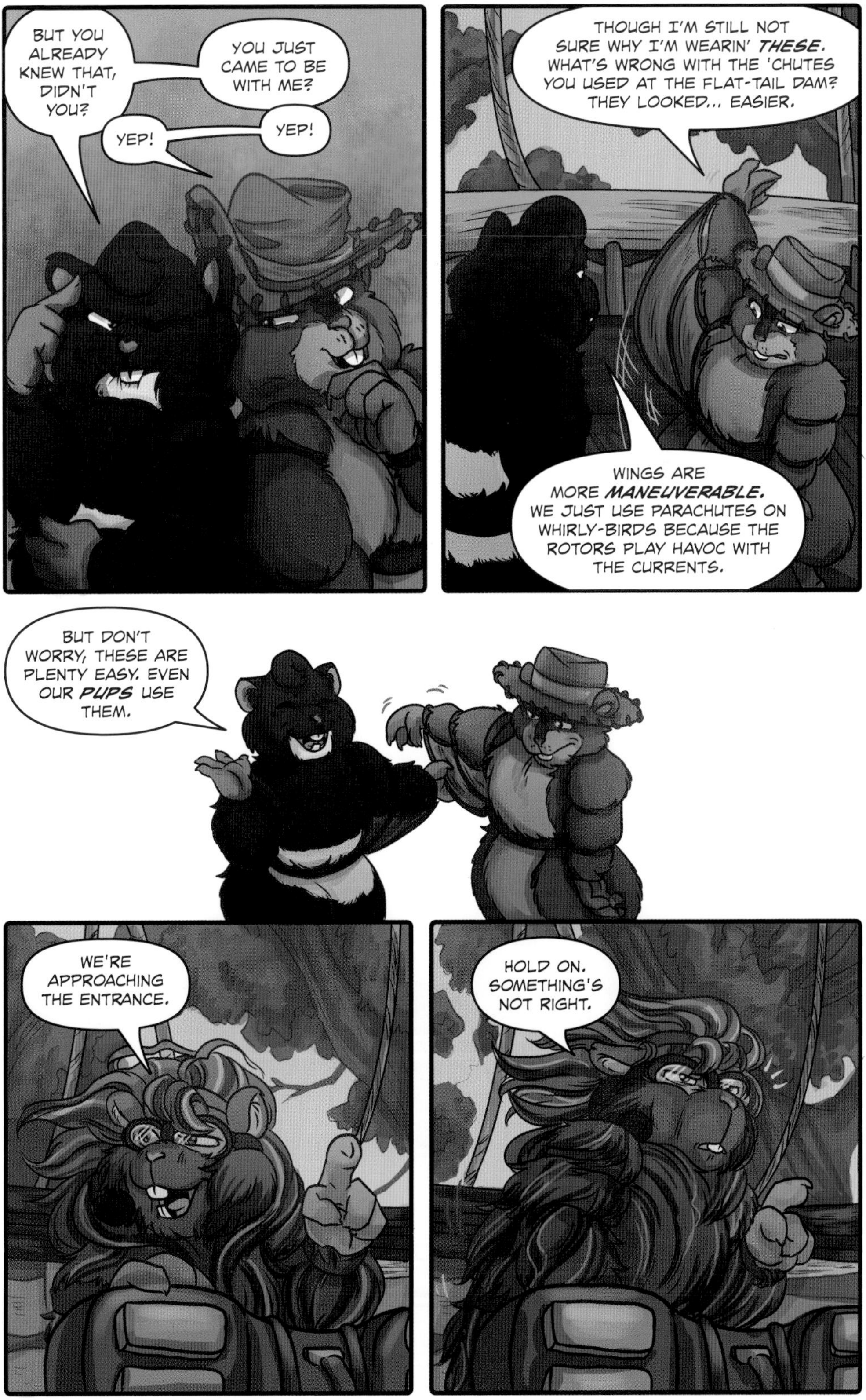
BUT YOU ALREADY KNEW THAT, DIDN'T YOU?
YOU JUST CAME TO BE WITH ME?
YEP!
YEP!
THOUGH I'M STILL NOT SURE WHY I'M WEARIN' *THESE.* WHAT'S WRONG WITH THE 'CHUTES YOU USED AT THE FLAT-TAIL DAM? THEY LOOKED... EASIER.
WINGS ARE MORE *MANEUVERABLE.* WE JUST USE PARACHUTES ON WHIRLY-BIRDS BECAUSE THE ROTORS PLAY HAVOC WITH THE CURRENTS.
BUT DON'T WORRY, THESE ARE PLENTY EASY. EVEN OUR *PUPS* USE THEM.
WE'RE APPROACHING THE ENTRANCE.
HOLD ON. SOMETHING'S NOT RIGHT.

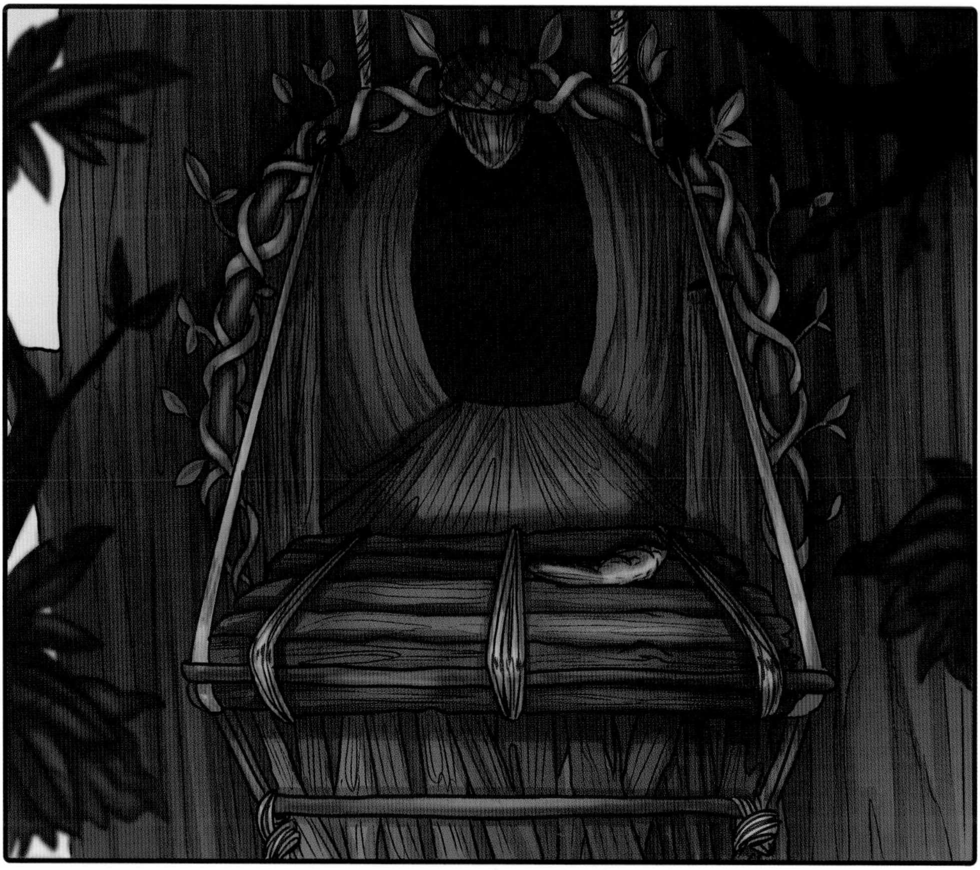

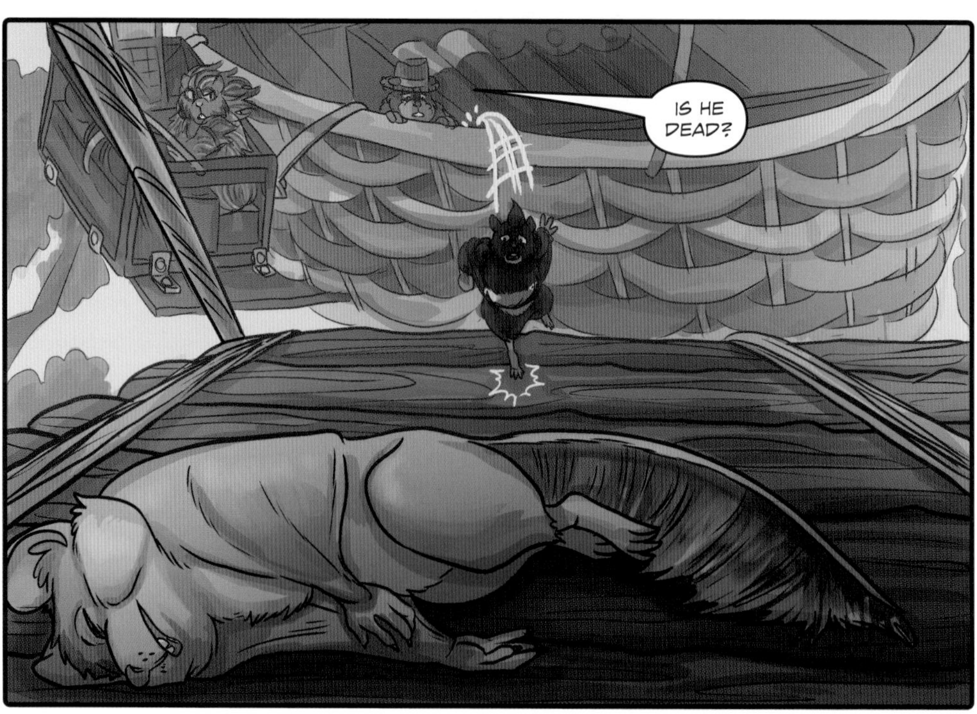
IS HE DEAD?

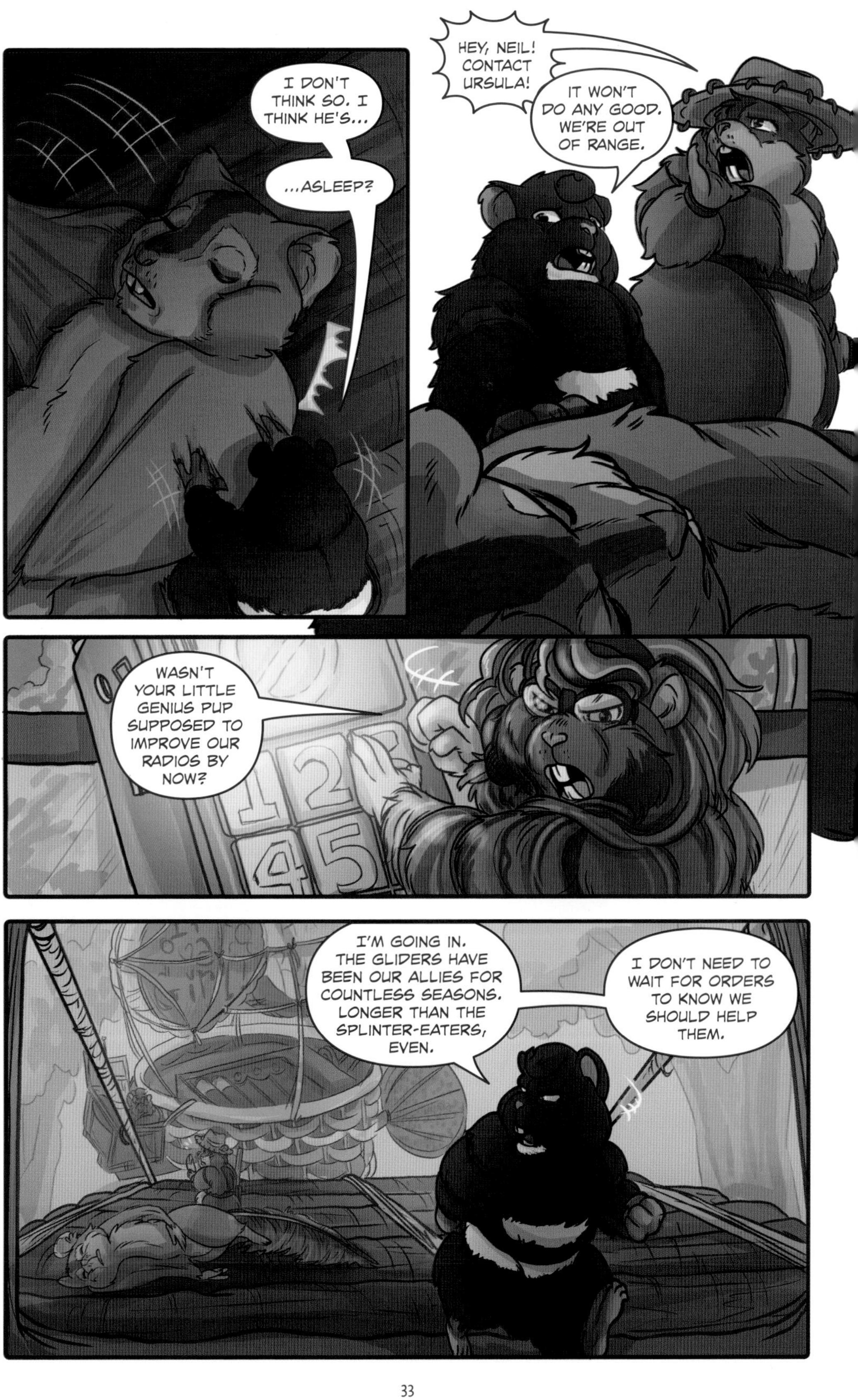
I DON'T THINK SO. I THINK HE'S...
...ASLEEP?
HEY, NEIL! CONTACT URSULA!
IT WON'T DO ANY GOOD. WE'RE OUT OF RANGE.
WASN'T YOUR LITTLE GENIUS PUP SUPPOSED TO IMPROVE OUR RADIOS BY NOW?
I'M GOING IN. THE GLIDERS HAVE BEEN OUR ALLIES FOR COUNTLESS SEASONS. LONGER THAN THE SPLINTER-EATERS, EVEN.
I DON'T NEED TO WAIT FOR ORDERS TO KNOW WE SHOULD HELP THEM.

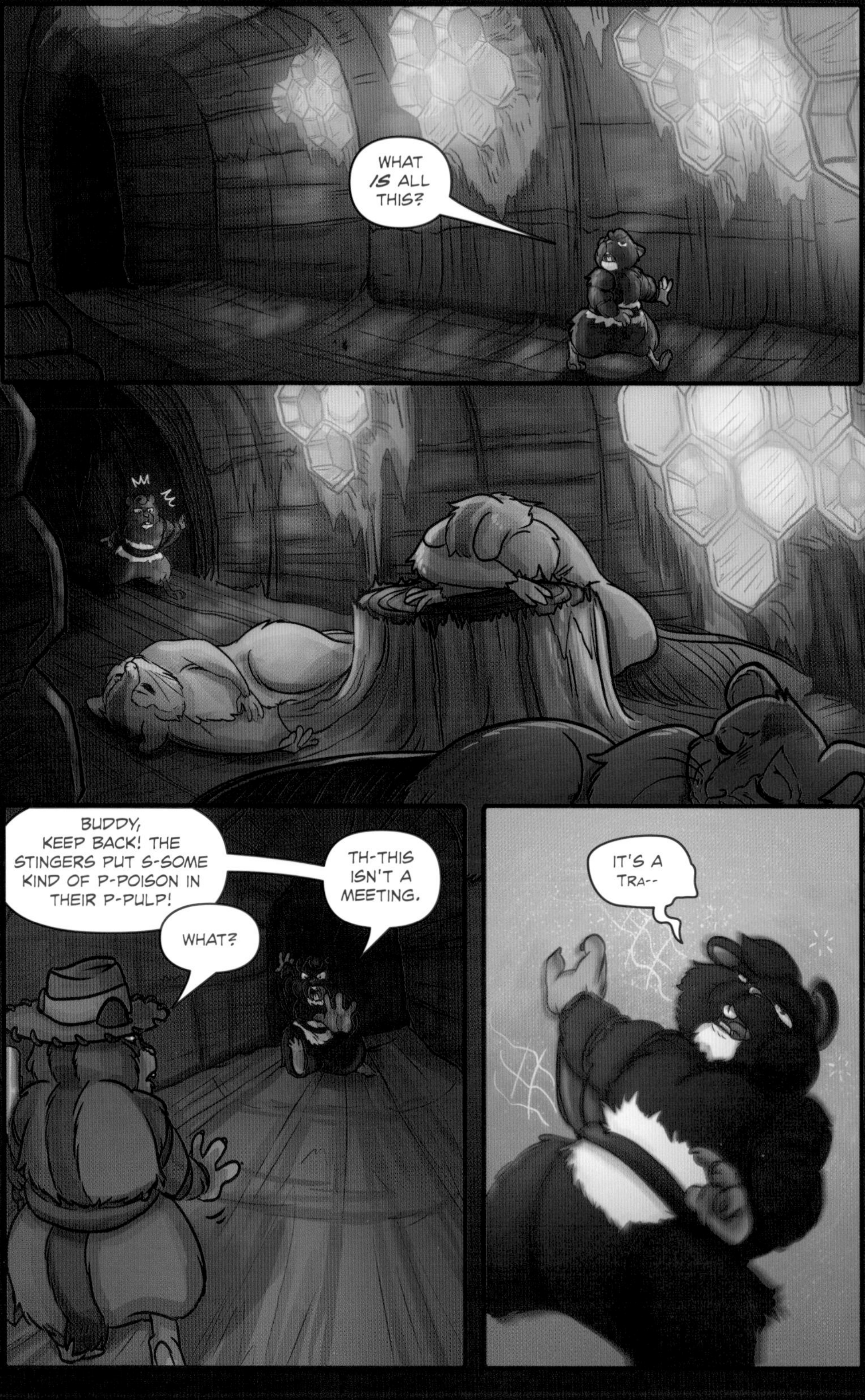
WHAT *IS* ALL THIS?
MM
BUDDY, KEEP BACK! THE STINGERS PUT S-SOME KIND OF P-POISON IN THEIR P-PULP!
TH-THIS ISN'T A MEETING.
WHAT?
IT'S A TRA--

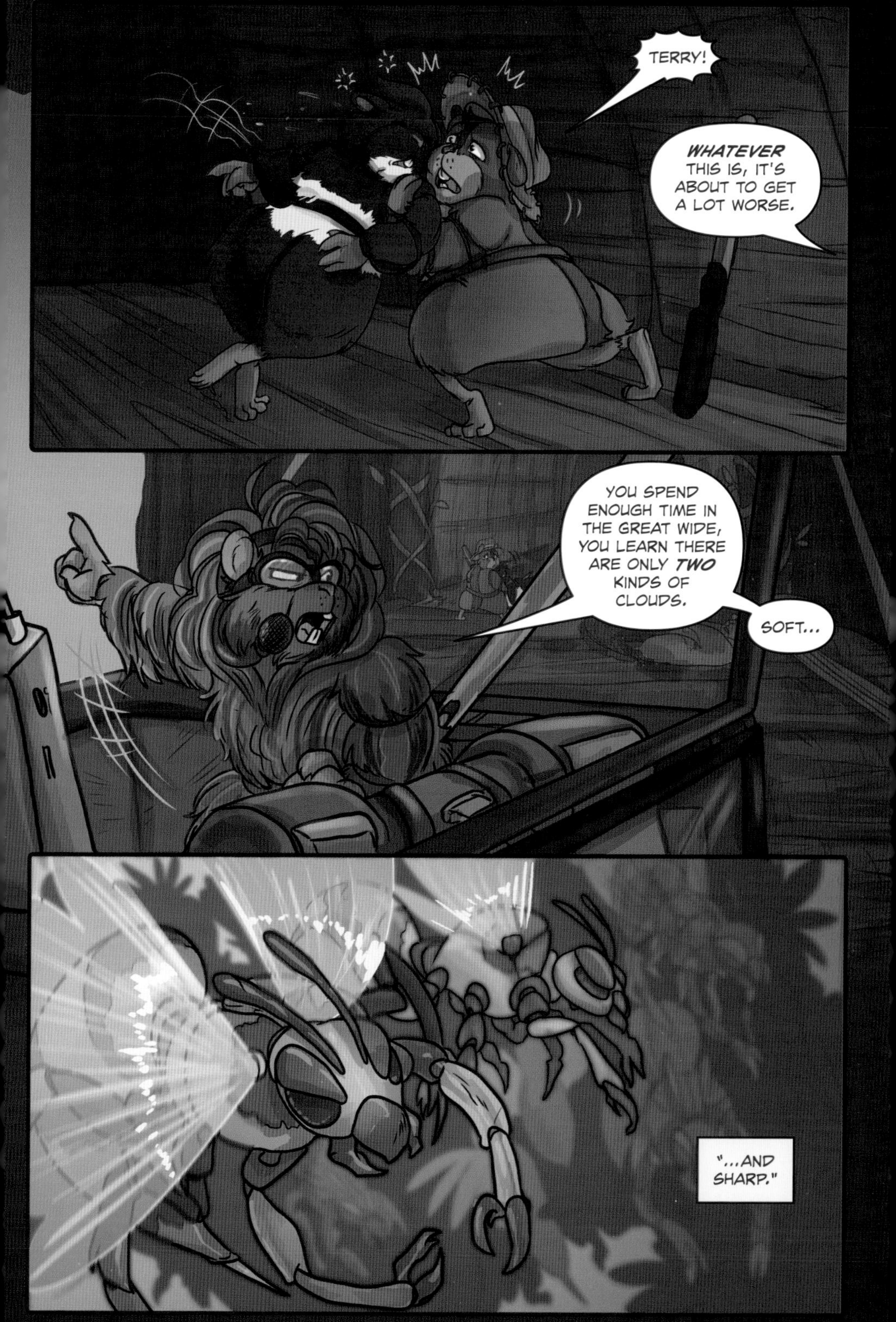
TERRY!
WHATEVER THIS IS, IT'S ABOUT TO GET A LOT WORSE.
YOU SPEND ENOUGH TIME IN THE GREAT WIDE, YOU LEARN THERE ARE ONLY TWO KINDS OF CLOUDS.
SOFT...
"...AND SHARP."

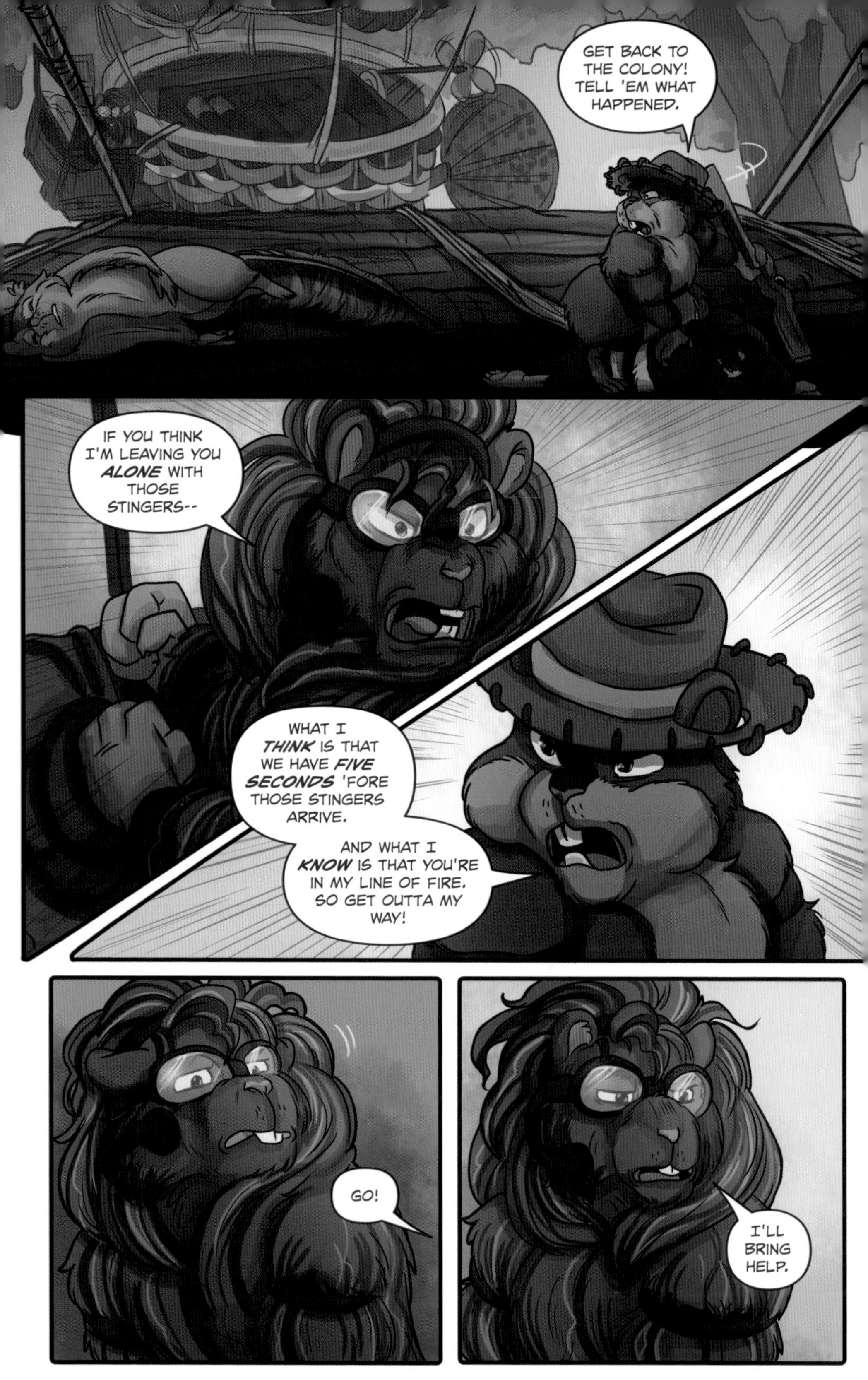
GET BACK TO THE COLONY! TELL 'EM WHAT HAPPENED.
IF YOU THINK I'M LEAVING YOU ALONE WITH THOSE STINGERS--
WHAT I THINK IS THAT WE HAVE FIVE SECONDS 'FORE THOSE STINGERS ARRIVE.
AND WHAT I KNOW IS THAT YOU'RE IN MY LINE OF FIRE. SO GET OUTTA MY WAY!
GO!
I'LL BRING HELP.

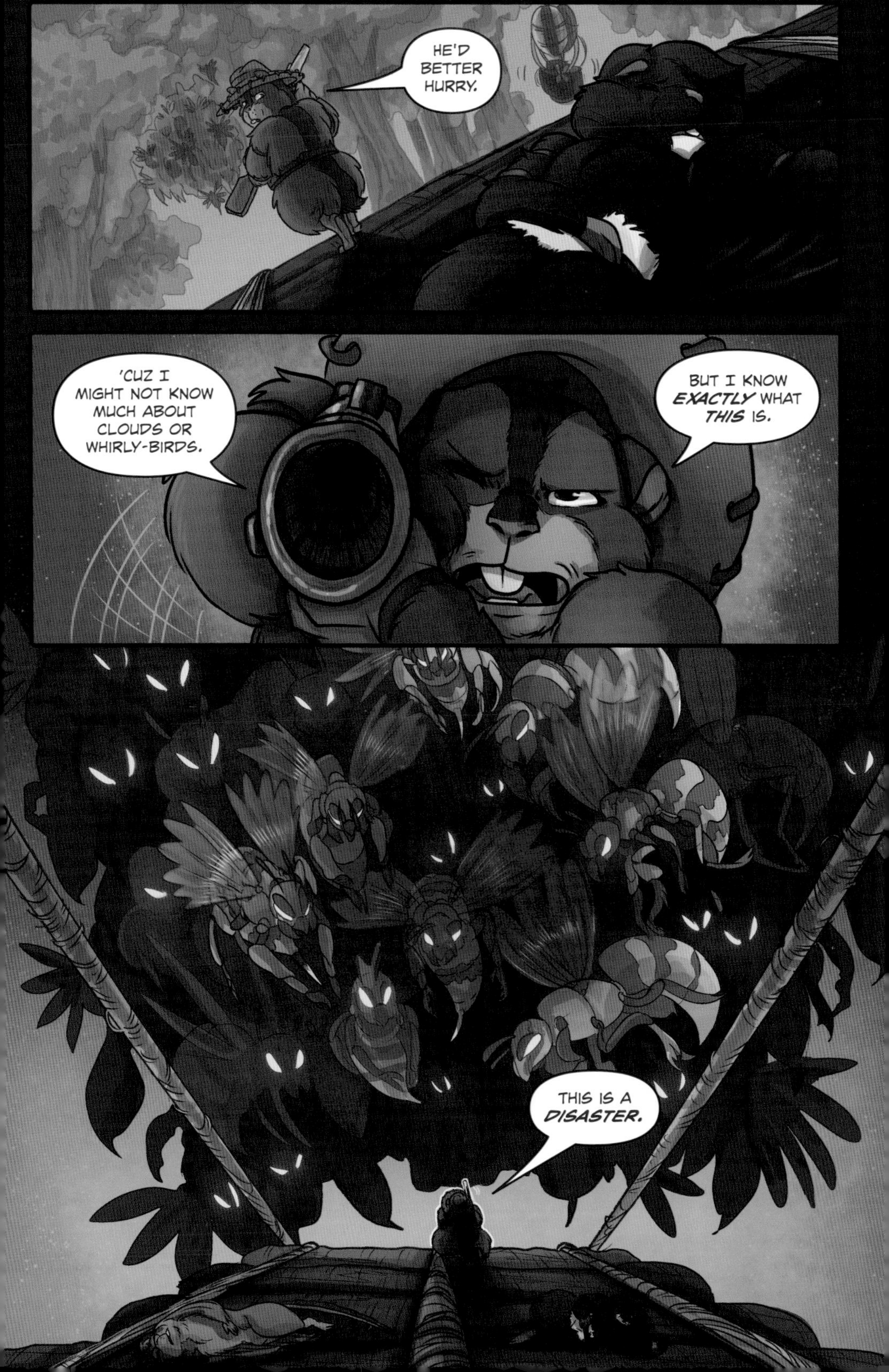
HE'D BETTER HURRY.
'CUZ I MIGHT NOT KNOW MUCH ABOUT CLOUDS OR WHIRLY-BIRDS.
BUT I KNOW *EXACTLY* WHAT *THIS* IS.
THIS IS A *DISASTER.*

Luciana

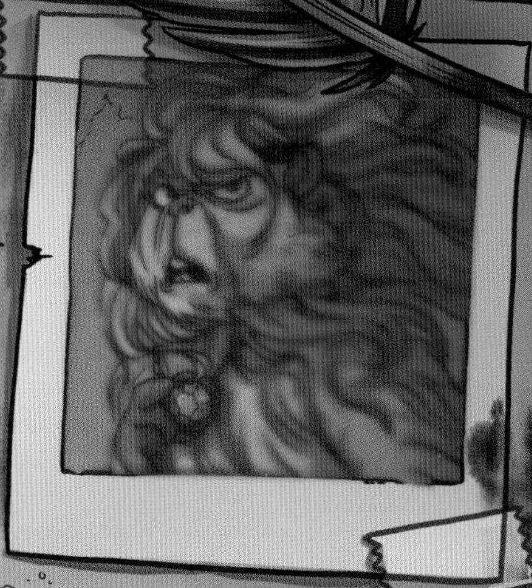

Appearance: Syrian – Teddy Bear (Mesocricetus auratus)
Title: H.A.M. Matriarch
Behavioral Patterns: Practical, authoritative, and exceedingly controlling. Understands sacrifice as necessary for the greater good. Accepts external-species' missions in exchange for future debt collection, i.e., "favors." It is unknown how or when she intends to collect payment.

Notes: Protective inclinations toward offspring at odds with ideology regarding practical use of assets.

Terry

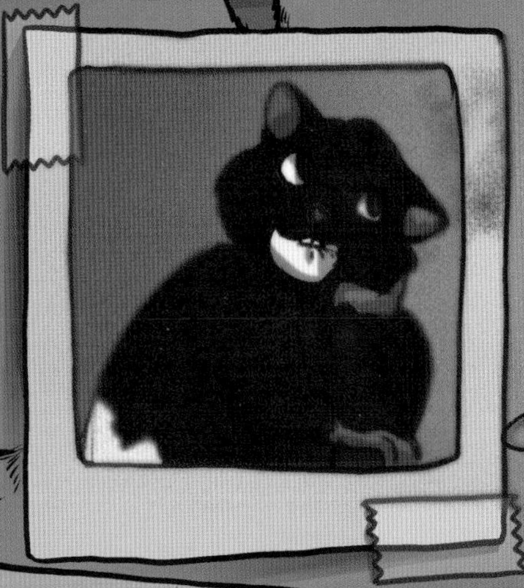

Appearance: Syrian (Mesocricetus auratus)
Title: H.A.P. Sharpshooter
Behavioral Patterns: Very competitive, with the talent to back it up. Cheerful, resourceful. Extraordinarily sharp observational skills and quick wit.

Luciana has requested Terry give a seminar at H.A.M. HQ due to her expertise with "specialized" ammunition.

Notes: Infuriated by injustice. Changes entire demeanor in such situations. Has bonded strongly with Buddy, who is working with H.A.P. temporarily to strengthen cross-team alliance.

Neil

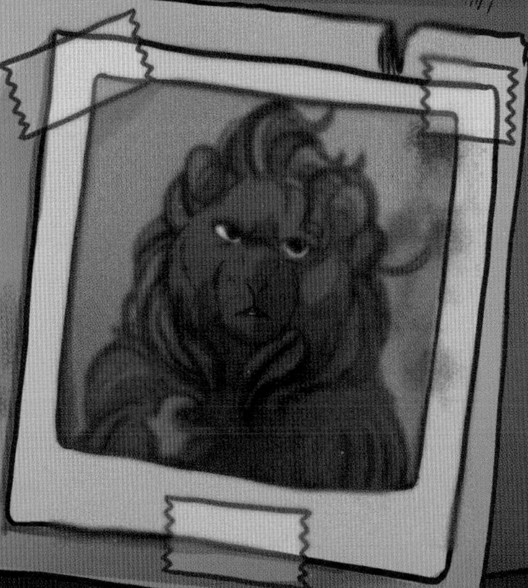

Appearance: Syrian – Teddy Bear (Mesocricetus auratus)
Title: H.A.P. Pilot
Behavioral Patterns: Adventurous, fearless. Has a focused enthusiasm for minutia of flying machines and controls. Neil is at such ease in the Great Wide that one could believe he is related to the Feathers. Currently teaching Ives how to pilot a whirly-bird.

Notes: When not flying, favorite hobby is reading in The Archives.

H.A.M. pups now emulating his hair.

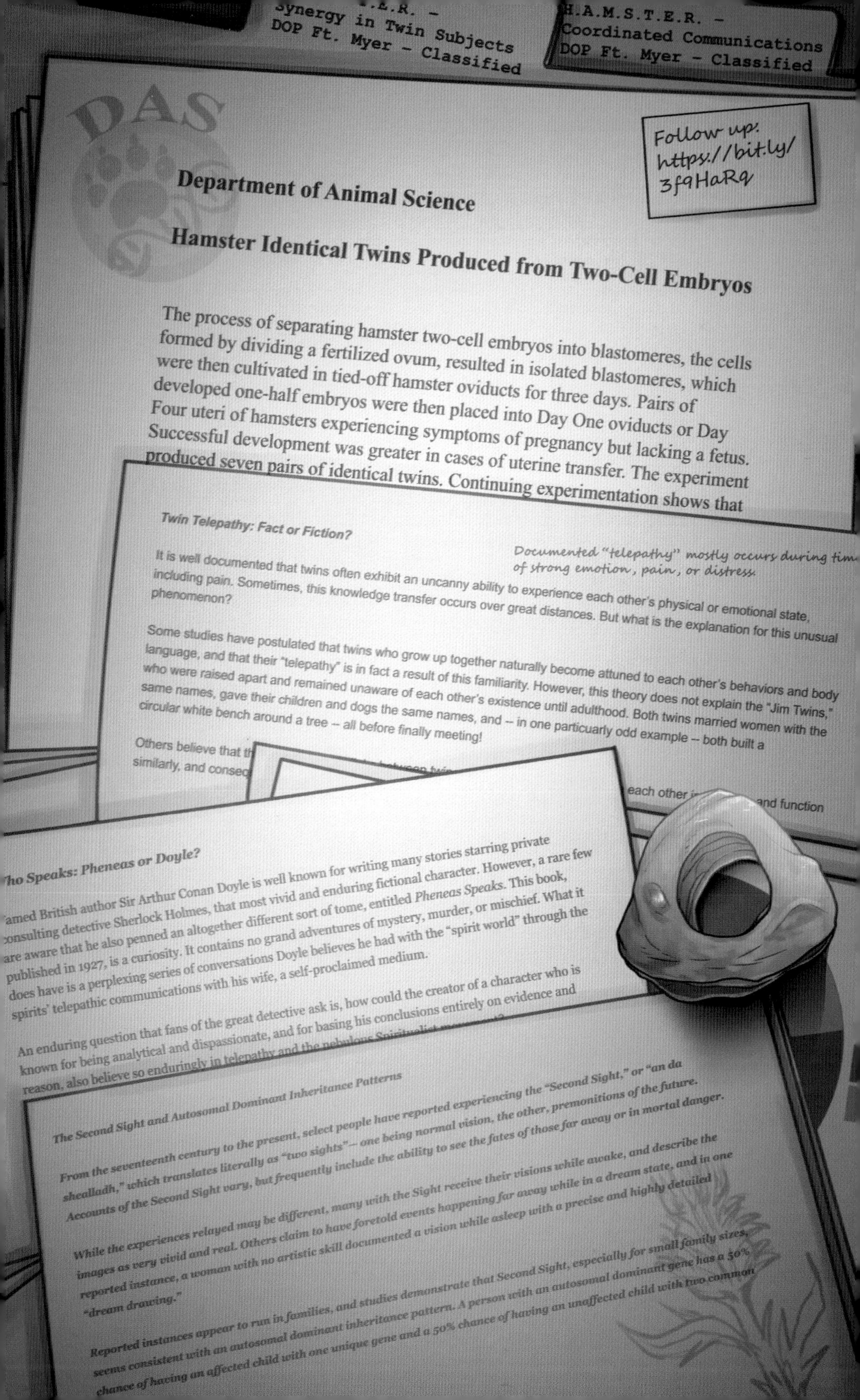

Synergy in Twin Subjects
DOP Ft. Myer - Classified
H.A.M.S.T.E.R. -
Coordinated Communications
DOP Ft. Myer - Classified
DAS
Follow up: https://bit.ly/3f9HaRq
Department of Animal Science
Hamster Identical Twins Produced from Two-Cell Embryos
The process of separating hamster two-cell embryos into blastomeres, the cells formed by dividing a fertilized ovum, resulted in isolated blastomeres, which were then cultivated in tied-off hamster oviducts for three days. Pairs of developed one-half embryos were then placed into Day One oviducts or Day Four uteri of hamsters experiencing symptoms of pregnancy but lacking a fetus. Successful development was greater in cases of uterine transfer. The experiment produced seven pairs of identical twins. Continuing experimentation shows that
Twin Telepathy: Fact or Fiction?
Documented "telepathy" mostly occurs during tim
of strong emotion, pain, or distress.
It is well documented that twins often exhibit an uncanny ability to experience each other's physical or emotional state, including pain. Sometimes, this knowledge transfer occurs over great distances. But what is the explanation for this unusual phenomenon?
Some studies have postulated that twins who grow up together naturally become attuned to each other's behaviors and body language, and that their "telepathy" is in fact a result of this familiarity. However, this theory does not explain the "Jim Twins," who were raised apart and remained unaware of each other's existence until adulthood. Both twins married women with the same names, gave their children and dogs the same names, and -- in one particularly odd example -- both built a circular white bench around a tree -- all before finally meeting!
Others believe that th
similarly, and conseq
each other
and function
Who Speaks: Pheneas or Doyle?
amed British author Sir Arthur Conan Doyle is well known for writing many stories starring private consulting detective Sherlock Holmes, that most vivid and enduring fictional character. However, a rare few are aware that he also penned an altogether different sort of tome, entitled Pheneas Speaks. This book, published in 1927, is a curiosity. It contains no grand adventures of mystery, murder, or mischief. What it does have is a perplexing series of conversations Doyle believes he had with the "spirit world" through the spirits' telepathic communications with his wife, a self-proclaimed medium.
An enduring question that fans of the great detective ask is, how could the creator of a character who is known for being analytical and dispassionate, and for basing his conclusions entirely on evidence and reason, also believe so enduringly in telepathy and the nebulous Spiritualist
The Second Sight and Autosomal Dominant Inheritance Patterns
From the seventeenth century to the present, select people have reported experiencing the "Second Sight," or "an da shealladh," which translates literally as "two sights"-- one being normal vision, the other, premonitions of the future. Accounts of the Second Sight vary, but frequently include the ability to see the fates of those far away or in mortal danger.
While the experiences relayed may be different, many with the Sight receive their visions while awake, and describe the images as very vivid and real. Others claim to have foretold events happening far away while in a dream state, and in one reported instance, a woman with no artistic skill documented a vision while asleep with a precise and highly detailed "dream drawing."
Reported instances appear to run in families, and studies demonstrate that Second Sight, especially for small family sizes, seems consistent with an autosomal dominant inheritance pattern. A person with an autosomal dominant gene has a 50% chance of having an affected child with one unique gene and a 50% chance of having an unaffected child with two common

CHAPTER TWO

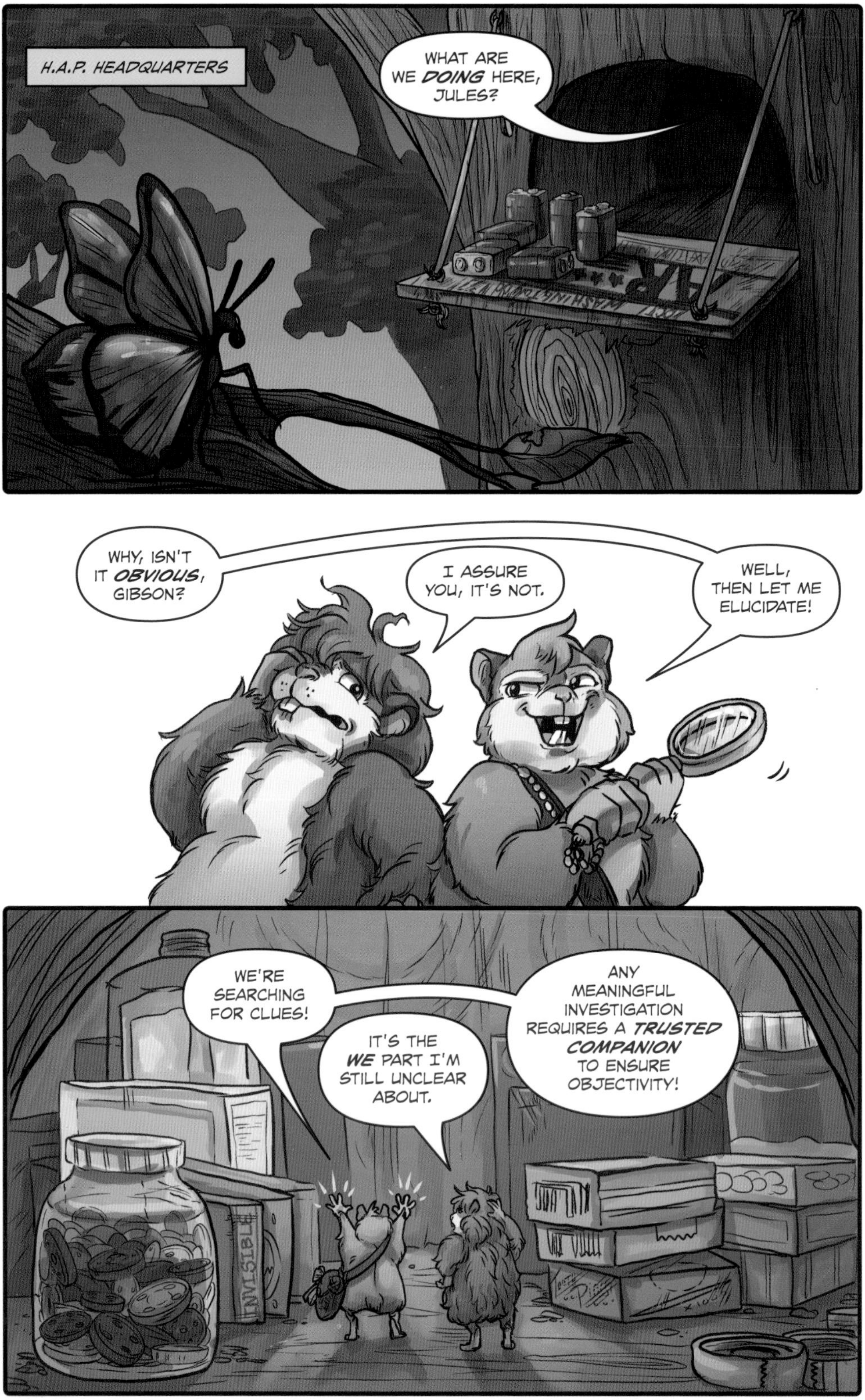
H.A.P. HEADQUARTERS
WHAT ARE WE DOING HERE, JULES?
WHY, ISN'T IT OBVIOUS, GIBSON?
I ASSURE YOU, IT'S NOT.
WELL, THEN LET ME ELUCIDATE!
WE'RE SEARCHING FOR CLUES!
IT'S THE WE PART I'M STILL UNCLEAR ABOUT.
ANY MEANINGFUL INVESTIGATION REQUIRES A TRUSTED COMPANION TO ENSURE OBJECTIVITY!
INVISIBLE

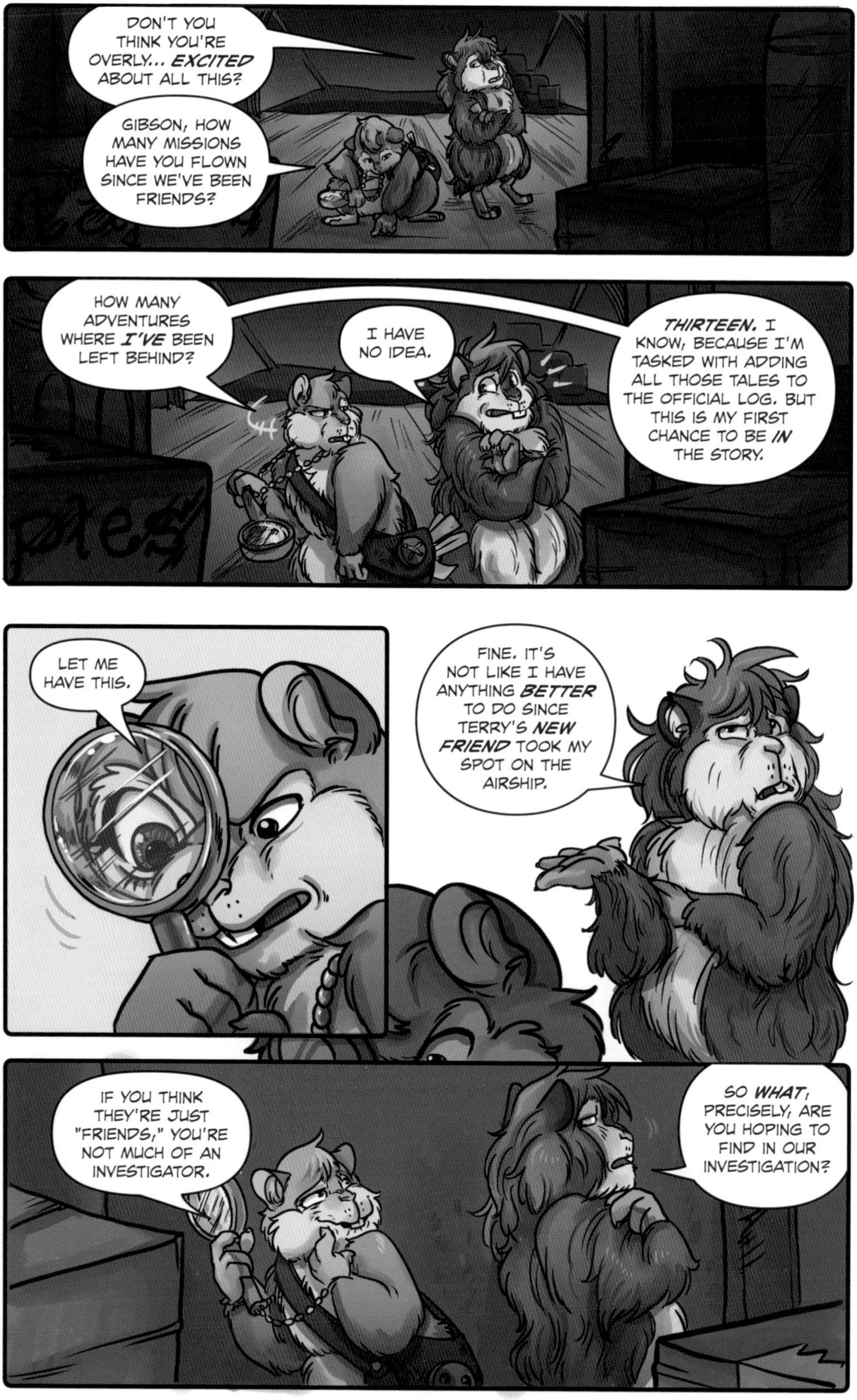
DON'T YOU THINK YOU'RE OVERLY... EXCITED ABOUT ALL THIS?
GIBSON, HOW MANY MISSIONS HAVE YOU FLOWN SINCE WE'VE BEEN FRIENDS?
HOW MANY ADVENTURES WHERE I'VE BEEN LEFT BEHIND?
I HAVE NO IDEA.
THIRTEEN. I KNOW, BECAUSE I'M TASKED WITH ADDING ALL THOSE TALES TO THE OFFICIAL LOG. BUT THIS IS MY FIRST CHANCE TO BE IN THE STORY.
LET ME HAVE THIS.
FINE. IT'S NOT LIKE I HAVE ANYTHING BETTER TO DO SINCE TERRY'S NEW FRIEND TOOK MY SPOT ON THE AIRSHIP.
IF YOU THINK THEY'RE JUST "FRIENDS," YOU'RE NOT MUCH OF AN INVESTIGATOR.
SO WHAT, PRECISELY, ARE YOU HOPING TO FIND IN OUR INVESTIGATION?

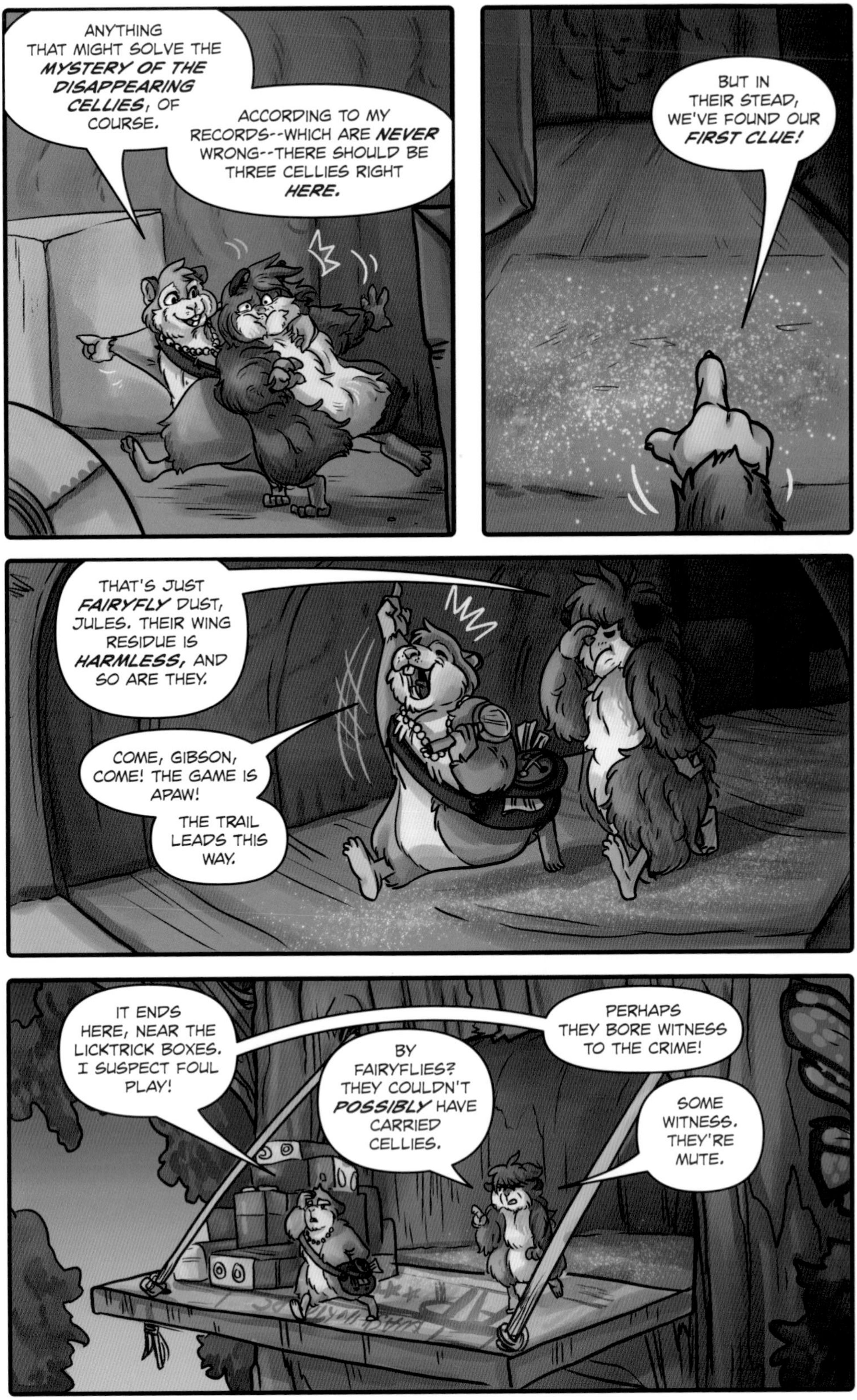
ANYTHING THAT MIGHT SOLVE THE MYSTERY OF THE DISAPPEARING CELLIES, OF COURSE.
ACCORDING TO MY RECORDS--WHICH ARE NEVER WRONG--THERE SHOULD BE THREE CELLIES RIGHT HERE.
BUT IN THEIR STEAD, WE'VE FOUND OUR FIRST CLUE!
THAT'S JUST FAIRYFLY DUST, JULES. THEIR WING RESIDUE IS HARMLESS, AND SO ARE THEY.
COME, GIBSON, COME! THE GAME IS APAW!
THE TRAIL LEADS THIS WAY.
IT ENDS HERE, NEAR THE LICKTRICK BOXES. I SUSPECT FOUL PLAY!
PERHAPS THEY BORE WITNESS TO THE CRIME!
BY FAIRYFLIES? THEY COULDN'T POSSIBLY HAVE CARRIED CELLIES.
SOME WITNESS. THEY'RE MUTE.

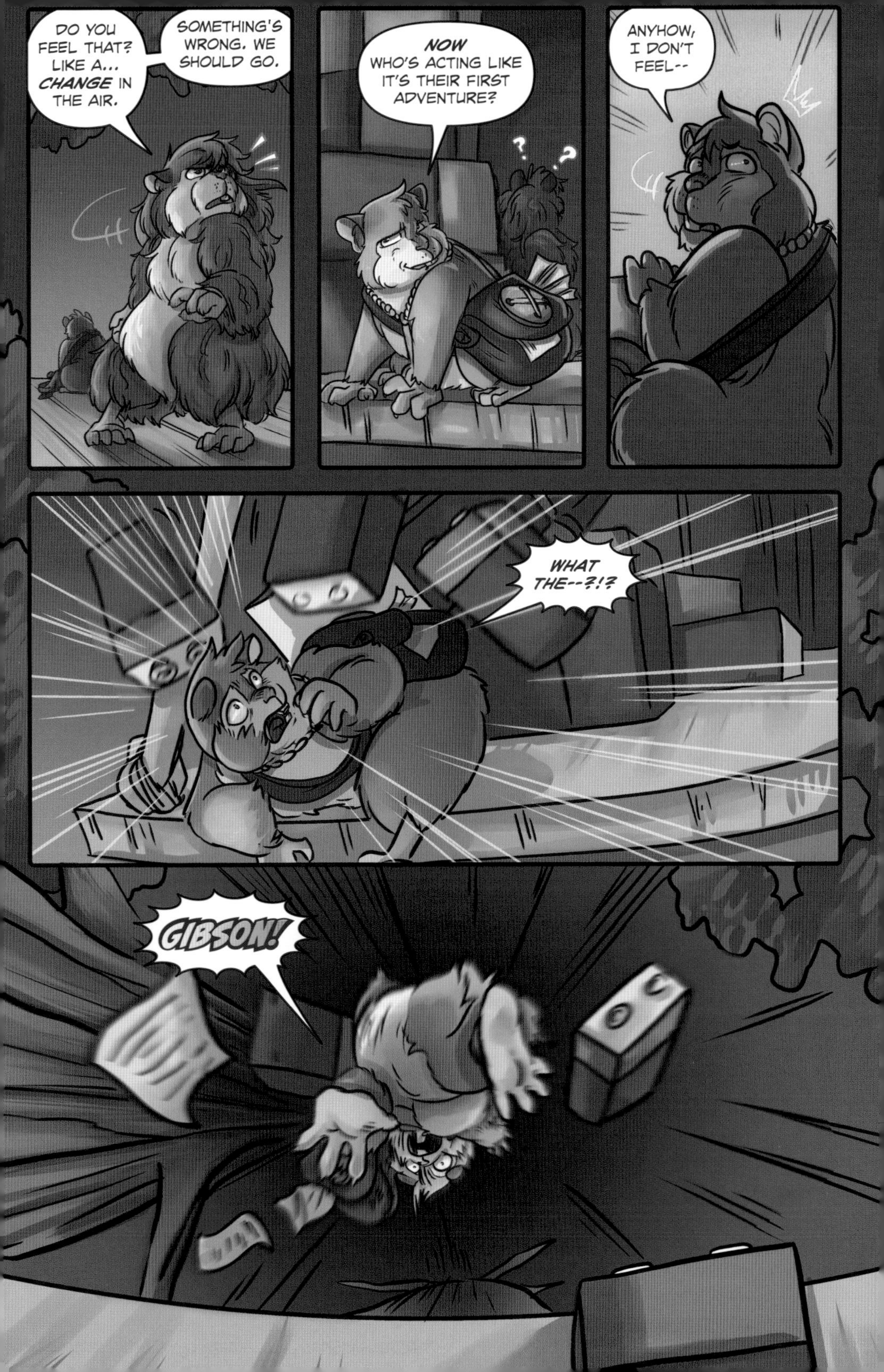
DO YOU FEEL THAT? LIKE A... CHANGE IN THE AIR.
SOMETHING'S WRONG. WE SHOULD GO.
NOW WHO'S ACTING LIKE IT'S THEIR FIRST ADVENTURE?
ANYHOW, I DON'T FEEL--
WHAT THE--?!?
GIBSON!

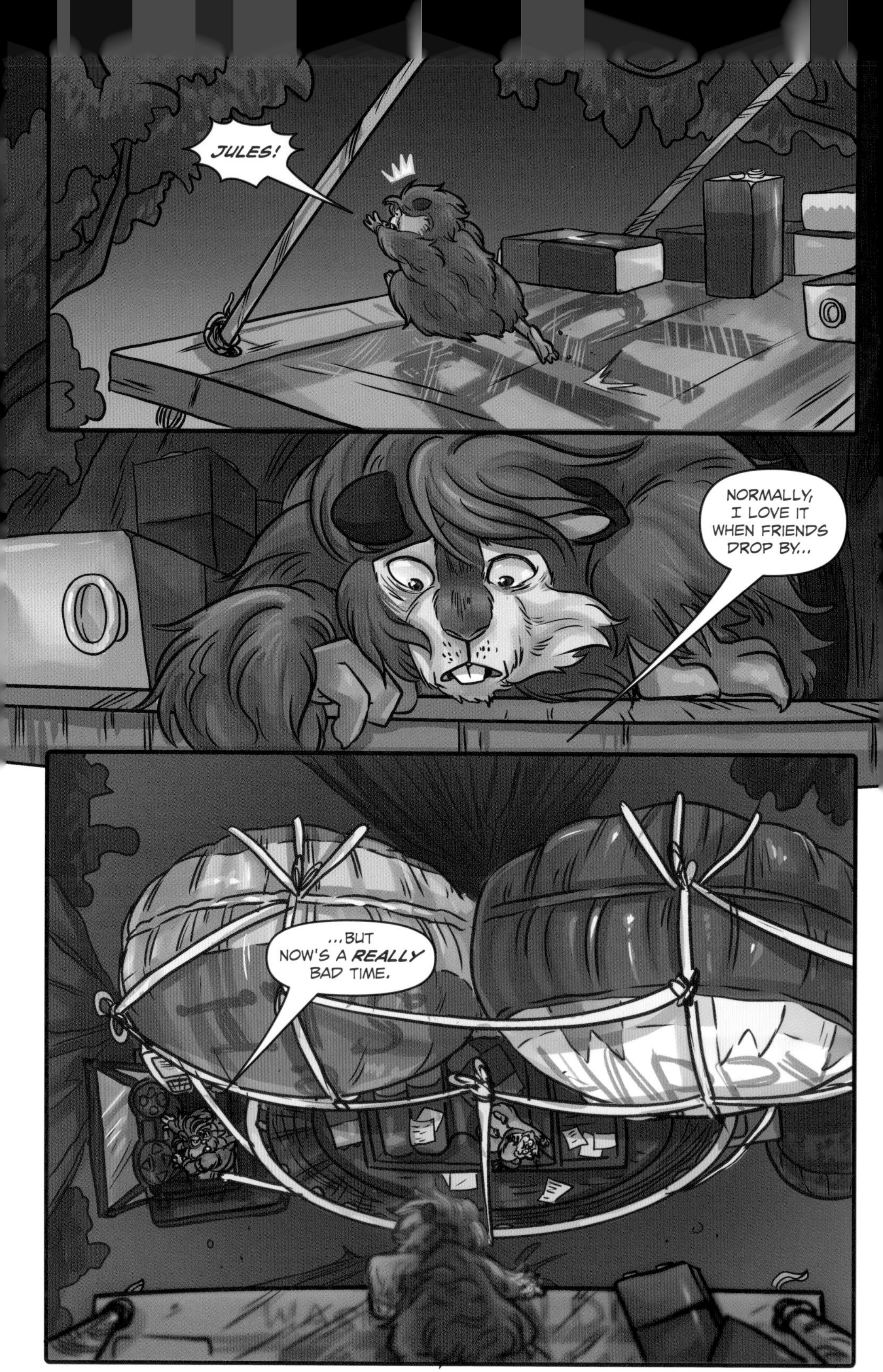
JULES!
NORMALLY, I LOVE IT WHEN FRIENDS DROP BY...
...BUT NOW'S A ***REALLY*** BAD TIME.

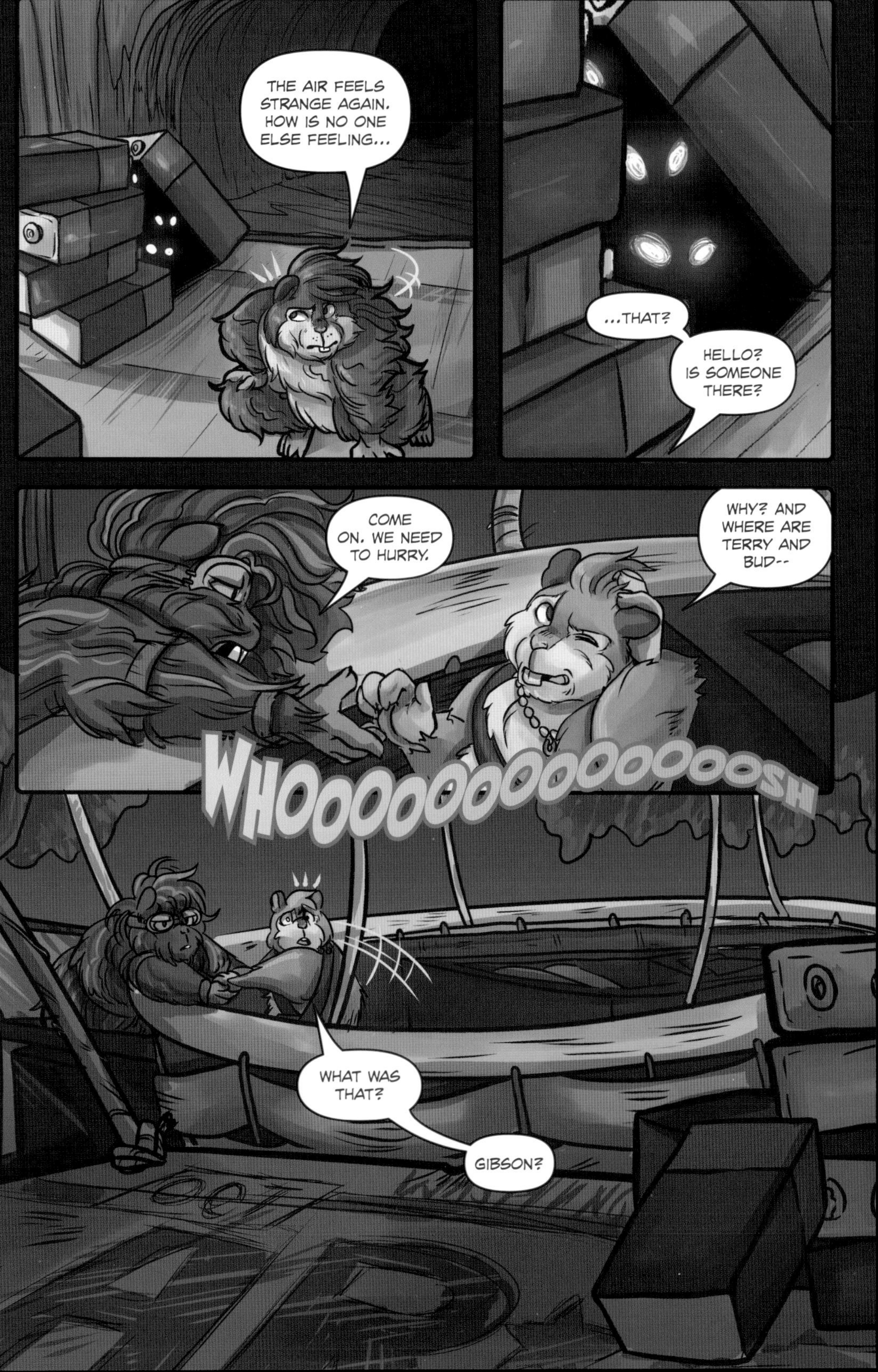
THE AIR FEELS STRANGE AGAIN. HOW IS NO ONE ELSE FEELING...
...THAT?
HELLO? IS SOMEONE THERE?
COME ON. WE NEED TO HURRY.
WHY? AND WHERE ARE TERRY AND BUD--
WHOOOOOOOOOOOOOOOSH
WHAT WAS THAT?
GIBSON?

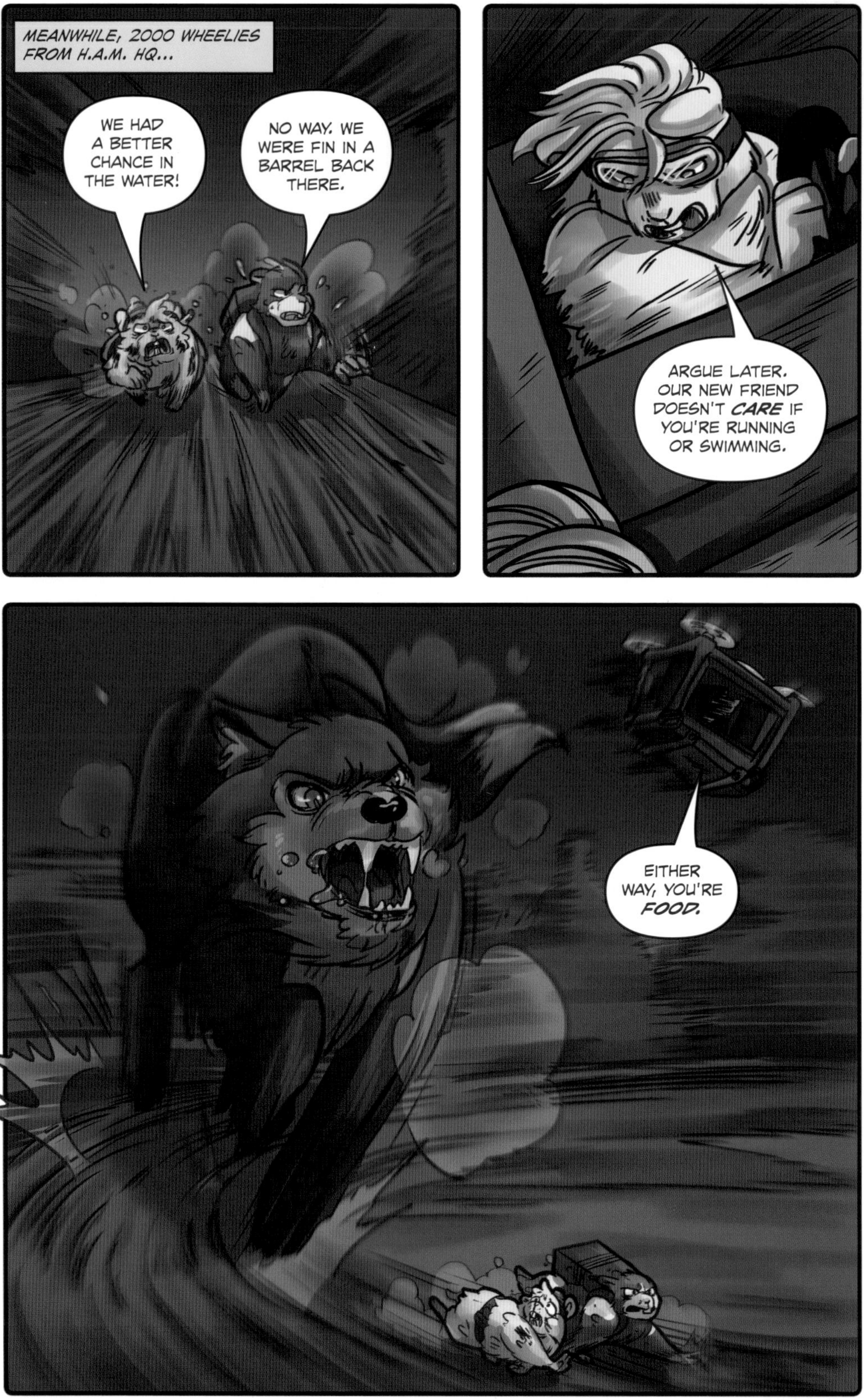
MEANWHILE, 2000 WHEELIES FROM H.A.M. HQ...
WE HAD A BETTER CHANCE IN THE WATER!
NO WAY. WE WERE FIN IN A BARREL BACK THERE.
ARGUE LATER. OUR NEW FRIEND DOESN'T *CARE* IF YOU'RE RUNNING OR SWIMMING.
EITHER WAY, YOU'RE *FOOD.*

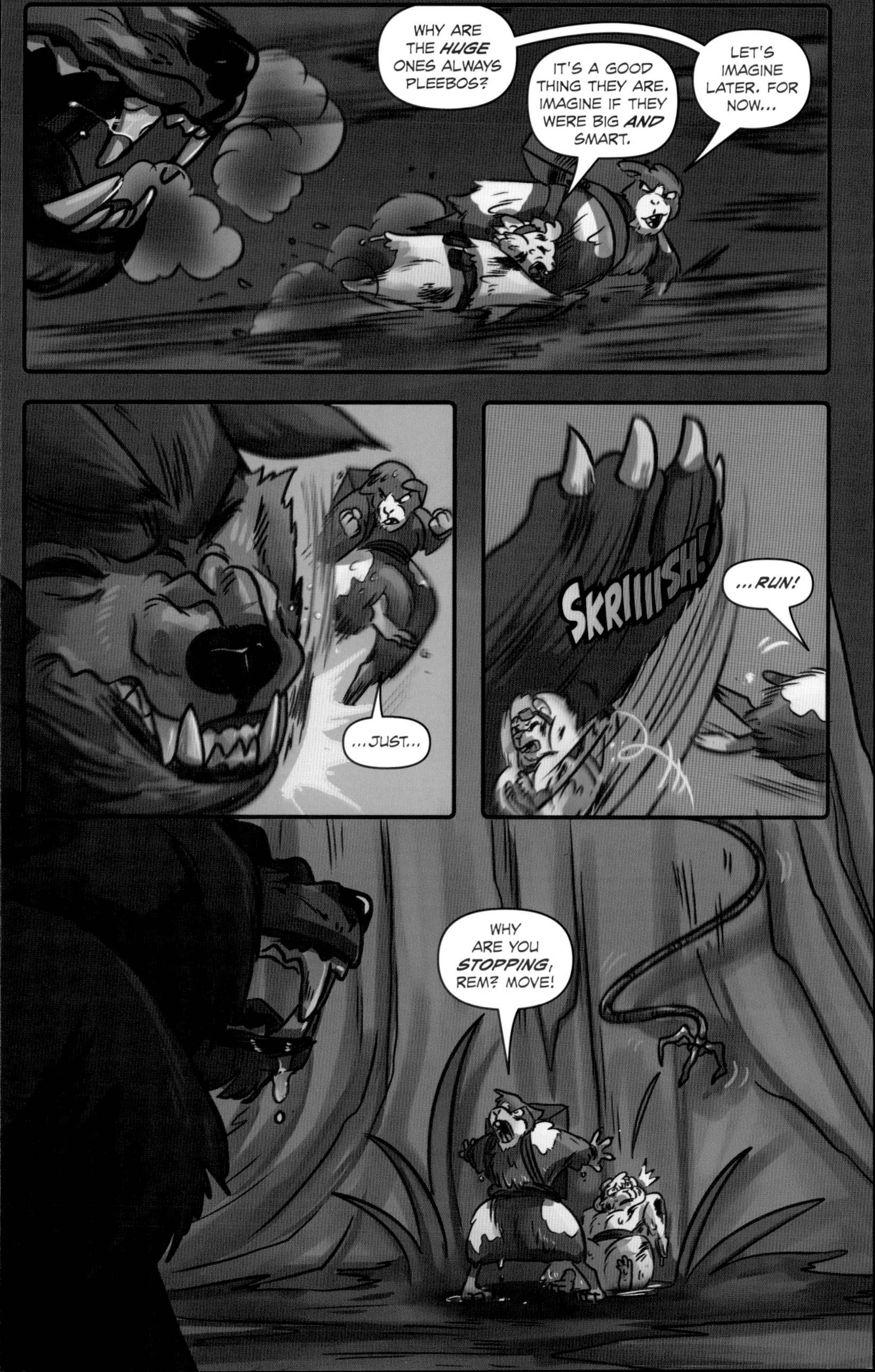
WHY ARE THE HUGE ONES ALWAYS PLEEBOS?
IT'S A GOOD THING THEY ARE. IMAGINE IF THEY WERE BIG AND SMART.
LET'S IMAGINE LATER. FOR NOW...
...JUST...
SKRIIIISH!
...RUN!
WHY ARE YOU STOPPING, REM? MOVE!

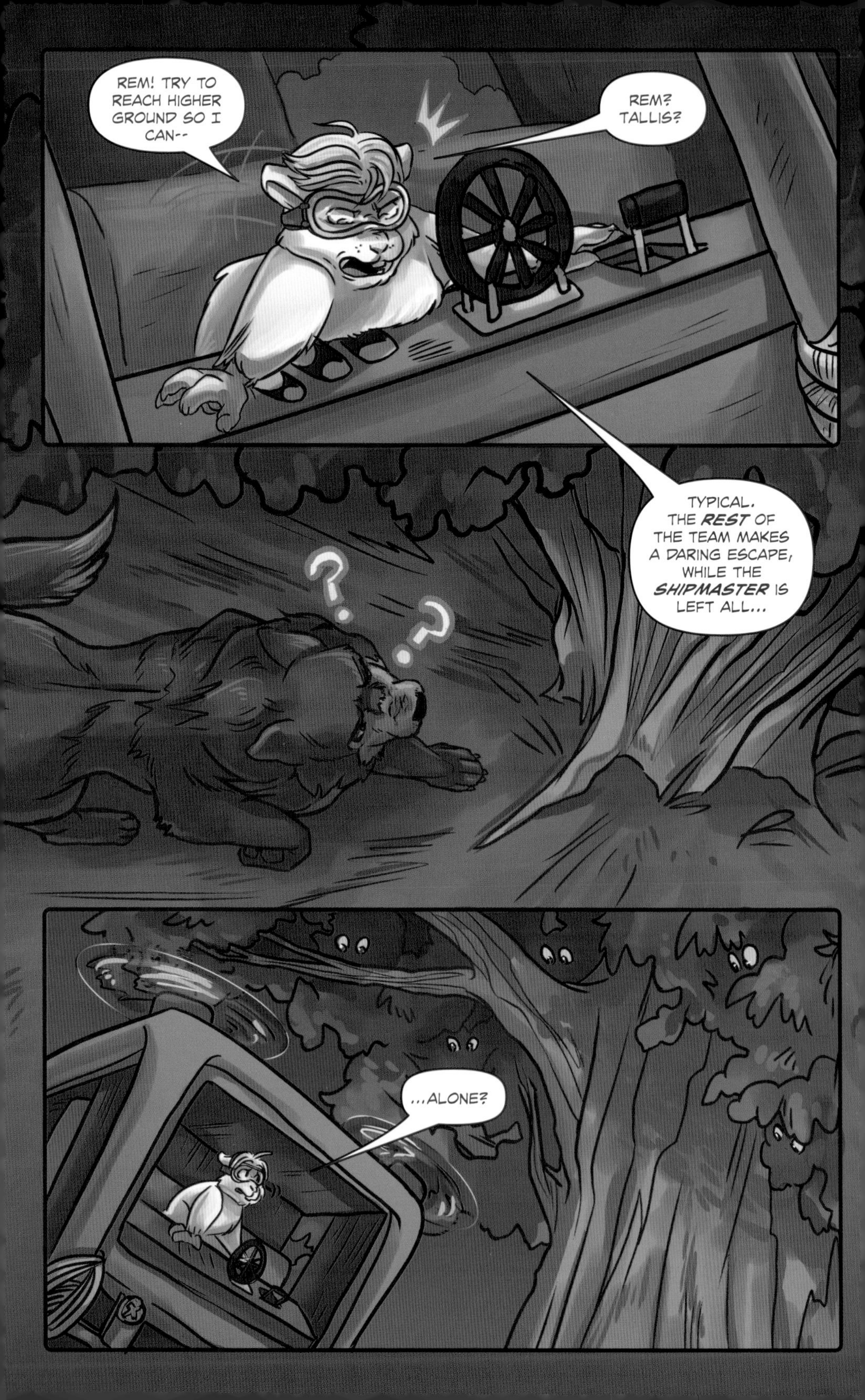
REM! TRY TO REACH HIGHER GROUND SO I CAN--
REM? TALLIS?
TYPICAL. THE REST OF THE TEAM MAKES A DARING ESCAPE, WHILE THE SHIPMASTER IS LEFT ALL...
...ALONE?

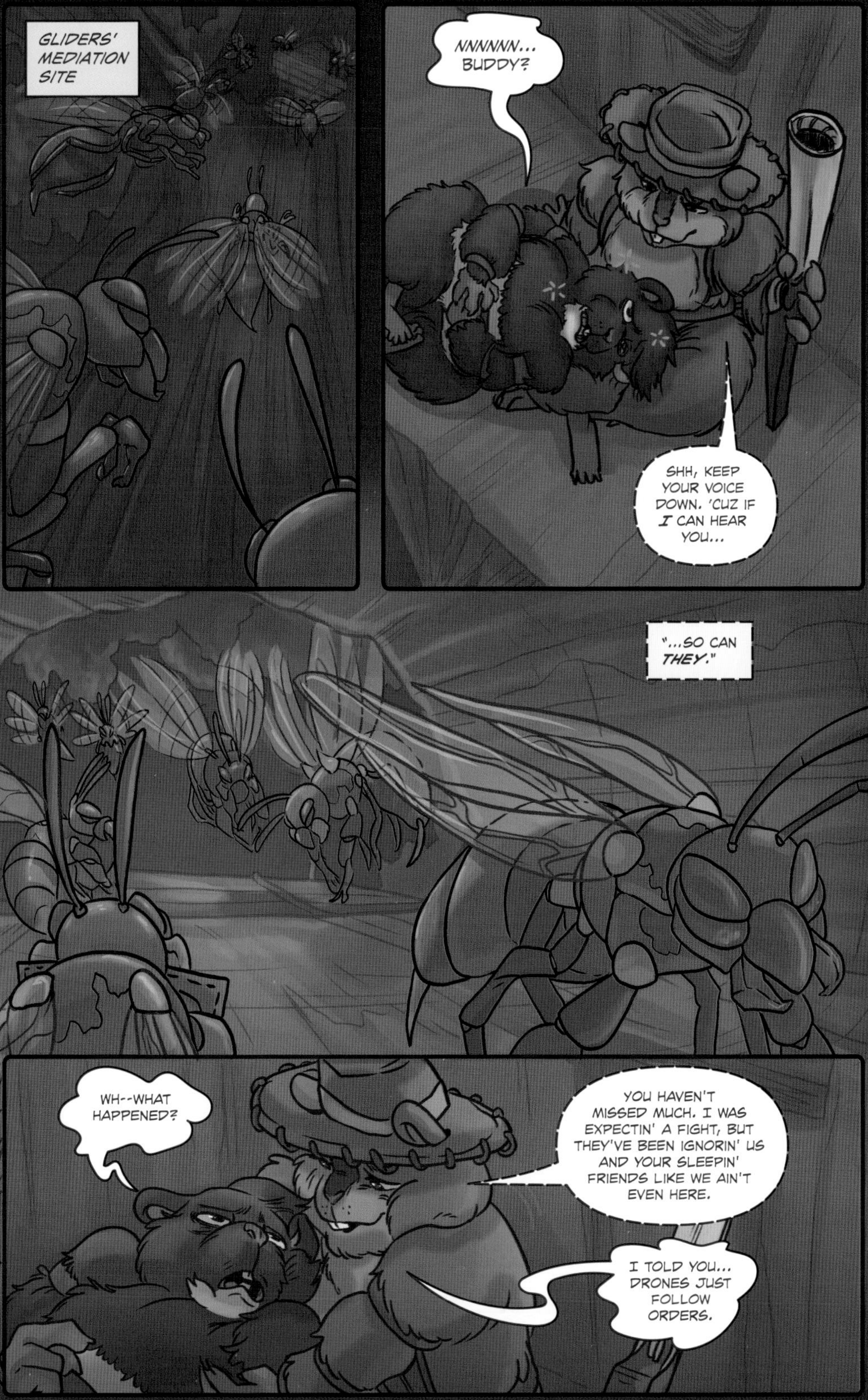
GLIDERS' MEDIATION SITE
NNNNNN... BUDDY?
SHH, KEEP YOUR VOICE DOWN. 'CUZ IF I CAN HEAR YOU...
"...SO CAN THEY."
WH--WHAT HAPPENED?
YOU HAVEN'T MISSED MUCH. I WAS EXPECTIN' A FIGHT, BUT THEY'VE BEEN IGNORIN' US AND YOUR SLEEPIN' FRIENDS LIKE WE AIN'T EVEN HERE.
I TOLD YOU... DRONES JUST FOLLOW ORDERS.

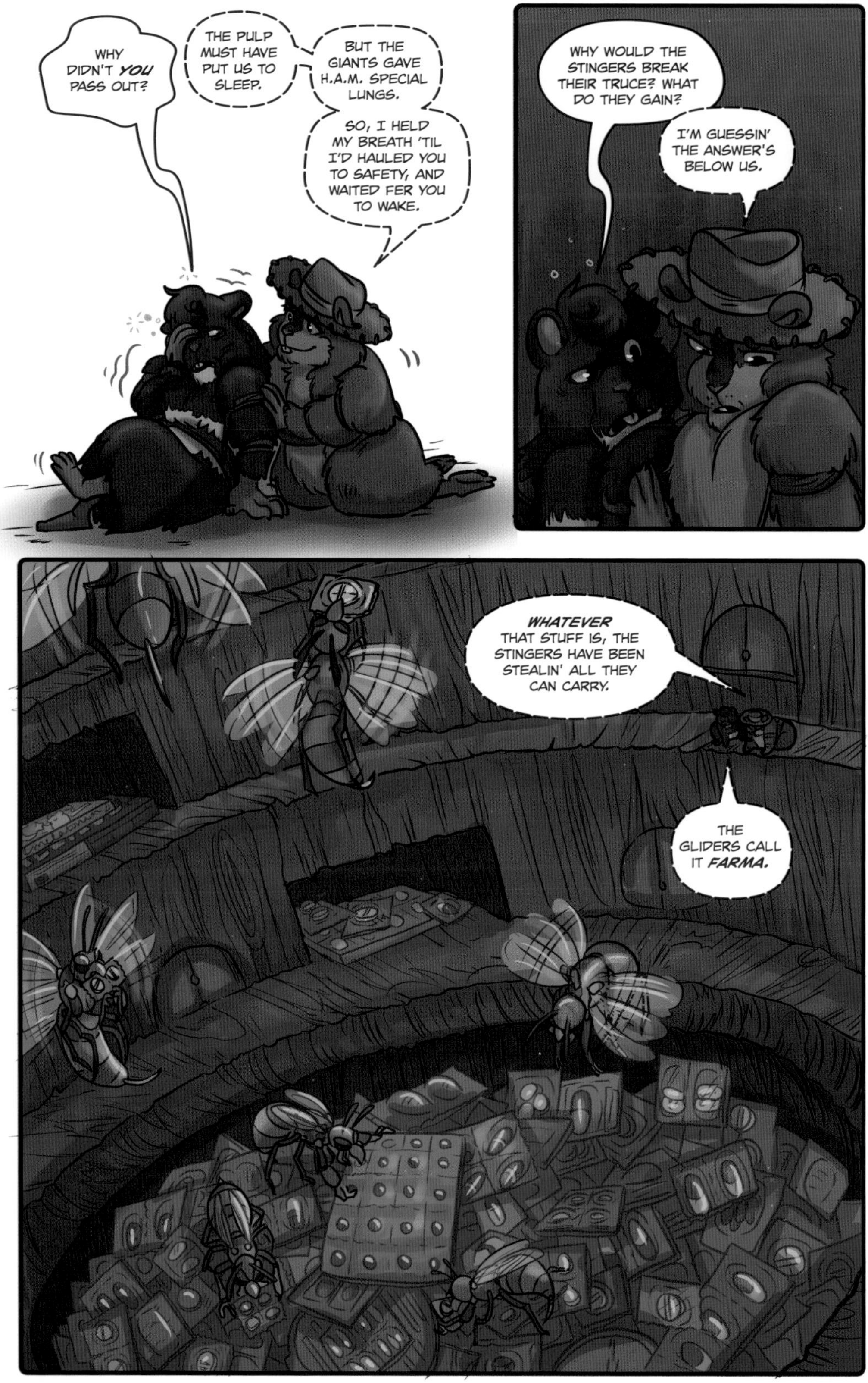
WHY DIDN'T *YOU* PASS OUT?
THE PULP MUST HAVE PUT US TO SLEEP.
BUT THE GIANTS GAVE H.A.M. SPECIAL LUNGS.
SO, I HELD MY BREATH 'TIL I'D HAULED YOU TO SAFETY, AND WAITED FER YOU TO WAKE.
WHY WOULD THE STINGERS BREAK THEIR TRUCE? WHAT DO THEY GAIN?
I'M GUESSIN' THE ANSWER'S *BELOW US.*
WHATEVER THAT STUFF IS, THE STINGERS HAVE BEEN STEALIN' ALL THEY CAN CARRY.
THE GLIDERS CALL IT ***FARMA.***

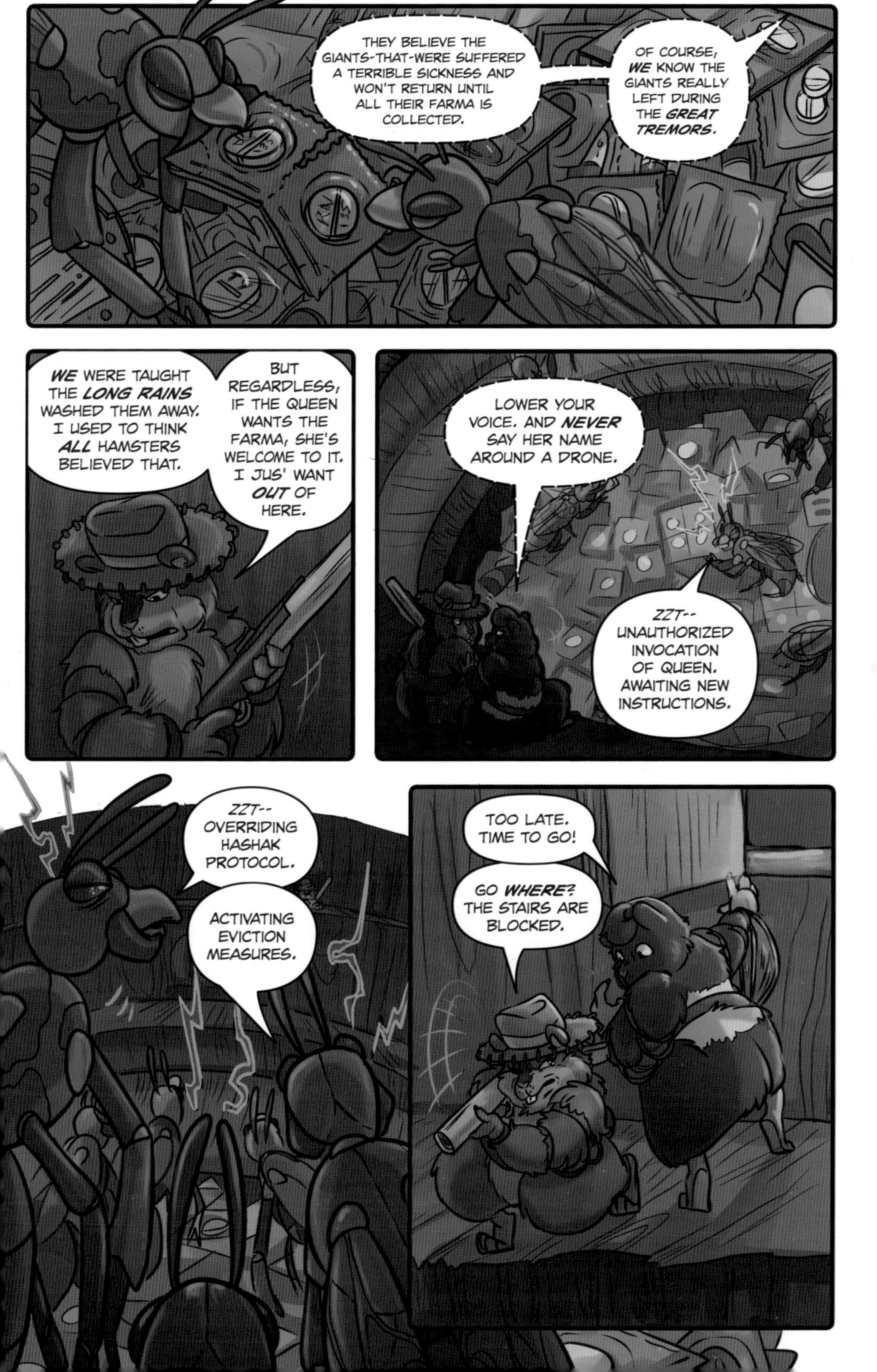
THEY BELIEVE THE GIANTS-THAT-WERE SUFFERED A TERRIBLE SICKNESS AND WON'T RETURN UNTIL ALL THEIR FARMA IS COLLECTED.
OF COURSE, *WE* KNOW THE GIANTS REALLY LEFT DURING THE *GREAT TREMORS.*
WE WERE TAUGHT THE *LONG RAINS* WASHED THEM AWAY. I USED TO THINK *ALL* HAMSTERS BELIEVED THAT.
BUT REGARDLESS, IF THE QUEEN WANTS THE FARMA, SHE'S WELCOME TO IT. I JUS' WANT *OUT* OF HERE.
LOWER YOUR VOICE. AND *NEVER* SAY HER NAME AROUND A DRONE.
ZZT-- UNAUTHORIZED INVOCATION OF QUEEN. AWAITING NEW INSTRUCTIONS.
ZZT-- OVERRIDING HASHAK PROTOCOL.
ACTIVATING EVICTION MEASURES.
TOO LATE. TIME TO GO!
GO *WHERE?* THE STAIRS ARE BLOCKED.

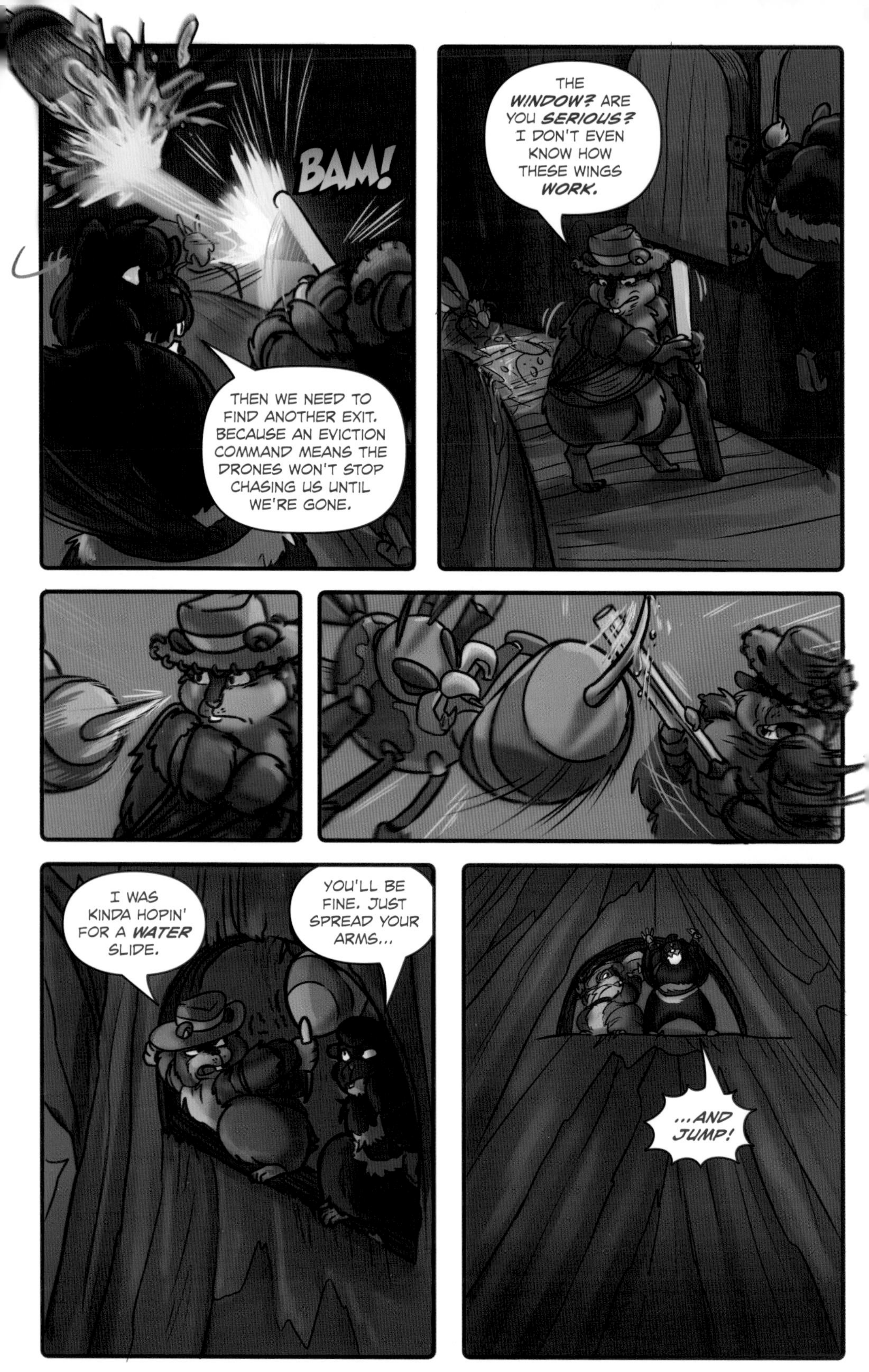
BAM!
THEN WE NEED TO FIND ANOTHER EXIT. BECAUSE AN EVICTION COMMAND MEANS THE DRONES WON'T STOP CHASING US UNTIL WE'RE GONE.
THE WINDOW? ARE YOU SERIOUS? I DON'T EVEN KNOW HOW THESE WINGS WORK.
I WAS KINDA HOPIN' FOR A WATER SLIDE.
YOU'LL BE FINE. JUST SPREAD YOUR ARMS...
...AND JUMP!

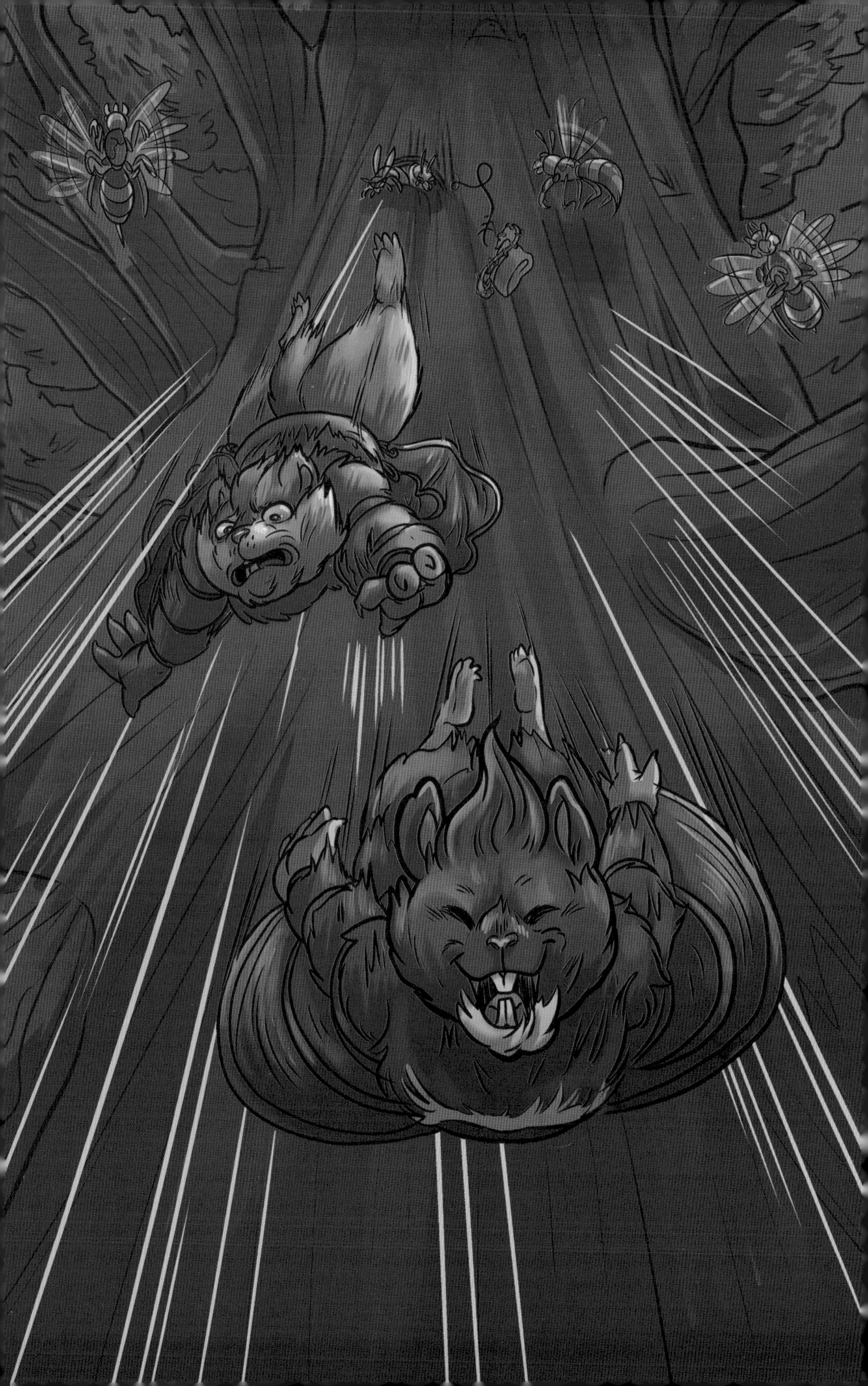

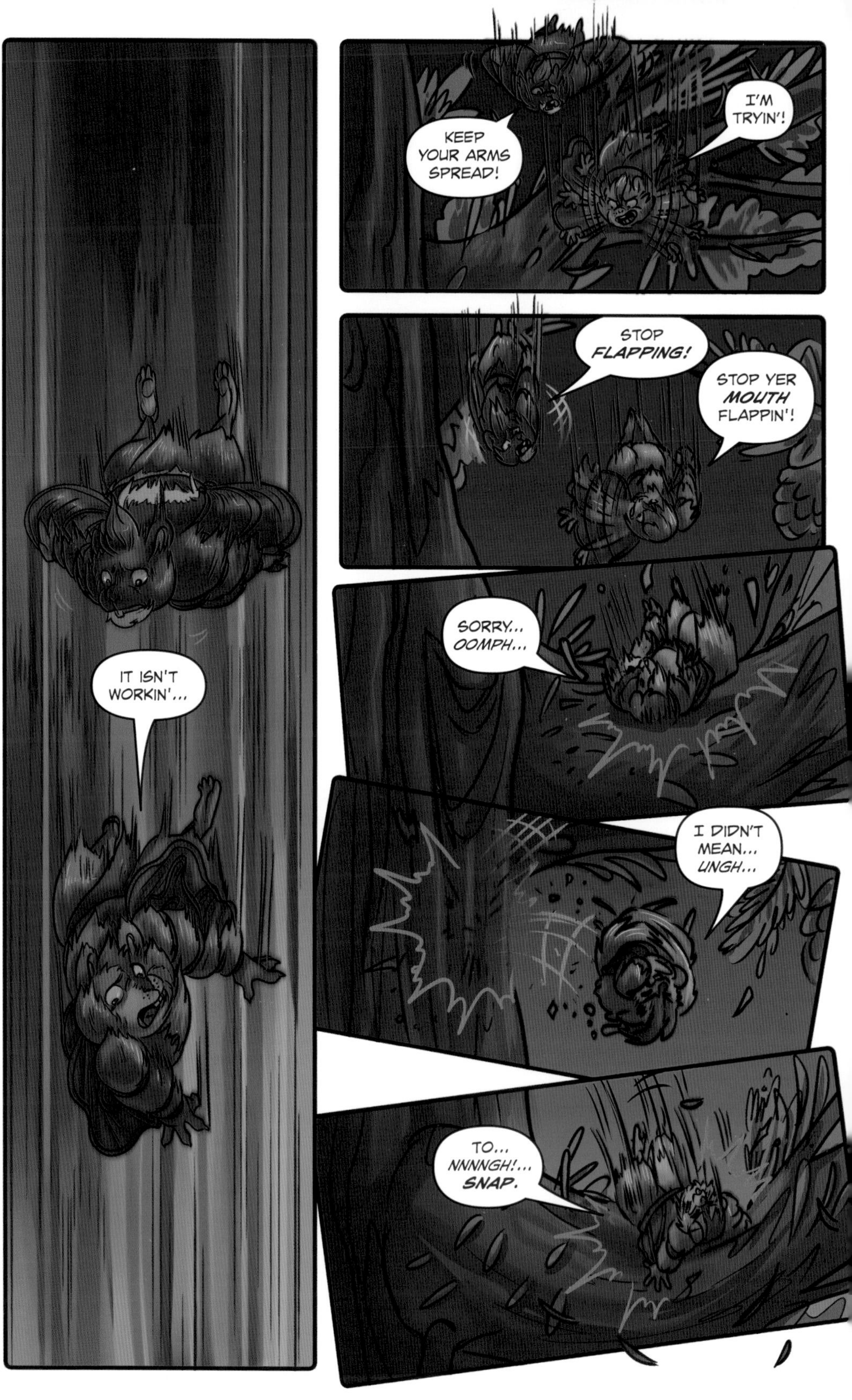
IT ISN'T WORKIN'...
KEEP YOUR ARMS SPREAD!
I'M TRYIN'!
STOP *FLAPPING!*
STOP YER *MOUTH* FLAPPIN'!
SORRY... *OOMPH...*
I DIDN'T MEAN... *UNGH...*
TO... *NNNNGH!...* ***SNAP.***

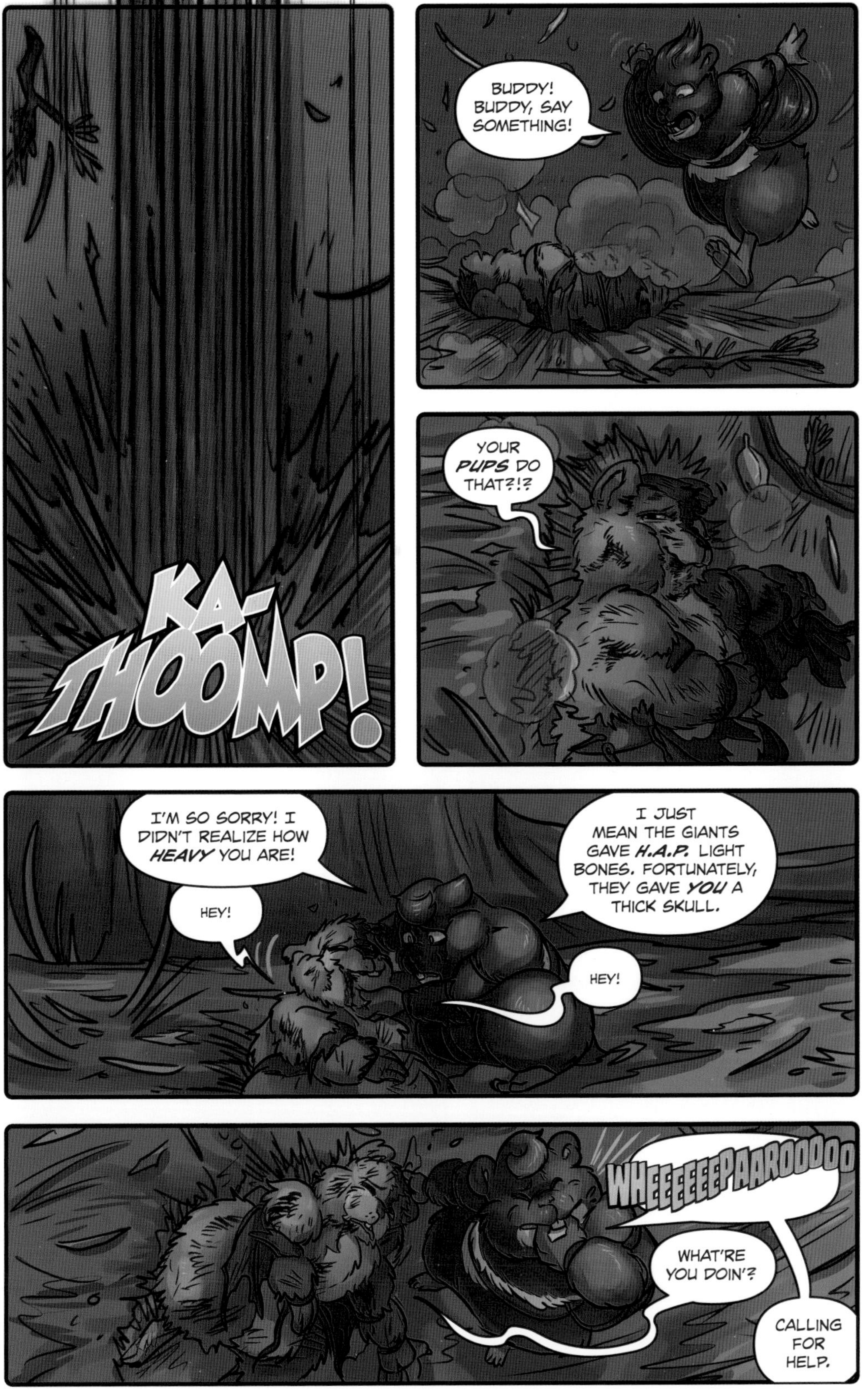
KA-THOOMP!
BUDDY! BUDDY, SAY SOMETHING!
YOUR PUPS DO THAT?!?
I'M SO SORRY! I DIDN'T REALIZE HOW HEAVY YOU ARE!
HEY!
I JUST MEAN THE GIANTS GAVE H.A.P. LIGHT BONES. FORTUNATELY, THEY GAVE YOU A THICK SKULL.
HEY!
WHEEEEEEPAAROOOOO
WHAT'RE YOU DOIN'?
CALLING FOR HELP.

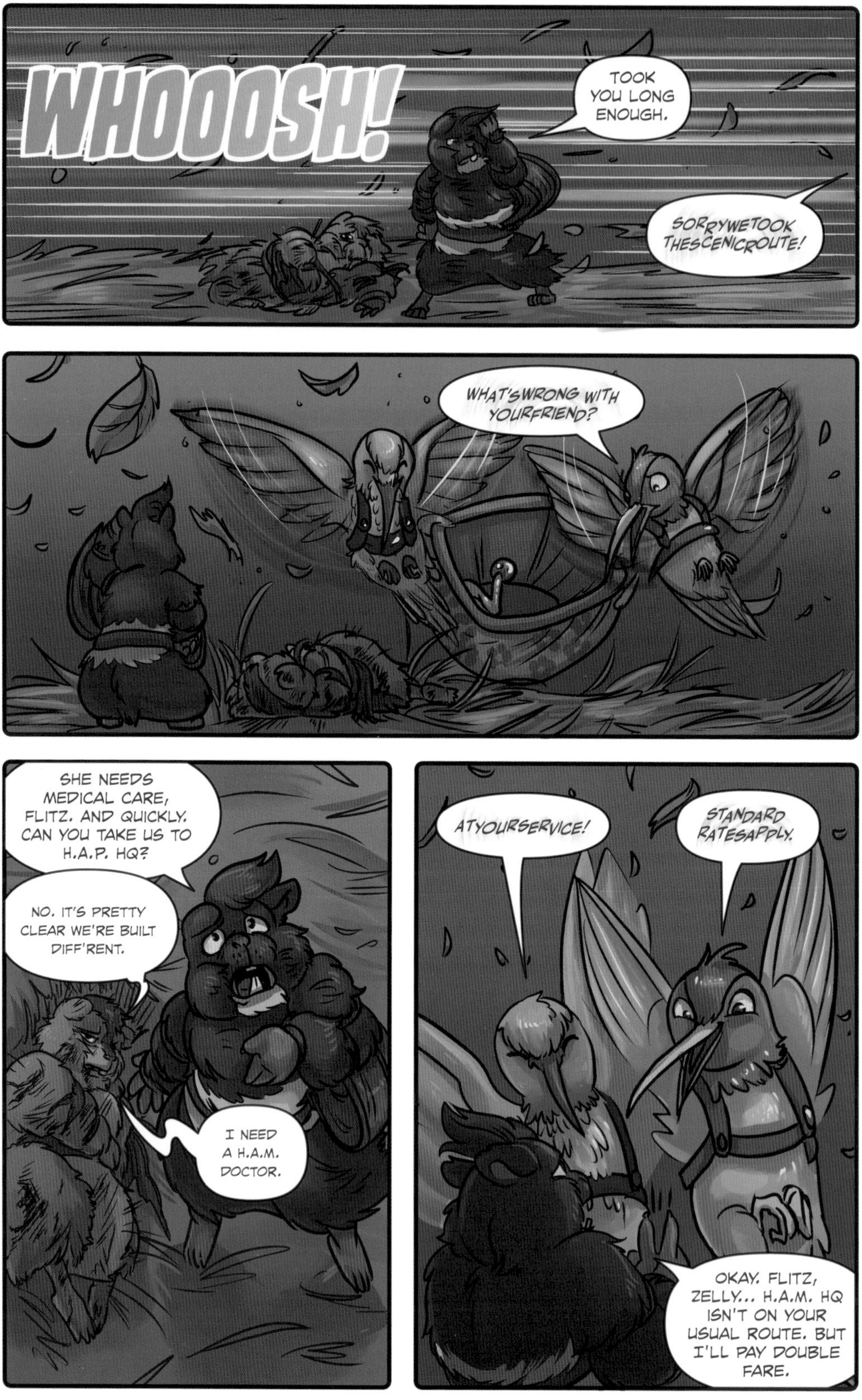
WHOOOOSH!
TOOK YOU LONG ENOUGH.
SORRYWETOOK THESCENICROUTE!
WHAT'SWRONG WITH YOURFRIEND?
SHE NEEDS MEDICAL CARE, FLITZ. AND QUICKLY. CAN YOU TAKE US TO H.A.P. HQ?
NO. IT'S PRETTY CLEAR WE'RE BUILT DIFF'RENT.
I NEED A H.A.M. DOCTOR.
ATYOURSERVICE!
STANDARD RATESAPPLY.
OKAY. FLITZ, ZELLY... H.A.M. HQ ISN'T ON YOUR USUAL ROUTE. BUT I'LL PAY DOUBLE FARE.

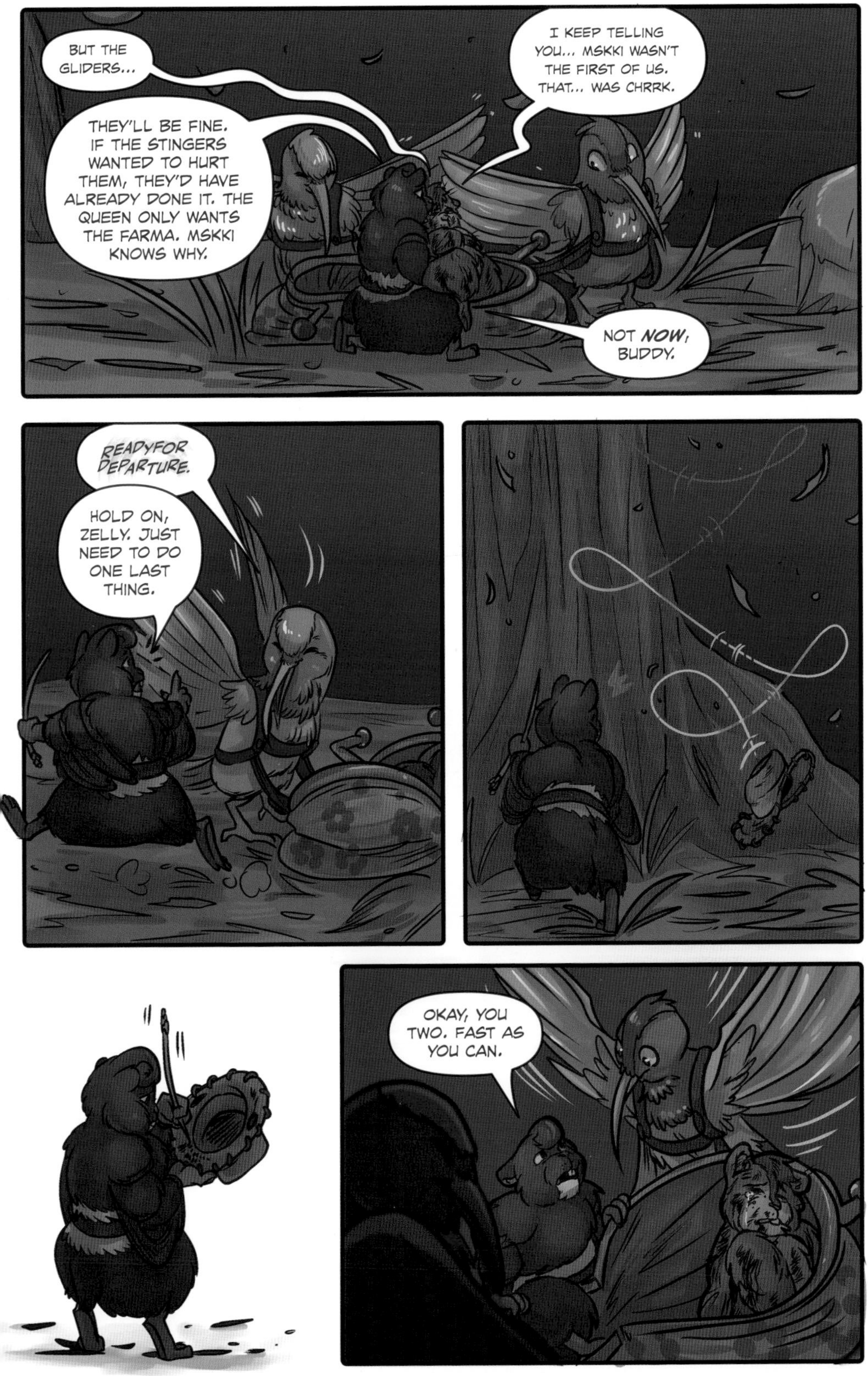
BUT THE GLIDERS...
THEY'LL BE FINE. IF THE STINGERS WANTED TO HURT THEM, THEY'D HAVE ALREADY DONE IT. THE QUEEN ONLY WANTS THE FARMA. MSKKI KNOWS WHY.
I KEEP TELLING YOU... MSKKI WASN'T THE FIRST OF US. THAT... WAS CHRRK.
NOT *NOW*, BUDDY.
READYFOR DEPARTURE.
HOLD ON, ZELLY. JUST NEED TO DO ONE LAST THING.
OKAY, YOU TWO. FAST AS YOU CAN.

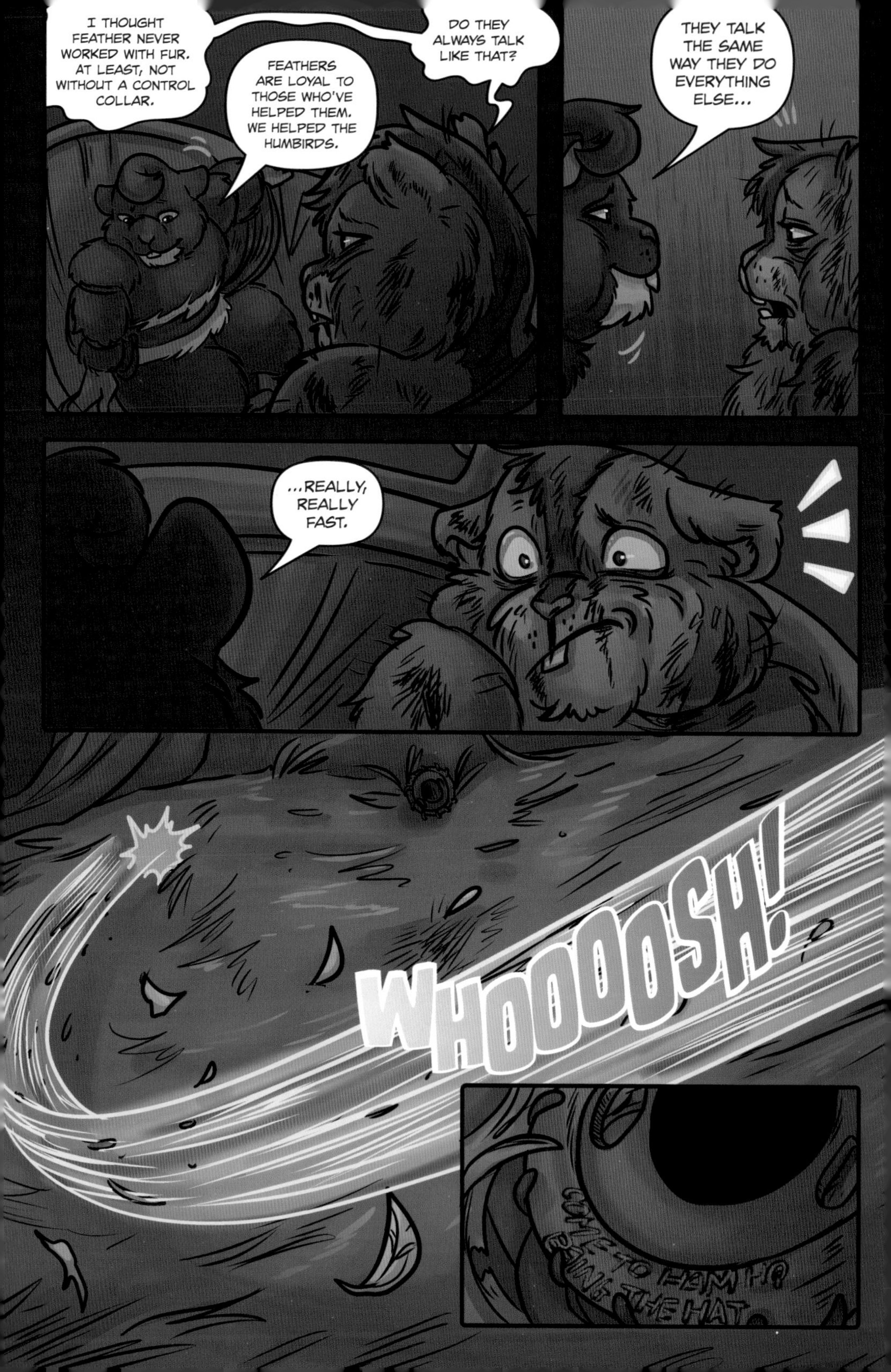
I THOUGHT FEATHER NEVER WORKED WITH FUR. AT LEAST, NOT WITHOUT A CONTROL COLLAR.
FEATHERS ARE LOYAL TO THOSE WHO'VE HELPED THEM. WE HELPED THE HUMBIRDS.
DO THEY ALWAYS TALK LIKE THAT?
THEY TALK THE SAME WAY THEY DO EVERYTHING ELSE...
...REALLY, REALLY FAST.
WHOOOOOSH!
COME TO FBM HQ
BRING THE HAT

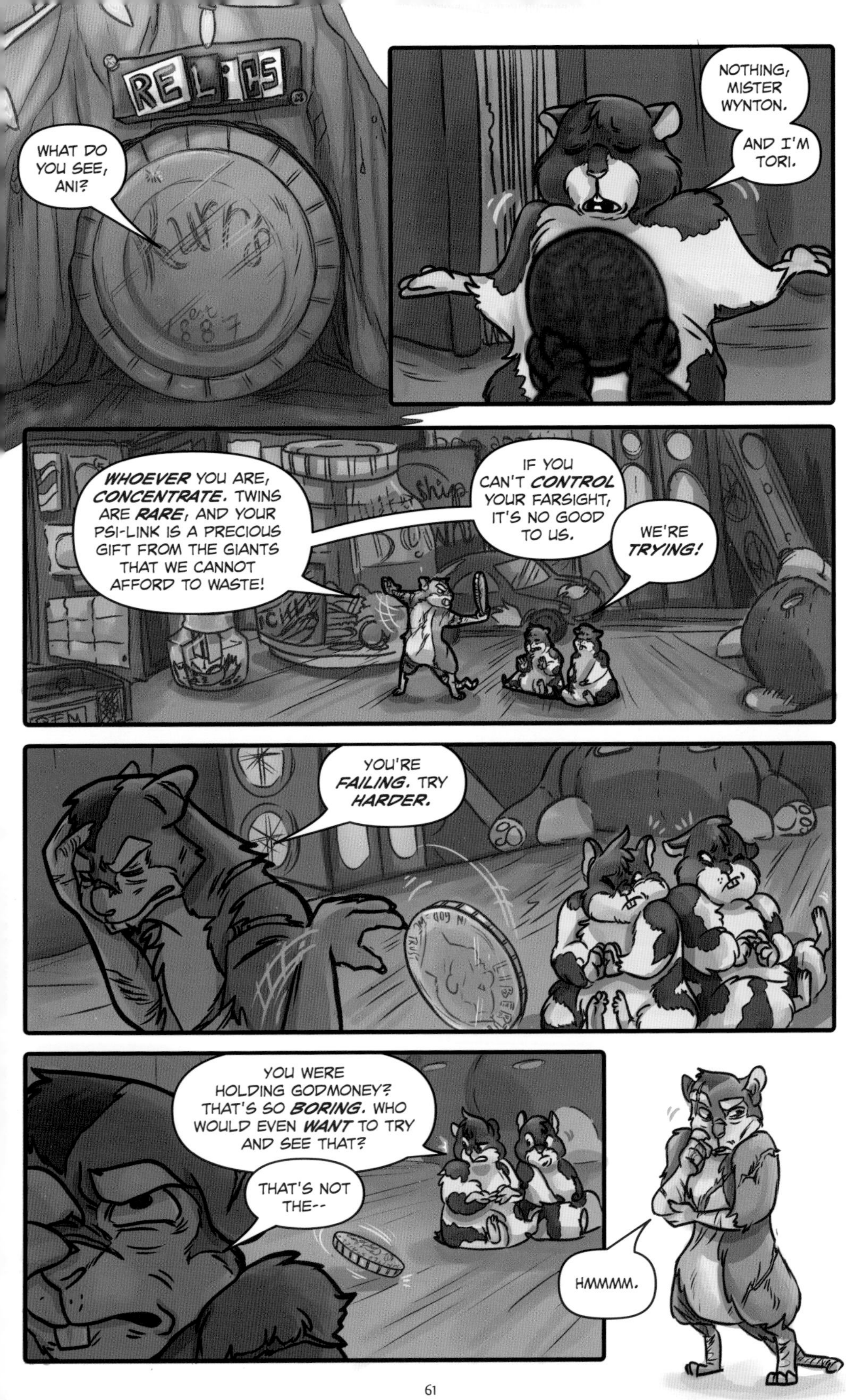
RELICS
WHAT DO YOU SEE, ANI?
NOTHING, MISTER WYNTON.
AND I'M TORI.
WHOEVER YOU ARE, CONCENTRATE. TWINS ARE RARE, AND YOUR PSI-LINK IS A PRECIOUS GIFT FROM THE GIANTS THAT WE CANNOT AFFORD TO WASTE!
IF YOU CAN'T CONTROL YOUR FARSIGHT, IT'S NO GOOD TO US.
WE'RE TRYING!
YOU'RE FAILING. TRY HARDER.
YOU WERE HOLDING GODMONEY? THAT'S SO BORING. WHO WOULD EVEN WANT TO TRY AND SEE THAT?
THAT'S NOT THE--
HMMMM.

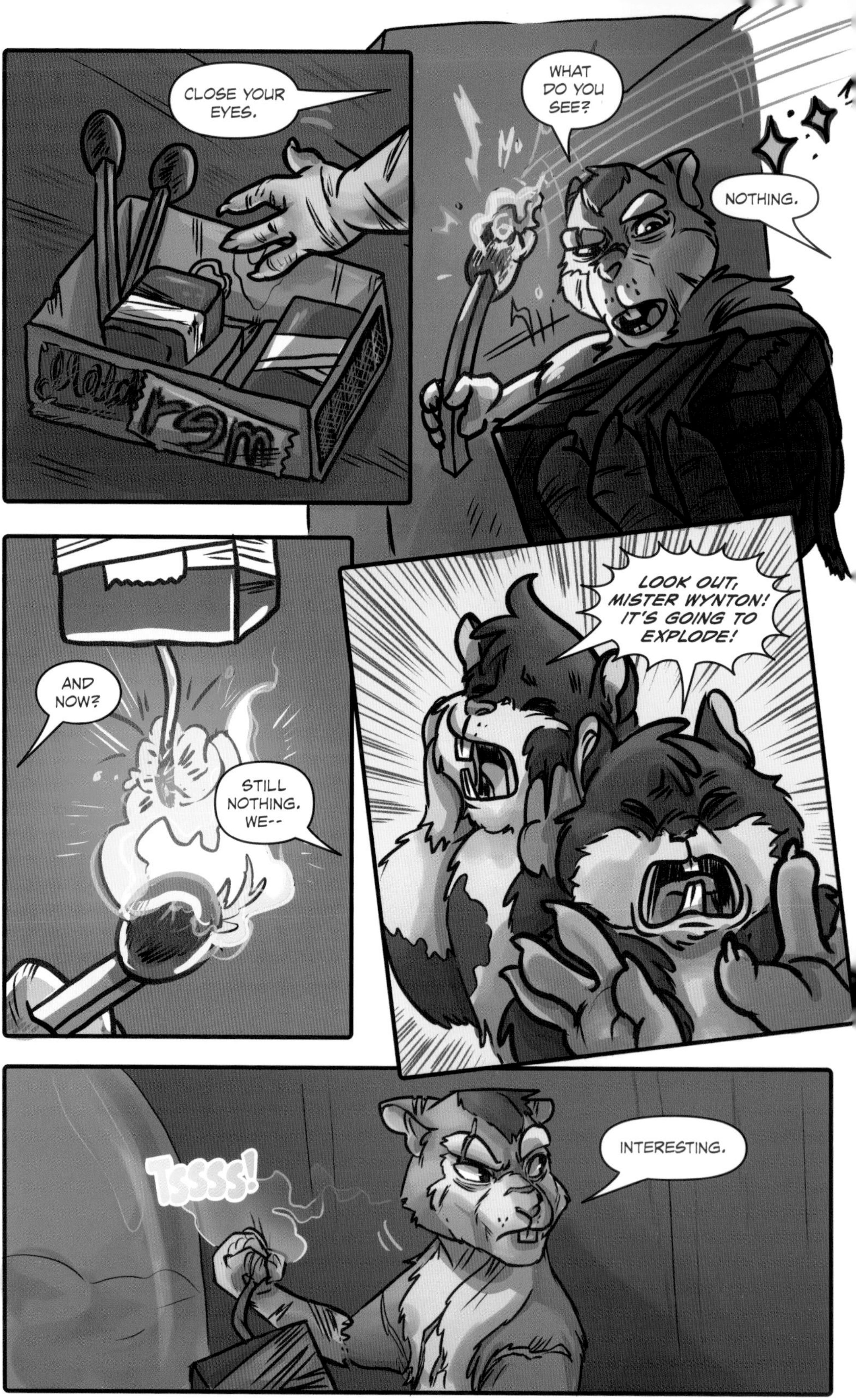
CLOSE YOUR EYES.
WHAT DO YOU SEE?
NOTHING.
AND NOW?
STILL NOTHING. WE--
LOOK OUT, MISTER WYNTON! IT'S GOING TO EXPLODE!
Tssss!
INTERESTING.

H.A.M. HEADQUARTERS

WHAT'S THE PROGNOSIS, HOLIDAY?

BUDDY'S AS TOUGH AS THEY COME. MULTIPLE CONTUSIONS, TWO CRACKED RIBS, AND A CONCUSSION. BUT SHE'LL LIVE.

WHAT HAPPENED OUT THERE, LUCIANA?

NEIL TOOK US TO THE MEDIATION SITE, BUT ALL WE FOUND WERE SLEEPING GLIDERS AND A HAT.

WE WERE HOPING JUNIP AND HIS DREY COULD FILL IN THE BLANKS, BUT THEY DON'T REMEMBER MUCH BEFORE FALLING ASLEEP.

I REMEMBER WE *USED* TO HAVE THREE GENERATIONS' WORTH OF GATHERED FARMA.

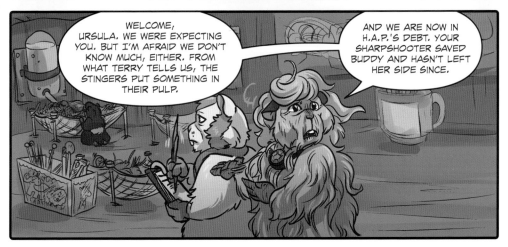

WELCOME, URSULA. WE WERE EXPECTING YOU. BUT I'M AFRAID WE DON'T KNOW MUCH, EITHER. FROM WHAT TERRY TELLS US, THE STINGERS PUT SOMETHING IN THEIR PULP.

AND WE ARE NOW IN H.A.P.'S DEBT. YOUR SHARPSHOOTER SAVED BUDDY AND HASN'T LEFT HER SIDE SINCE.

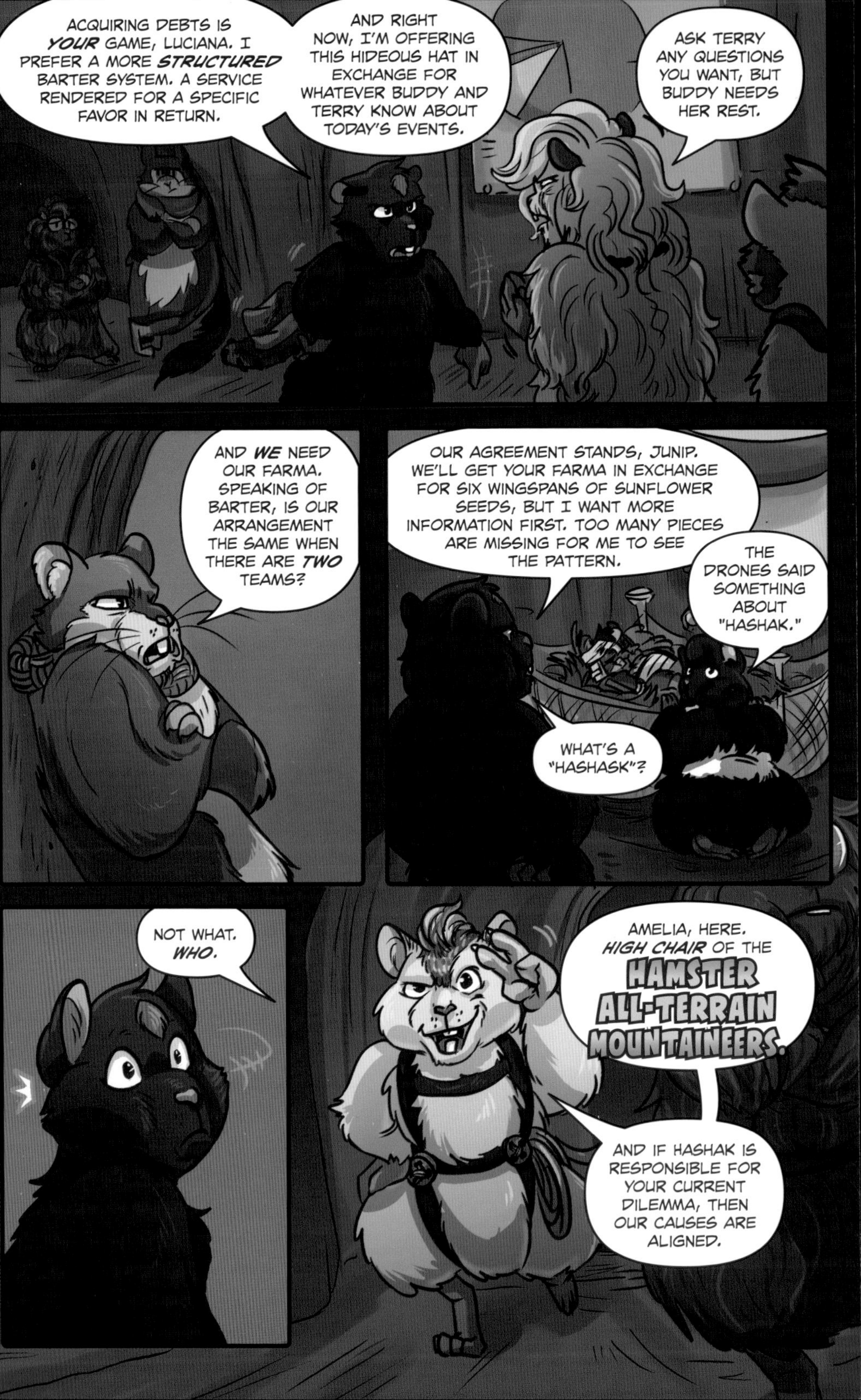
ACQUIRING DEBTS IS *YOUR* GAME, LUCIANA. I PREFER A MORE *STRUCTURED* BARTER SYSTEM. A SERVICE RENDERED FOR A SPECIFIC FAVOR IN RETURN.
AND RIGHT NOW, I'M OFFERING THIS HIDEOUS HAT IN EXCHANGE FOR WHATEVER BUDDY AND TERRY KNOW ABOUT TODAY'S EVENTS.
ASK TERRY ANY QUESTIONS YOU WANT, BUT BUDDY NEEDS HER REST.
AND *WE* NEED OUR FARMA. SPEAKING OF BARTER, IS OUR ARRANGEMENT THE SAME WHEN THERE ARE *TWO* TEAMS?
OUR AGREEMENT STANDS, JUNIP. WE'LL GET YOUR FARMA IN EXCHANGE FOR SIX WINGSPANS OF SUNFLOWER SEEDS, BUT I WANT MORE INFORMATION FIRST. TOO MANY PIECES ARE MISSING FOR ME TO SEE THE PATTERN.
THE DRONES SAID SOMETHING ABOUT "HASHAK."
WHAT'S A "HASHASK"?
NOT WHAT. *WHO*.
AMELIA, HERE. *HIGH CHAIR* OF THE
HAMSTER ALL-TERRAIN MOUNTAINEERS.
AND IF HASHAK IS RESPONSIBLE FOR YOUR CURRENT DILEMMA, THEN OUR CAUSES ARE ALIGNED.

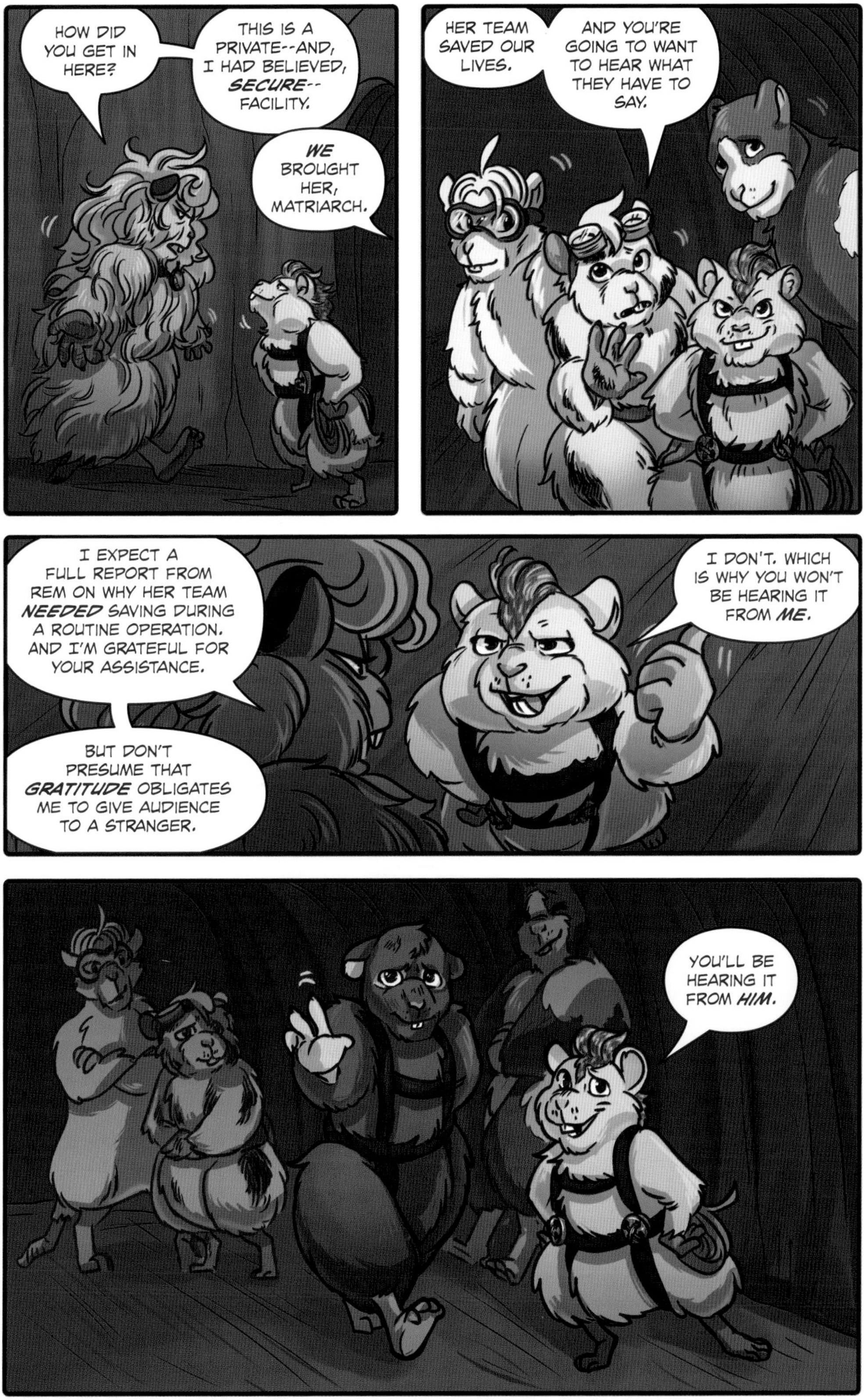
HOW DID YOU GET IN HERE?
THIS IS A PRIVATE--AND, I HAD BELIEVED, SECURE--FACILITY.
WE BROUGHT HER, MATRIARCH.
HER TEAM SAVED OUR LIVES.
AND YOU'RE GOING TO WANT TO HEAR WHAT THEY HAVE TO SAY.
I EXPECT A FULL REPORT FROM REM ON WHY HER TEAM NEEDED SAVING DURING A ROUTINE OPERATION. AND I'M GRATEFUL FOR YOUR ASSISTANCE.
BUT DON'T PRESUME THAT GRATITUDE OBLIGATES ME TO GIVE AUDIENCE TO A STRANGER.
I DON'T. WHICH IS WHY YOU WON'T BE HEARING IT FROM ME.
YOU'LL BE HEARING IT FROM HIM.

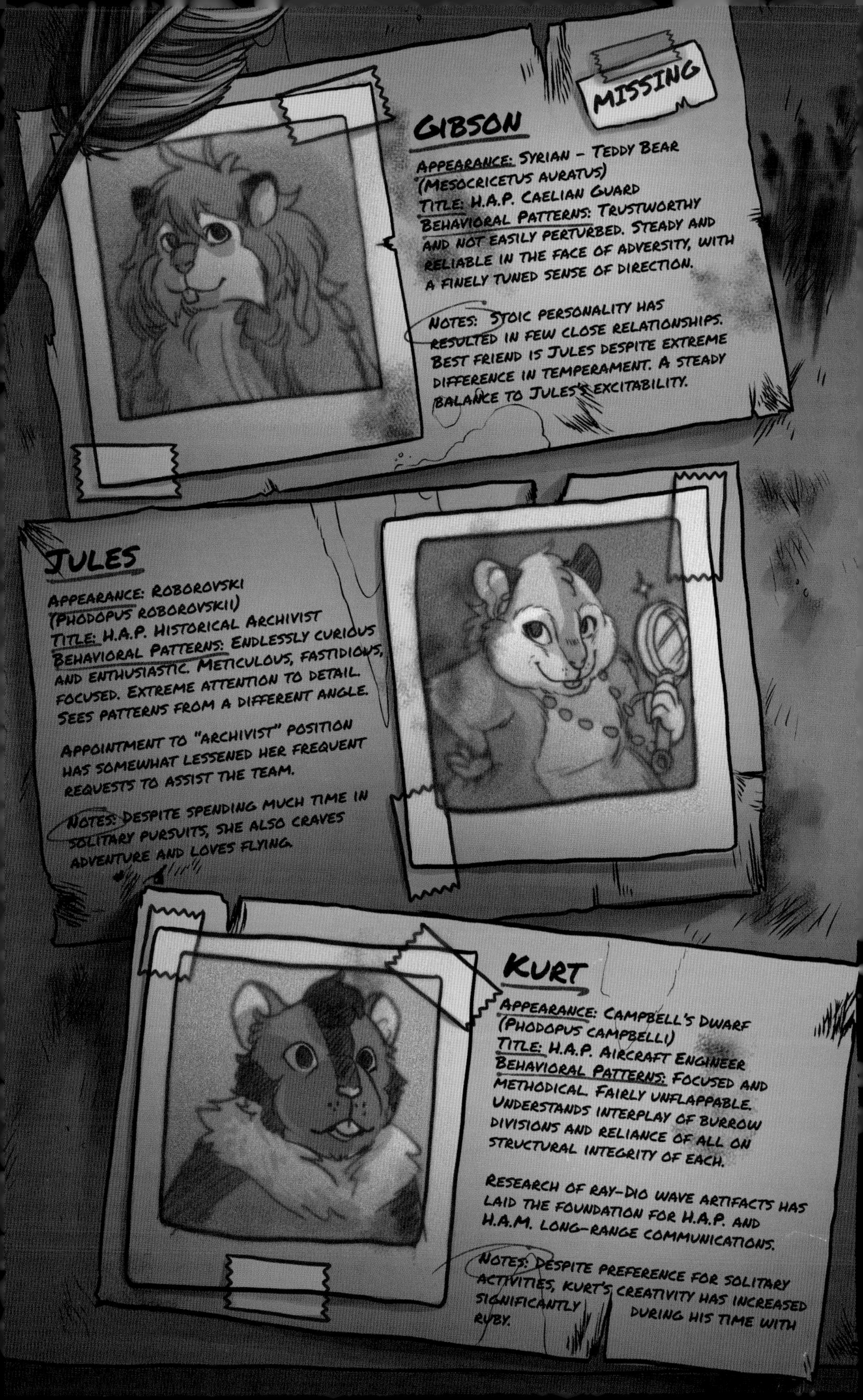
MISSING
GIBSON
APPEARANCE: SYRIAN – TEDDY BEAR (MESOCRICETUS AURATUS)
TITLE: H.A.P. CAELIAN GUARD
BEHAVIORAL PATTERNS: TRUSTWORTHY AND NOT EASILY PERTURBED. STEADY AND RELIABLE IN THE FACE OF ADVERSITY, WITH A FINELY TUNED SENSE OF DIRECTION.
NOTES: STOIC PERSONALITY HAS RESULTED IN FEW CLOSE RELATIONSHIPS. BEST FRIEND IS JULES DESPITE EXTREME DIFFERENCE IN TEMPERAMENT. A STEADY BALANCE TO JULES'S EXCITABILITY.
JULES
APPEARANCE: ROBOROVSKI (PHODOPUS ROBOROVSKII)
TITLE: H.A.P. HISTORICAL ARCHIVIST
BEHAVIORAL PATTERNS: ENDLESSLY CURIOUS AND ENTHUSIASTIC. METICULOUS, FASTIDIOUS, FOCUSED. EXTREME ATTENTION TO DETAIL. SEES PATTERNS FROM A DIFFERENT ANGLE.
APPOINTMENT TO "ARCHIVIST" POSITION HAS SOMEWHAT LESSENED HER FREQUENT REQUESTS TO ASSIST THE TEAM.
NOTES: DESPITE SPENDING MUCH TIME IN SOLITARY PURSUITS, SHE ALSO CRAVES ADVENTURE AND LOVES FLYING.
KURT
APPEARANCE: CAMPBELL'S DWARF (PHODOPUS CAMPBELLI)
TITLE: H.A.P. AIRCRAFT ENGINEER
BEHAVIORAL PATTERNS: FOCUSED AND METHODICAL. FAIRLY UNFLAPPABLE. UNDERSTANDS INTERPLAY OF BURROW DIVISIONS AND RELIANCE OF ALL ON STRUCTURAL INTEGRITY OF EACH.
RESEARCH OF RAY-DIO WAVE ARTIFACTS HAS LAID THE FOUNDATION FOR H.A.P. AND H.A.M. LONG-RANGE COMMUNICATIONS.
NOTES: DESPITE PREFERENCE FOR SOLITARY ACTIVITIES, KURT'S CREATIVITY HAS INCREASED SIGNIFICANTLY DURING HIS TIME WITH RUBY.

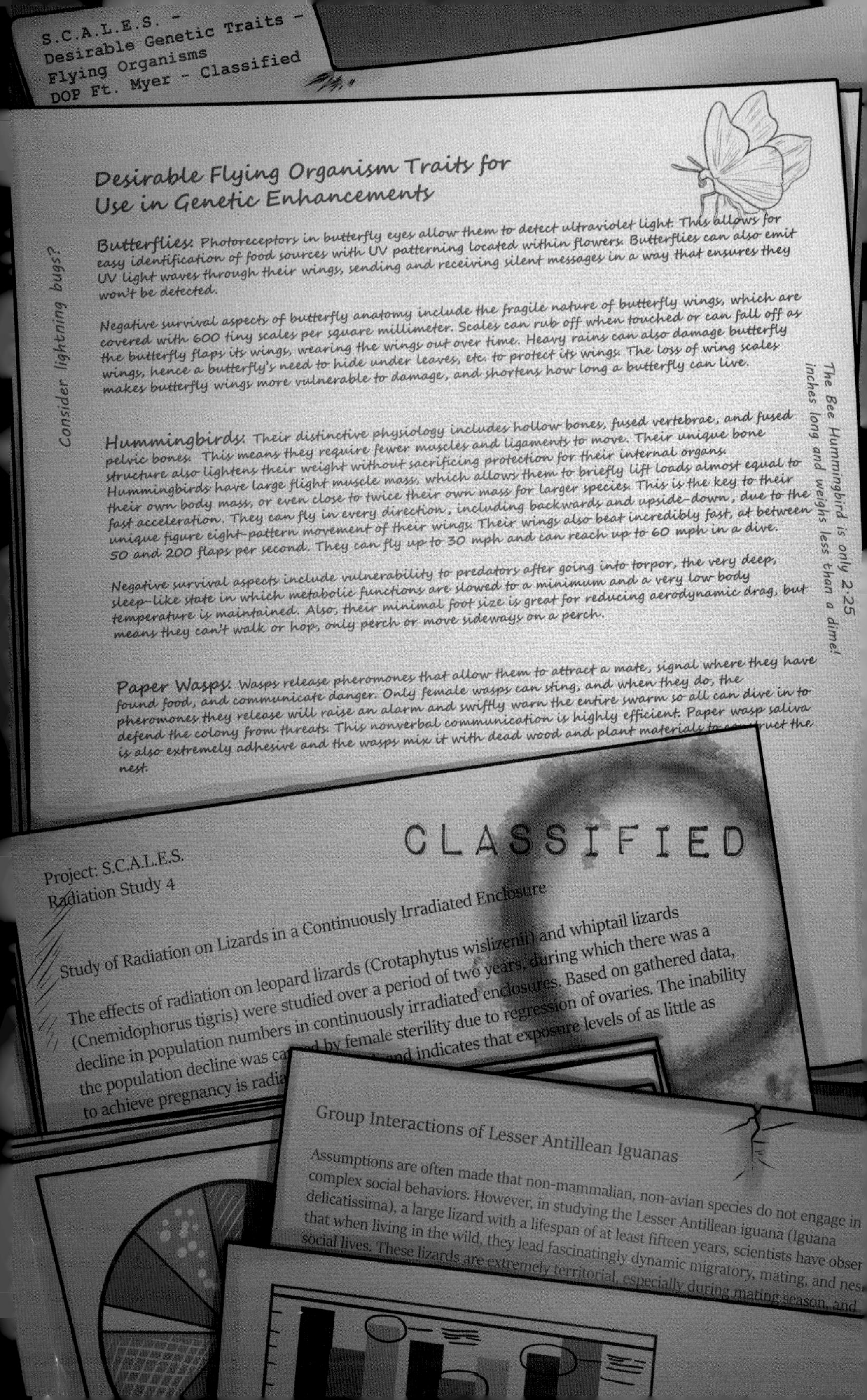
S.C.A.L.E.S. –
Desirable Genetic Traits –
Flying Organisms
DOP Ft. Myer – Classified
Desirable Flying Organism Traits for Use in Genetic Enhancements
Butterflies: Photoreceptors in butterfly eyes allow them to detect ultraviolet light. This allows for easy identification of food sources with UV patterning located within flowers. Butterflies can also emit UV light waves through their wings, sending and receiving silent messages in a way that ensures they won't be detected.
Negative survival aspects of butterfly anatomy include the fragile nature of butterfly wings, which are covered with 600 tiny scales per square millimeter. Scales can rub off when touched or can fall off as the butterfly flaps its wings, wearing the wings out over time. Heavy rains can also damage butterfly wings, hence a butterfly's need to hide under leaves, etc. to protect its wings. The loss of wing scales makes butterfly wings more vulnerable to damage, and shortens how long a butterfly can live.
Consider lightning bugs?
Hummingbirds: Their distinctive physiology includes hollow bones, fused vertebrae, and fused pelvic bones. This means they require fewer muscles and ligaments to move. Their unique bone structure also lightens their weight without sacrificing protection for their internal organs. Hummingbirds have large flight muscle mass, which allows them to briefly lift loads almost equal to their own body mass, or even close to twice their own mass for larger species. This is the key to their fast acceleration. They can fly in every direction, including backwards and upside-down, due to the unique figure eight-pattern movement of their wings. Their wings also beat incredibly fast, at between 50 and 200 flaps per second. They can fly up to 30 mph and can reach up to 60 mph in a dive.
Negative survival aspects include vulnerability to predators after going into torpor, the very deep, sleep-like state in which metabolic functions are slowed to a minimum and a very low body temperature is maintained. Also, their minimal foot size is great for reducing aerodynamic drag, but means they can't walk or hop, only perch or move sideways on a perch.
The Bee Hummingbird is only 2.25 inches long and weighs less than a dime!
Paper Wasps: Wasps release pheromones that allow them to attract a mate, signal where they have found food, and communicate danger. Only female wasps can sting, and when they do, the pheromones they release will raise an alarm and swiftly warn the entire swarm so all can dive in to defend the colony from threats. This nonverbal communication is highly efficient. Paper wasp saliva is also extremely adhesive and the wasps mix it with dead wood and plant materials to construct the nest.
CLASSIFIED
Project: S.C.A.L.E.S.
Radiation Study 4
Study of Radiation on Lizards in a Continuously Irradiated Enclosure
The effects of radiation on leopard lizards (Crotaphytus wislizenii) and whiptail lizards
(Cnemidophorus tigris) were studied over a period of two years, during which there was a
decline in population numbers in continuously irradiated enclosures. Based on gathered data,
the population decline was ca
to achieve pregnancy is radia
Group Interactions of Lesser Antillean Iguanas
Assumptions are often made that non-mammalian, non-avian species do not engage in
complex social behaviors. However, in studying the Lesser Antillean iguana (Iguana
delicatissima), a large lizard with a lifespan of at least fifteen years, scientists have obser
that when living in the wild, they lead fascinatingly dynamic migratory, mating, and nes
social lives. These lizards are extremely territorial, especially during mating season, and

CHAPTER THREE

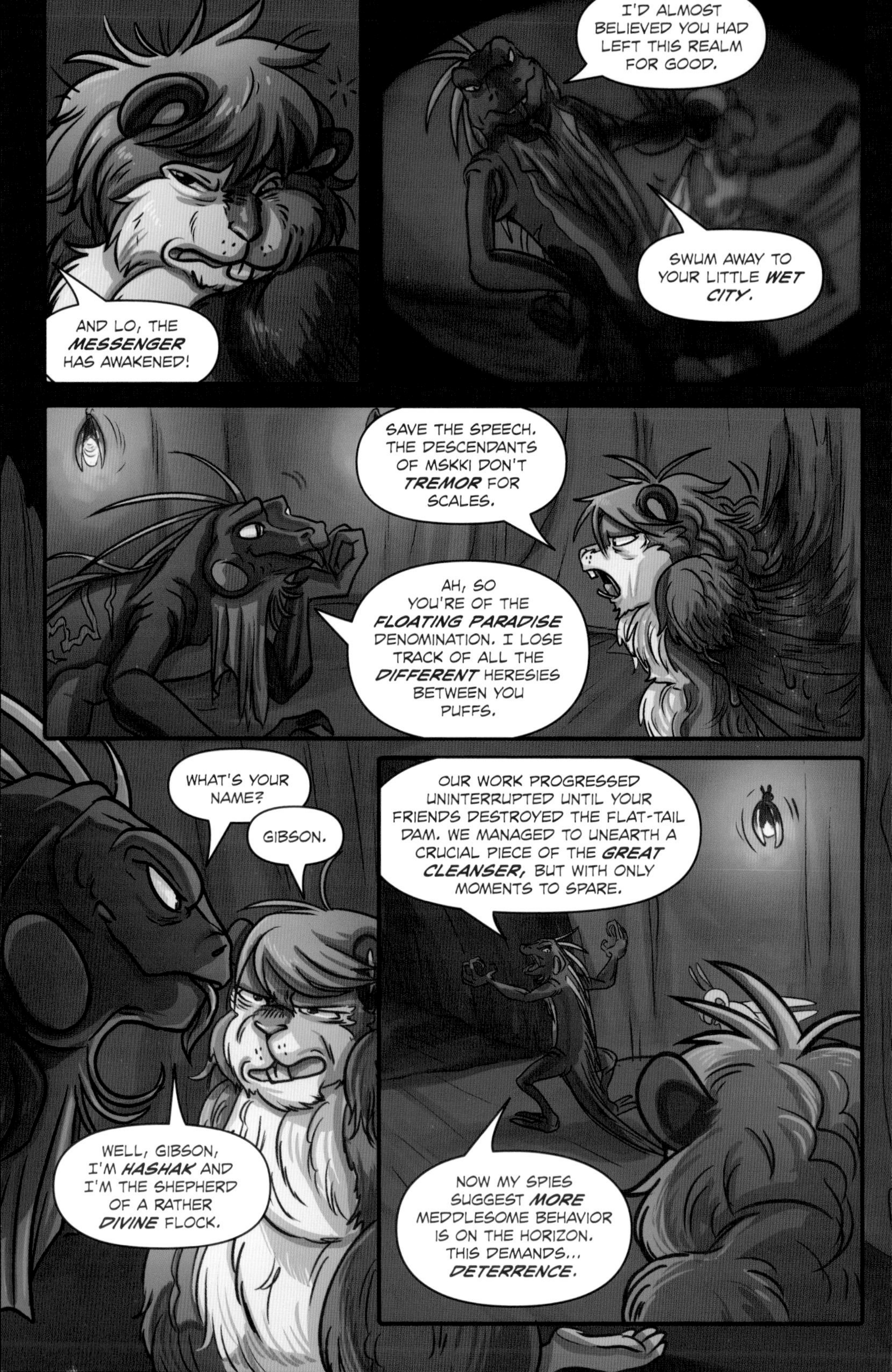
AND LO, THE *MESSENGER* HAS AWAKENED!
I'D ALMOST BELIEVED YOU HAD LEFT THIS REALM FOR GOOD.
SWUM AWAY TO YOUR LITTLE *WET CITY*.
SAVE THE SPEECH. THE DESCENDANTS OF MSKKI DON'T *TREMOR* FOR SCALES.
AH, SO YOU'RE OF THE *FLOATING PARADISE* DENOMINATION. I LOSE TRACK OF ALL THE *DIFFERENT* HERESIES BETWEEN YOU PUFFS.
WHAT'S YOUR NAME?
GIBSON.
WELL, GIBSON, I'M *HASHAK* AND I'M THE SHEPHERD OF A RATHER *DIVINE* FLOCK.
OUR WORK PROGRESSED UNINTERRUPTED UNTIL YOUR FRIENDS DESTROYED THE FLAT-TAIL DAM. WE MANAGED TO UNEARTH A CRUCIAL PIECE OF THE *GREAT CLEANSER,* BUT WITH ONLY MOMENTS TO SPARE.
NOW MY SPIES SUGGEST *MORE* MEDDLESOME BEHAVIOR IS ON THE HORIZON. THIS DEMANDS... *DETERRENCE*.

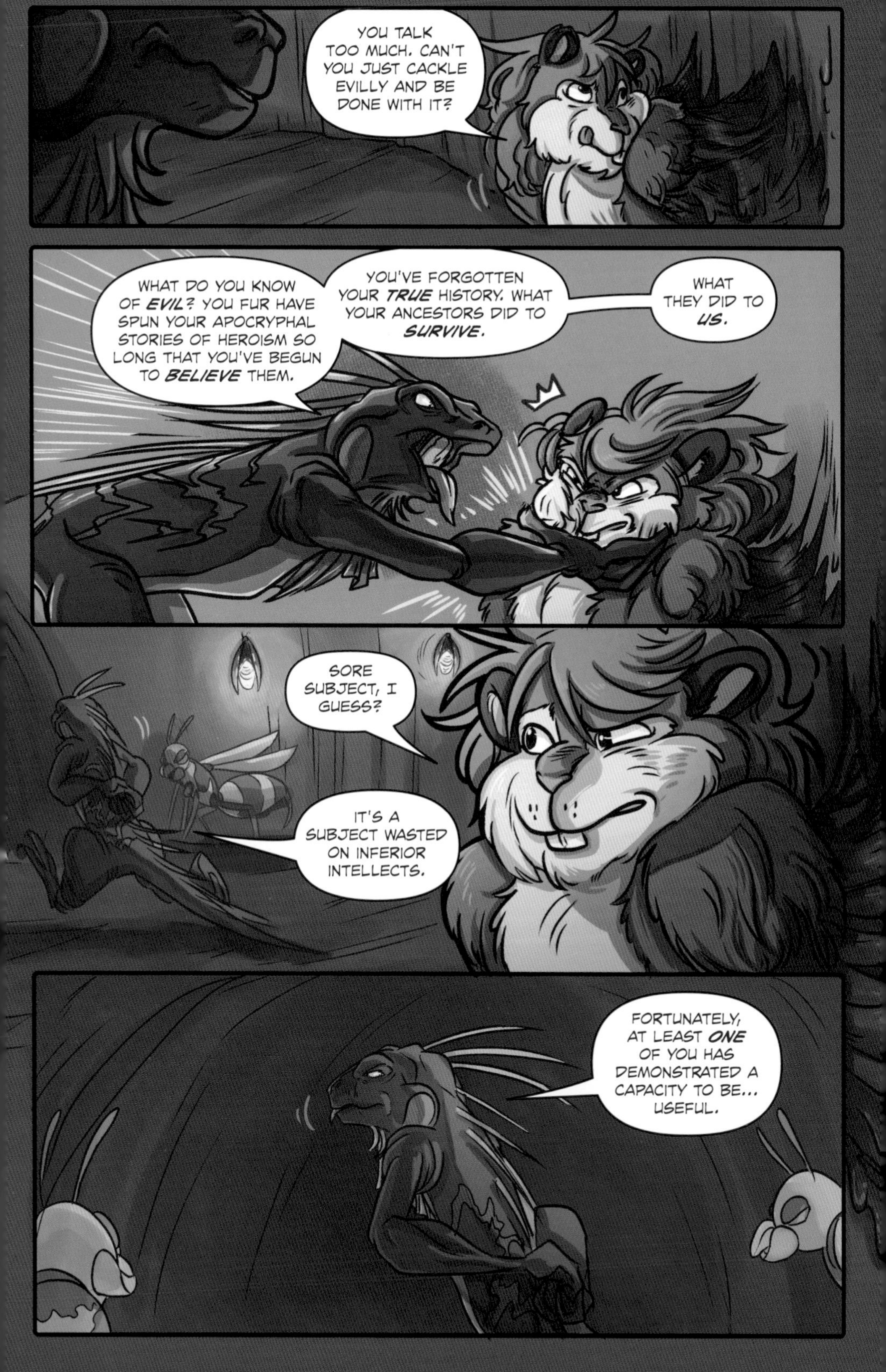
YOU TALK TOO MUCH. CAN'T YOU JUST CACKLE EVILLY AND BE DONE WITH IT?
WHAT DO YOU KNOW OF EVIL? YOU FUR HAVE SPUN YOUR APOCRYPHAL STORIES OF HEROISM SO LONG THAT YOU'VE BEGUN TO BELIEVE THEM.
YOU'VE FORGOTTEN YOUR TRUE HISTORY. WHAT YOUR ANCESTORS DID TO SURVIVE.
WHAT THEY DID TO US.
SORE SUBJECT, I GUESS?
IT'S A SUBJECT WASTED ON INFERIOR INTELLECTS.
FORTUNATELY, AT LEAST ONE OF YOU HAS DEMONSTRATED A CAPACITY TO BE... USEFUL.

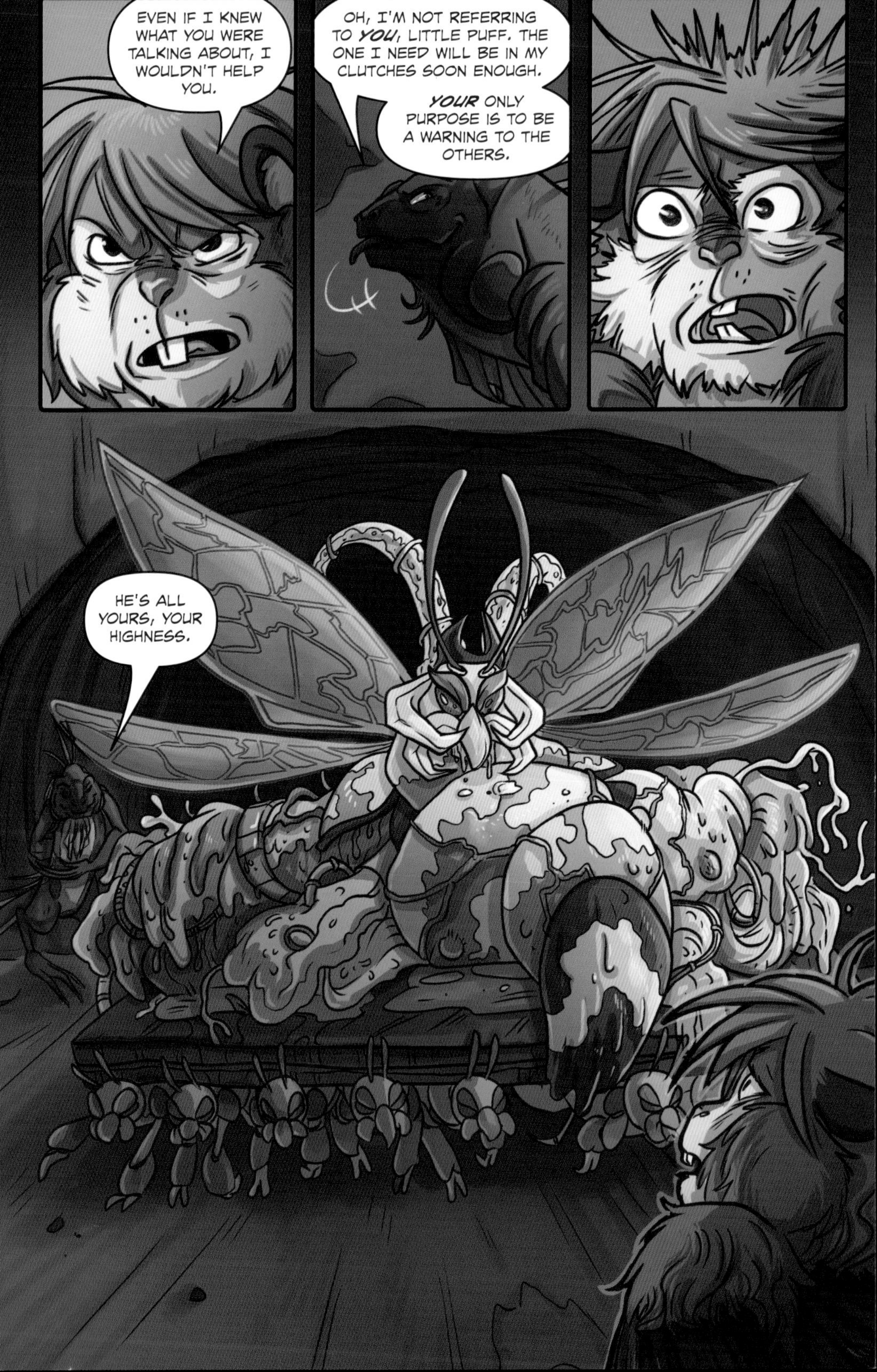
EVEN IF I KNEW WHAT YOU WERE TALKING ABOUT, I WOULDN'T HELP YOU.
OH, I'M NOT REFERRING TO *YOU*, LITTLE PUFF. THE ONE I NEED WILL BE IN MY CLUTCHES SOON ENOUGH.
YOUR ONLY PURPOSE IS TO BE A WARNING TO THE OTHERS.
HE'S ALL YOURS, YOUR HIGHNESS.

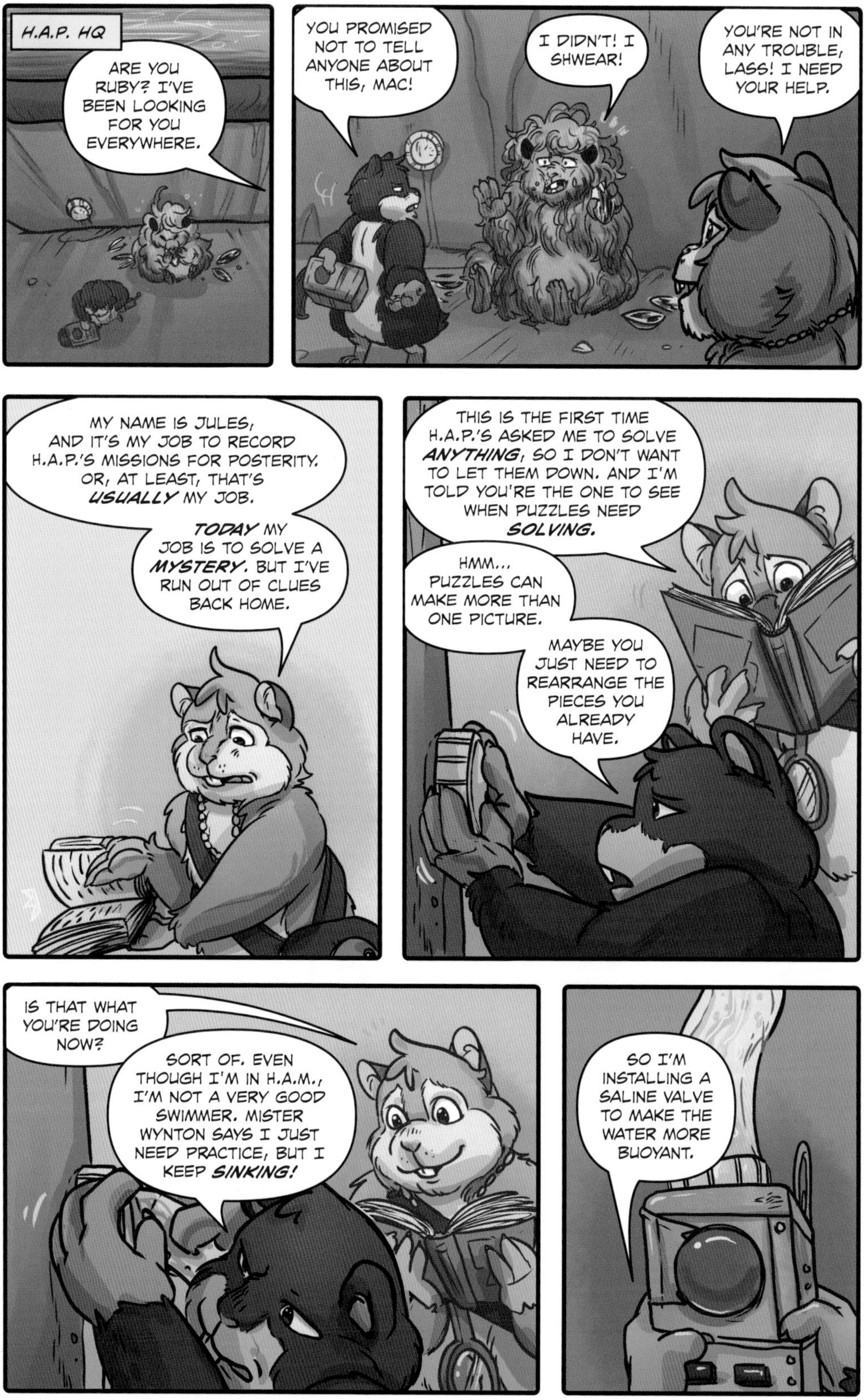
H.A.P. HQ
ARE YOU RUBY? I'VE BEEN LOOKING FOR YOU EVERYWHERE.
YOU PROMISED NOT TO TELL ANYONE ABOUT THIS, MAC!
I DIDN'T! I SHWEAR!
YOU'RE NOT IN ANY TROUBLE, LASS! I NEED YOUR HELP.
MY NAME IS JULES, AND IT'S MY JOB TO RECORD H.A.P.'S MISSIONS FOR POSTERITY. OR, AT LEAST, THAT'S USUALLY MY JOB.
TODAY MY JOB IS TO SOLVE A MYSTERY. BUT I'VE RUN OUT OF CLUES BACK HOME.
THIS IS THE FIRST TIME H.A.P.'S ASKED ME TO SOLVE ANYTHING, SO I DON'T WANT TO LET THEM DOWN. AND I'M TOLD YOU'RE THE ONE TO SEE WHEN PUZZLES NEED SOLVING.
HMM... PUZZLES CAN MAKE MORE THAN ONE PICTURE.
MAYBE YOU JUST NEED TO REARRANGE THE PIECES YOU ALREADY HAVE.
IS THAT WHAT YOU'RE DOING NOW?
SORT OF. EVEN THOUGH I'M IN H.A.M., I'M NOT A VERY GOOD SWIMMER. MISTER WYNTON SAYS I JUST NEED PRACTICE, BUT I KEEP SINKING!
SO I'M INSTALLING A SALINE VALVE TO MAKE THE WATER MORE BUOYANT.

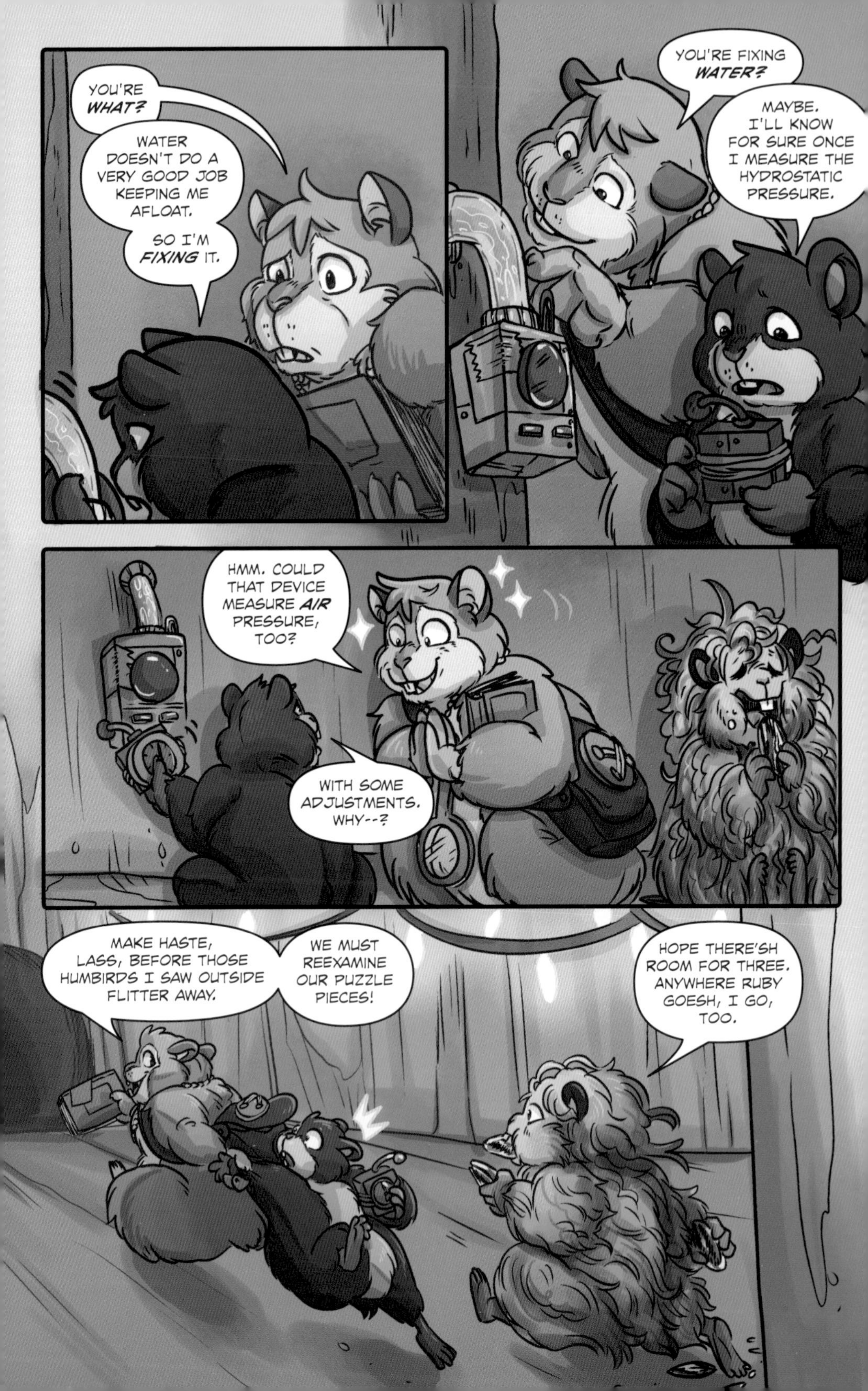
YOU'RE *WHAT?*
WATER DOESN'T DO A VERY GOOD JOB KEEPING ME AFLOAT.
SO I'M *FIXING* IT.
YOU'RE FIXING *WATER?*
MAYBE. I'LL KNOW FOR SURE ONCE I MEASURE THE HYDROSTATIC PRESSURE.
HMM. COULD THAT DEVICE MEASURE *AIR* PRESSURE, TOO?
WITH SOME ADJUSTMENTS. WHY--?
MAKE HASTE, LASS, BEFORE THOSE HUMBIRDS I SAW OUTSIDE FLITTER AWAY.
WE MUST REEXAMINE OUR PUZZLE PIECES!
HOPE THERE'SH ROOM FOR THREE. ANYWHERE RUBY GOESH, I GO, TOO.

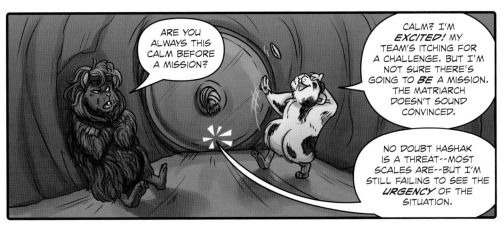

ARE YOU ALWAYS THIS CALM BEFORE A MISSION?

CALM? I'M *EXCITED!* MY TEAM'S ITCHING FOR A CHALLENGE. BUT I'M NOT SURE THERE'S GOING TO *BE* A MISSION. THE MATRIARCH DOESN'T SOUND CONVINCED.

NO DOUBT HASHAK IS A THREAT--MOST SCALES ARE--BUT I'M STILL FAILING TO SEE THE *URGENCY* OF THE SITUATION.

I AGREE WITH LUCIANA. ASSUMING HASHAK STOLE THE GLIDERS' FARMA, SHE'LL NEED TO BE DEALT WITH, BUT WHY THE RUSH?

BECAUSE OF WHAT I SUSPECT SHE'S PLANNING TO *DO* WITH THE FARMA. AND YOUR MISSING CELLIES.

WE DON'T EVEN KNOW SHE STOLE THE CELLIES. WE KEEP TALKING ABOUT MISSING ITEMS AND HAMSTERS, BUT I'M STILL WAITING TO HEAR A *CONNECTION.*

THEN YOU HAVEN'T BEEN LISTENING! HASHAK CONNECTS IT *ALL!*

SHE COMMISSIONED THE FLAT-TAILS TO UNEARTH A STRANGE TUBE WITH THEIR DAM. SHE CONVINCED THE STINGERS TO STEAL FARMA. AND NOW H.A.P.'S CELLIES ARE MISSING.

ALL OF WHICH HAPPEN TO BE ARTIFACTS LEFT BEHIND BY THE GIANTS. YOU REALLY THINK THAT'S A COINCIDENCE?

MIND YOUR PLACE, BECK. YOU'RE HERE AS AN *INTERMEDIARY,* NOTHING MORE.

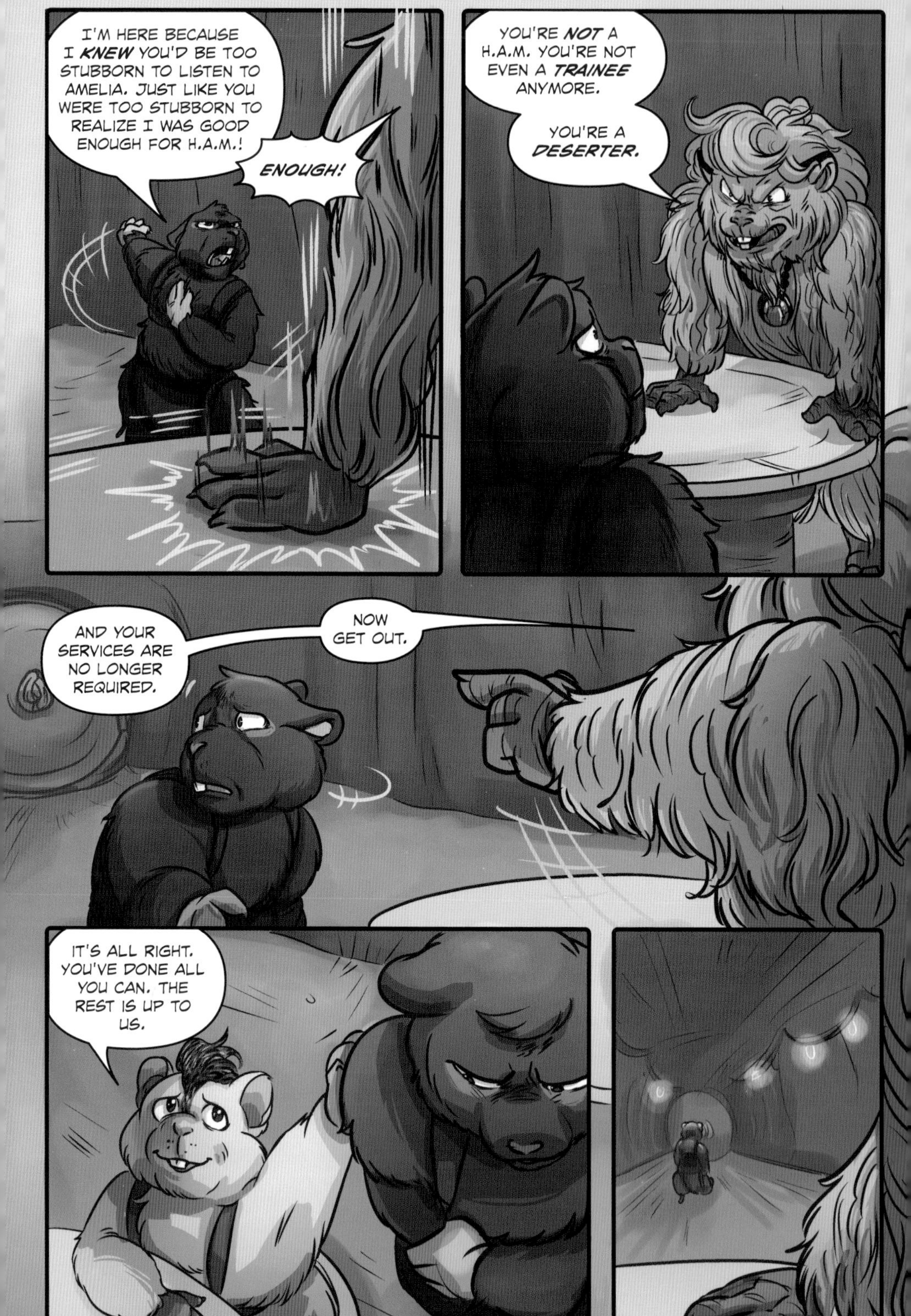
I'M HERE BECAUSE I KNEW YOU'D BE TOO STUBBORN TO LISTEN TO AMELIA. JUST LIKE YOU WERE TOO STUBBORN TO REALIZE I WAS GOOD ENOUGH FOR H.A.M.!
ENOUGH!
YOU'RE NOT A H.A.M. YOU'RE NOT EVEN A TRAINEE ANYMORE.
YOU'RE A DESERTER.
AND YOUR SERVICES ARE NO LONGER REQUIRED.
NOW GET OUT.
IT'S ALL RIGHT. YOU'VE DONE ALL YOU CAN. THE REST IS UP TO US.

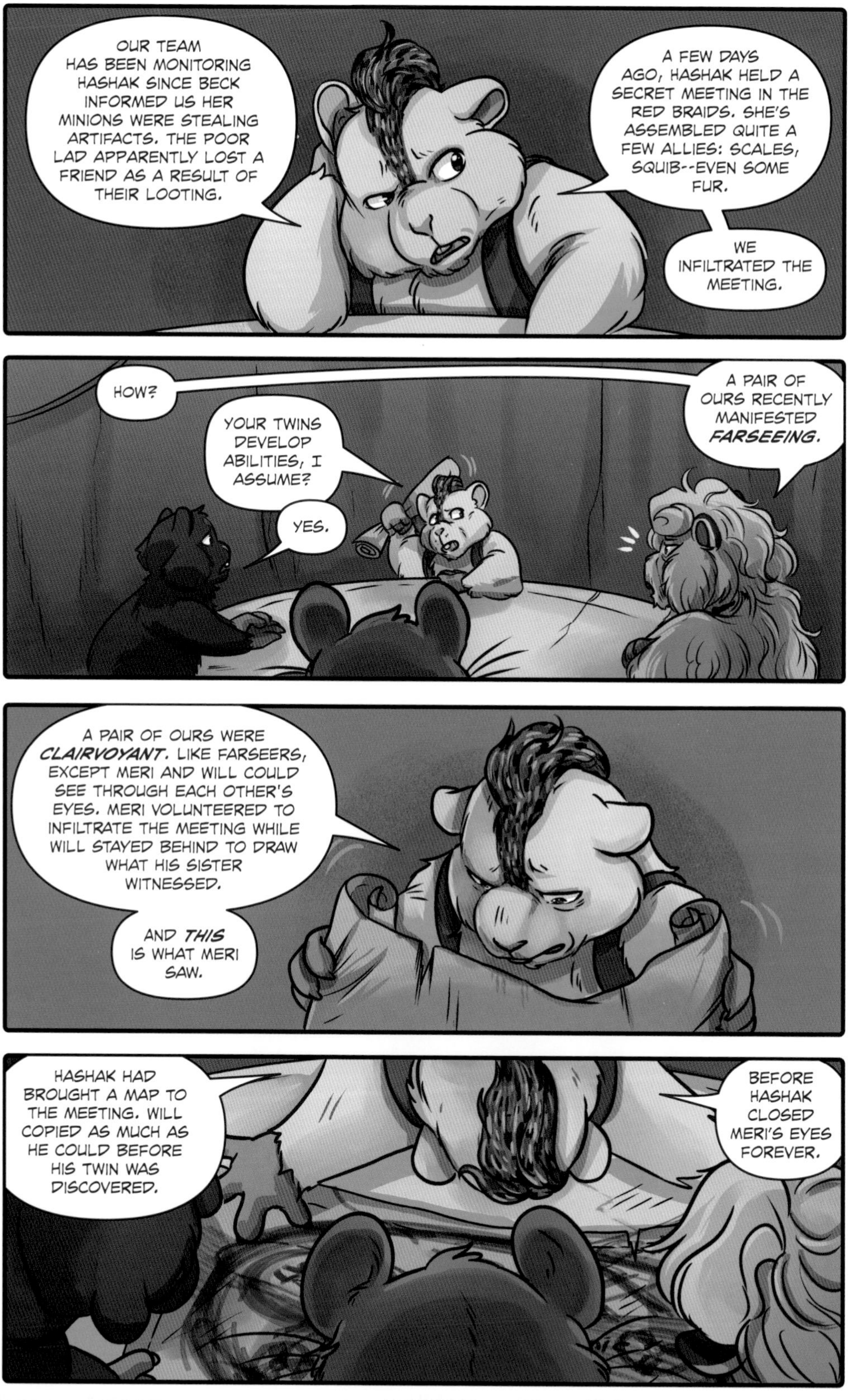
OUR TEAM HAS BEEN MONITORING HASHAK SINCE BECK INFORMED US HER MINIONS WERE STEALING ARTIFACTS. THE POOR LAD APPARENTLY LOST A FRIEND AS A RESULT OF THEIR LOOTING.
A FEW DAYS AGO, HASHAK HELD A SECRET MEETING IN THE RED BRAIDS. SHE'S ASSEMBLED QUITE A FEW ALLIES: SCALES, SQUIB--EVEN SOME FUR.
WE INFILTRATED THE MEETING.
HOW?
A PAIR OF OURS RECENTLY MANIFESTED *FARSEEING*.
YOUR TWINS DEVELOP ABILITIES, I ASSUME?
YES.
A PAIR OF OURS WERE *CLAIRVOYANT*. LIKE FARSEERS, EXCEPT MERI AND WILL COULD SEE THROUGH EACH OTHER'S EYES. MERI VOLUNTEERED TO INFILTRATE THE MEETING WHILE WILL STAYED BEHIND TO DRAW WHAT HIS SISTER WITNESSED.
AND *THIS* IS WHAT MERI SAW.
HASHAK HAD BROUGHT A MAP TO THE MEETING. WILL COPIED AS MUCH AS HE COULD BEFORE HIS TWIN WAS DISCOVERED.
BEFORE HASHAK CLOSED MERI'S EYES FOREVER.

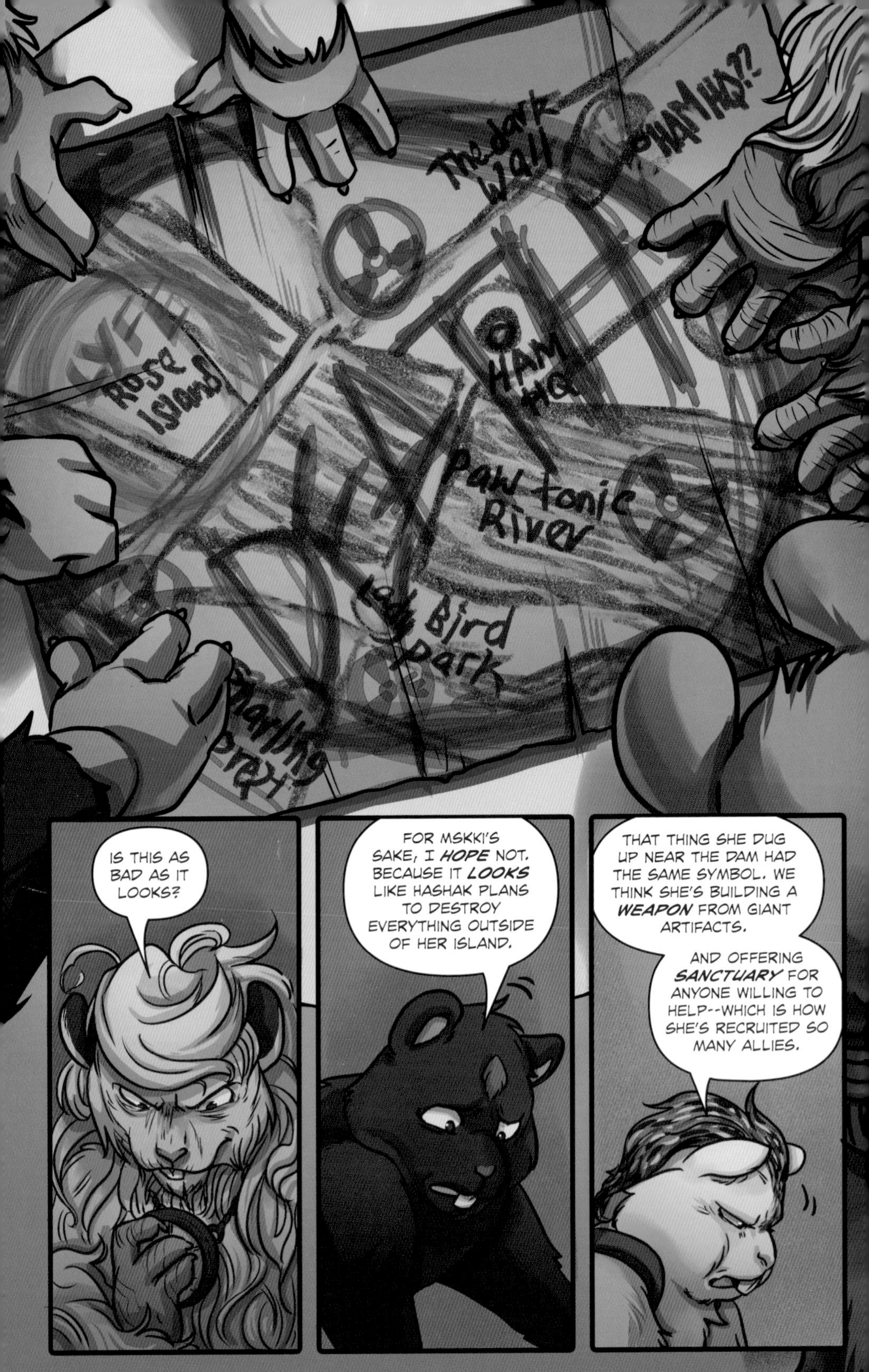

The dark Wall
HAM HQ??
Rose Island
HAM HQ
Paw tonic River
lady Bird park
IS THIS AS BAD AS IT LOOKS?
FOR MSKKI'S SAKE, I HOPE NOT. BECAUSE IT LOOKS LIKE HASHAK PLANS TO DESTROY EVERYTHING OUTSIDE OF HER ISLAND.
THAT THING SHE DUG UP NEAR THE DAM HAD THE SAME SYMBOL. WE THINK SHE'S BUILDING A WEAPON FROM GIANT ARTIFACTS.
AND OFFERING SANCTUARY FOR ANYONE WILLING TO HELP--WHICH IS HOW SHE'S RECRUITED SO MANY ALLIES.

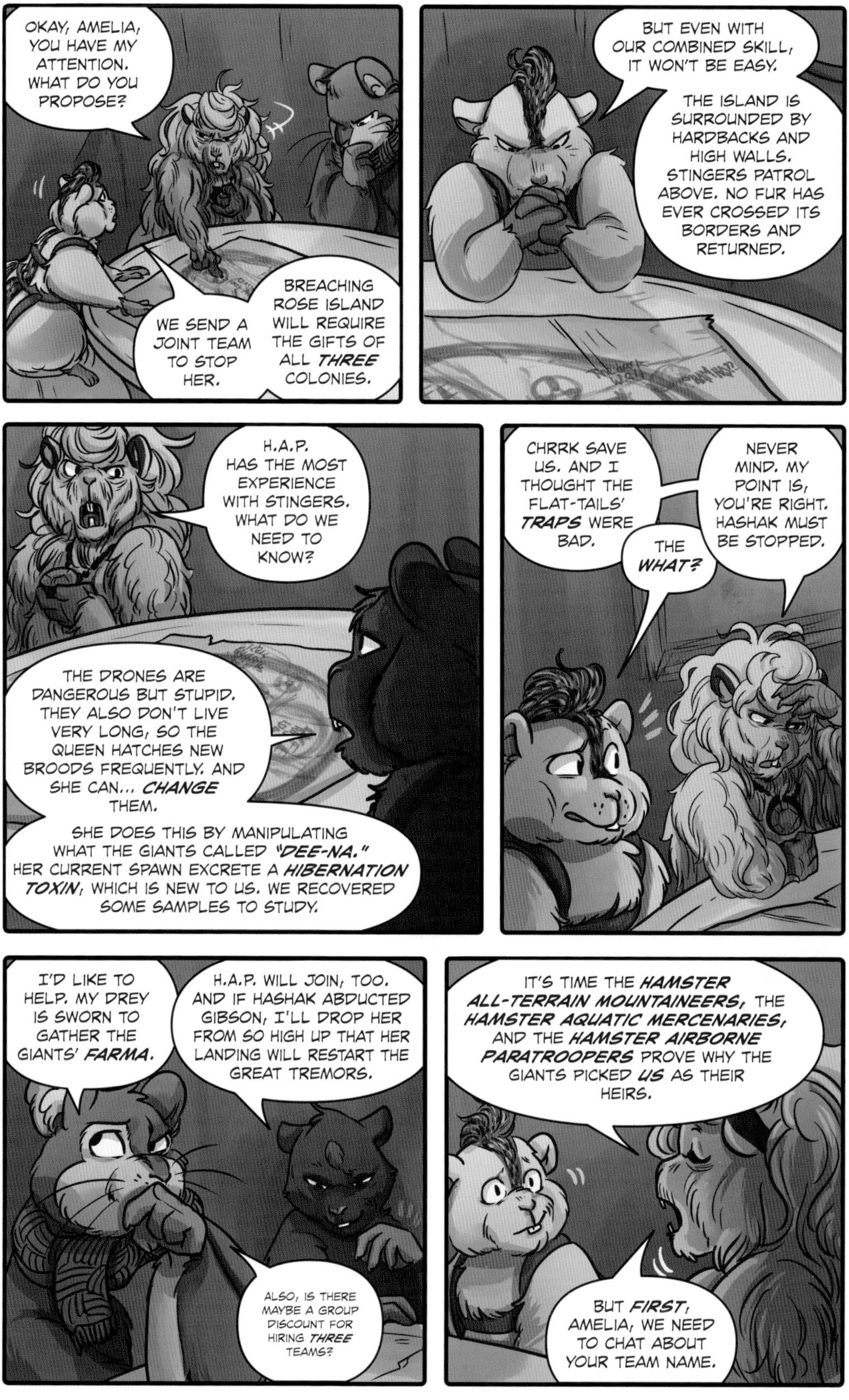
OKAY, AMELIA, YOU HAVE MY ATTENTION. WHAT DO YOU PROPOSE?
BREACHING ROSE ISLAND WILL REQUIRE THE GIFTS OF ALL *THREE* COLONIES.
WE SEND A JOINT TEAM TO STOP HER.
BUT EVEN WITH OUR COMBINED SKILL, IT WON'T BE EASY.
THE ISLAND IS SURROUNDED BY HARDBACKS AND HIGH WALLS. STINGERS PATROL ABOVE. NO FUR HAS EVER CROSSED ITS BORDERS AND RETURNED.
H.A.P. HAS THE MOST EXPERIENCE WITH STINGERS. WHAT DO WE NEED TO KNOW?
THE DRONES ARE DANGEROUS BUT STUPID. THEY ALSO DON'T LIVE VERY LONG, SO THE QUEEN HATCHES NEW BROODS FREQUENTLY. AND SHE CAN... *CHANGE* THEM.
SHE DOES THIS BY MANIPULATING WHAT THE GIANTS CALLED *"DEE-NA."* HER CURRENT SPAWN EXCRETE A *HIBERNATION TOXIN*, WHICH IS NEW TO US. WE RECOVERED SOME SAMPLES TO STUDY.
CHRRK SAVE US. AND I THOUGHT THE FLAT-TAILS' *TRAPS* WERE BAD.
THE *WHAT?*
NEVER MIND. MY POINT IS, YOU'RE RIGHT. HASHAK MUST BE STOPPED.
I'D LIKE TO HELP. MY DREY IS SWORN TO GATHER THE GIANTS' *FARMA*.
H.A.P. WILL JOIN, TOO. AND IF HASHAK ABDUCTED GIBSON, I'LL DROP HER FROM SO HIGH UP THAT HER LANDING WILL RESTART THE GREAT TREMORS.
ALSO, IS THERE MAYBE A GROUP DISCOUNT FOR HIRING *THREE* TEAMS?
IT'S TIME THE *HAMSTER ALL-TERRAIN MOUNTAINEERS*, THE *HAMSTER AQUATIC MERCENARIES*, AND THE *HAMSTER AIRBORNE PARATROOPERS* PROVE WHY THE GIANTS PICKED *US* AS THEIR HEIRS.
BUT *FIRST*, AMELIA, WE NEED TO CHAT ABOUT YOUR TEAM NAME.

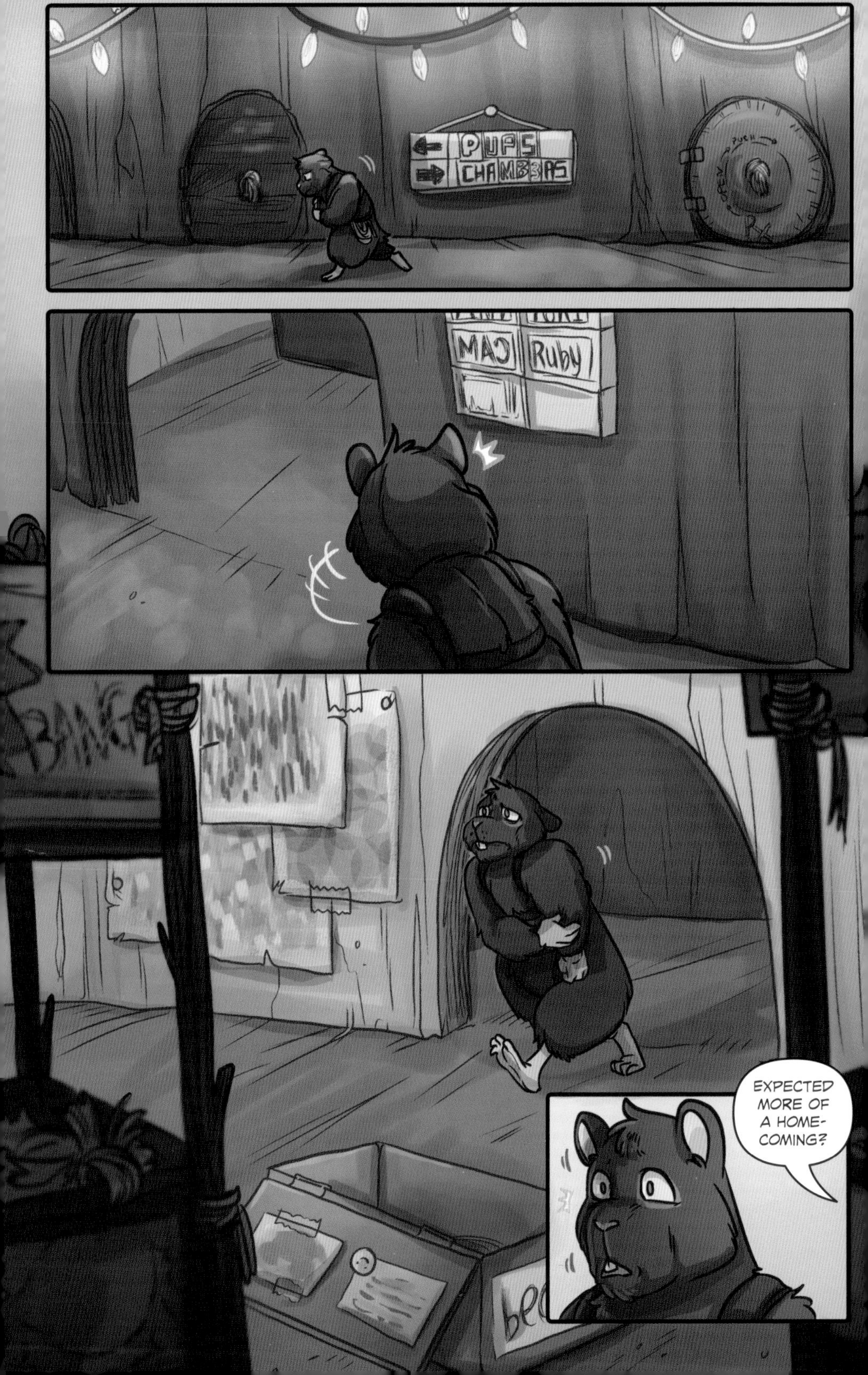
PUPS
CHAMB3AS
PUSH
MAC
Ruby
EXPECTED MORE OF A HOME-COMING?

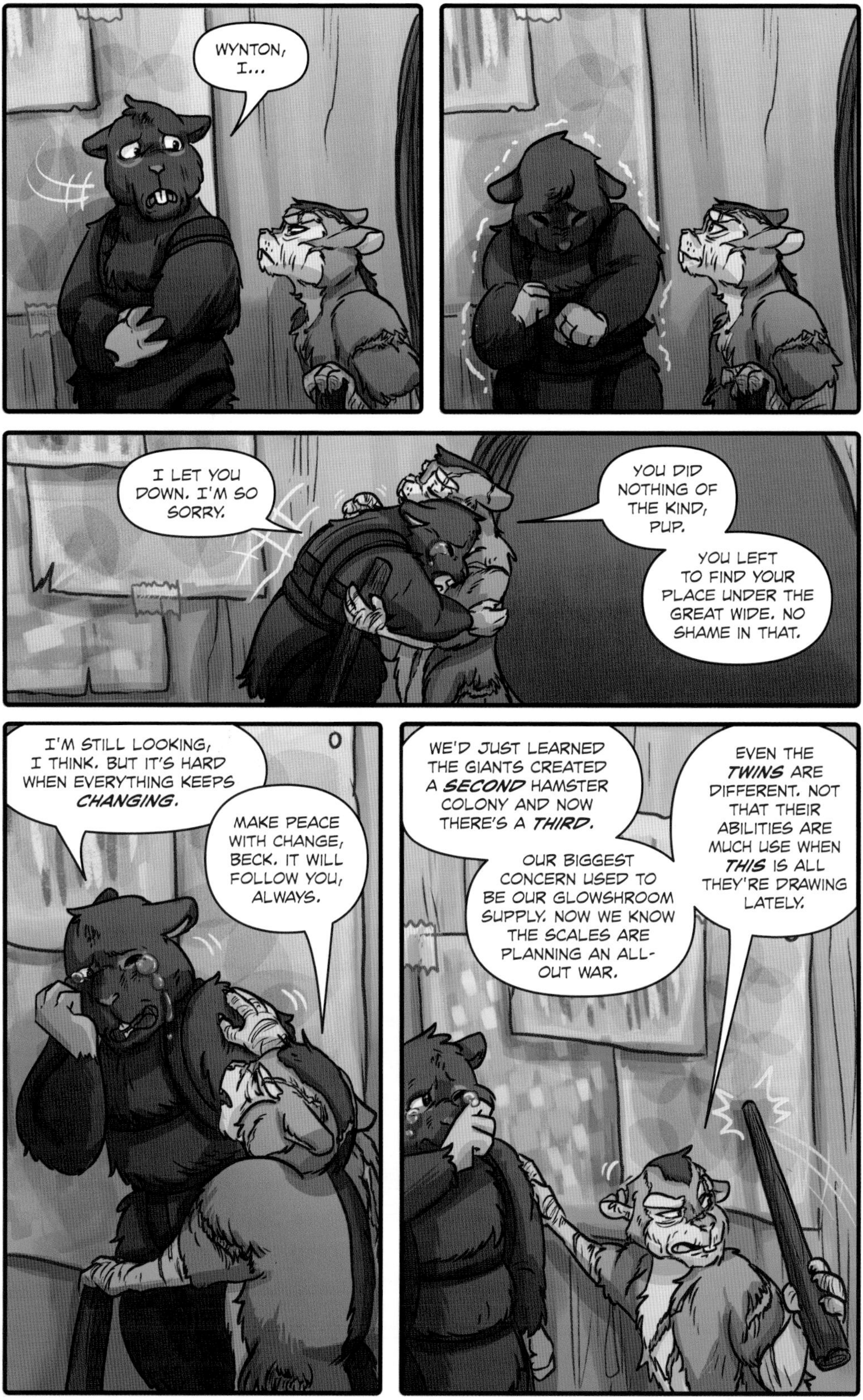
WYNTON, I...
I LET YOU DOWN. I'M SO SORRY.
YOU DID NOTHING OF THE KIND, PUP.
YOU LEFT TO FIND YOUR PLACE UNDER THE GREAT WIDE. NO SHAME IN THAT.
I'M STILL LOOKING, I THINK. BUT IT'S HARD WHEN EVERYTHING KEEPS CHANGING.
MAKE PEACE WITH CHANGE, BECK. IT WILL FOLLOW YOU, ALWAYS.
WE'D JUST LEARNED THE GIANTS CREATED A SECOND HAMSTER COLONY AND NOW THERE'S A THIRD.
OUR BIGGEST CONCERN USED TO BE OUR GLOWSHROOM SUPPLY. NOW WE KNOW THE SCALES ARE PLANNING AN ALL-OUT WAR.
EVEN THE TWINS ARE DIFFERENT. NOT THAT THEIR ABILITIES ARE MUCH USE WHEN THIS IS ALL THEY'RE DRAWING LATELY.

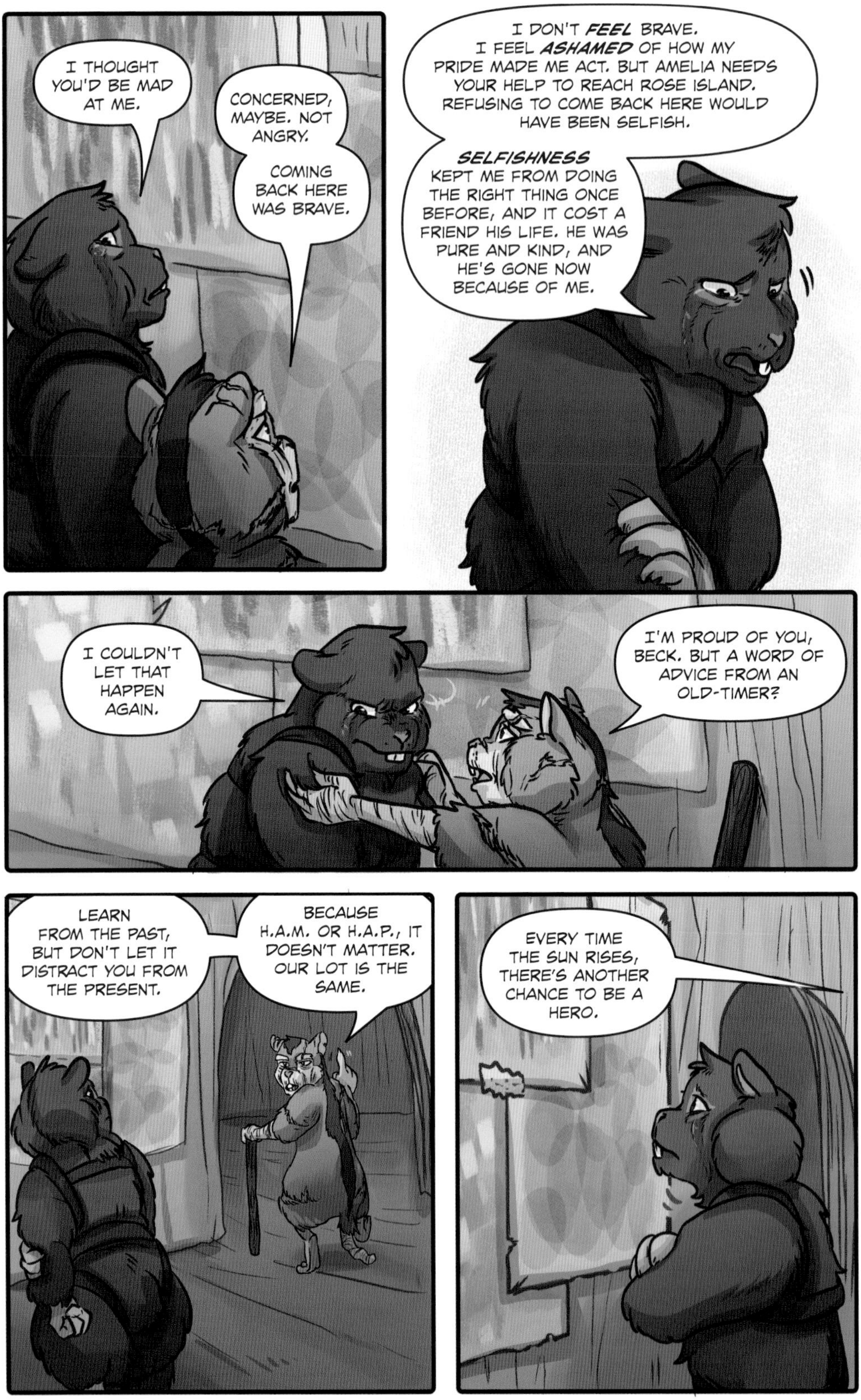
I THOUGHT YOU'D BE MAD AT ME.
CONCERNED, MAYBE. NOT ANGRY.
COMING BACK HERE WAS BRAVE.
I DON'T FEEL BRAVE. I FEEL ASHAMED OF HOW MY PRIDE MADE ME ACT. BUT AMELIA NEEDS YOUR HELP TO REACH ROSE ISLAND. REFUSING TO COME BACK HERE WOULD HAVE BEEN SELFISH.
SELFISHNESS KEPT ME FROM DOING THE RIGHT THING ONCE BEFORE, AND IT COST A FRIEND HIS LIFE. HE WAS PURE AND KIND, AND HE'S GONE NOW BECAUSE OF ME.
I COULDN'T LET THAT HAPPEN AGAIN.
I'M PROUD OF YOU, BECK. BUT A WORD OF ADVICE FROM AN OLD-TIMER?
LEARN FROM THE PAST, BUT DON'T LET IT DISTRACT YOU FROM THE PRESENT.
BECAUSE H.A.M. OR H.A.P., IT DOESN'T MATTER. OUR LOT IS THE SAME.
EVERY TIME THE SUN RISES, THERE'S ANOTHER CHANCE TO BE A HERO.

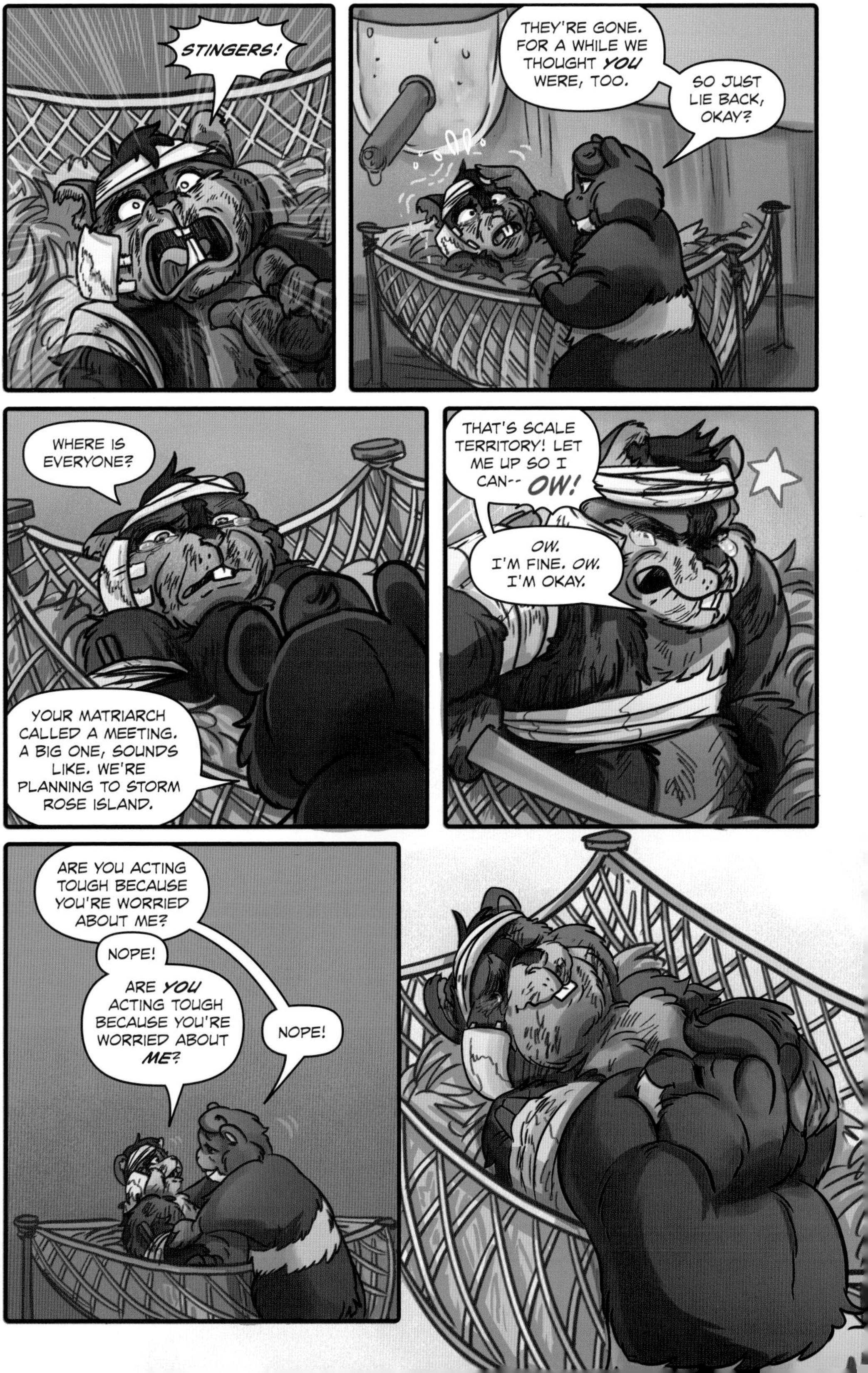
STINGERS!
THEY'RE GONE. FOR A WHILE WE THOUGHT YOU WERE, TOO.
SO JUST LIE BACK, OKAY?
WHERE IS EVERYONE?
YOUR MATRIARCH CALLED A MEETING. A BIG ONE, SOUNDS LIKE. WE'RE PLANNING TO STORM ROSE ISLAND.
THAT'S SCALE TERRITORY! LET ME UP SO I CAN-- OW!
OW. I'M FINE. OW. I'M OKAY.
ARE YOU ACTING TOUGH BECAUSE YOU'RE WORRIED ABOUT ME?
NOPE!
ARE YOU ACTING TOUGH BECAUSE YOU'RE WORRIED ABOUT ME?
NOPE!

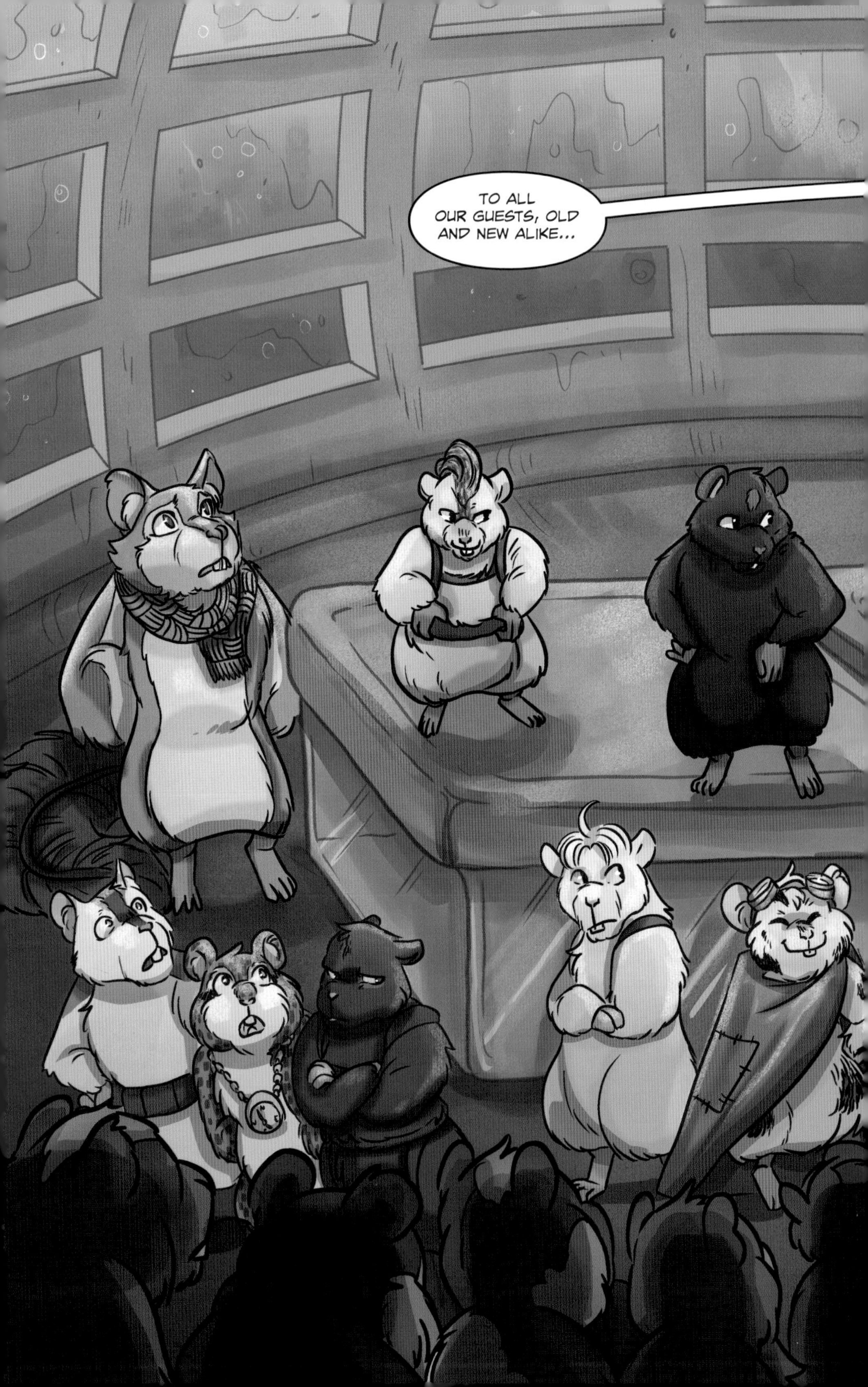
TO ALL OUR GUESTS, OLD AND NEW ALIKE...

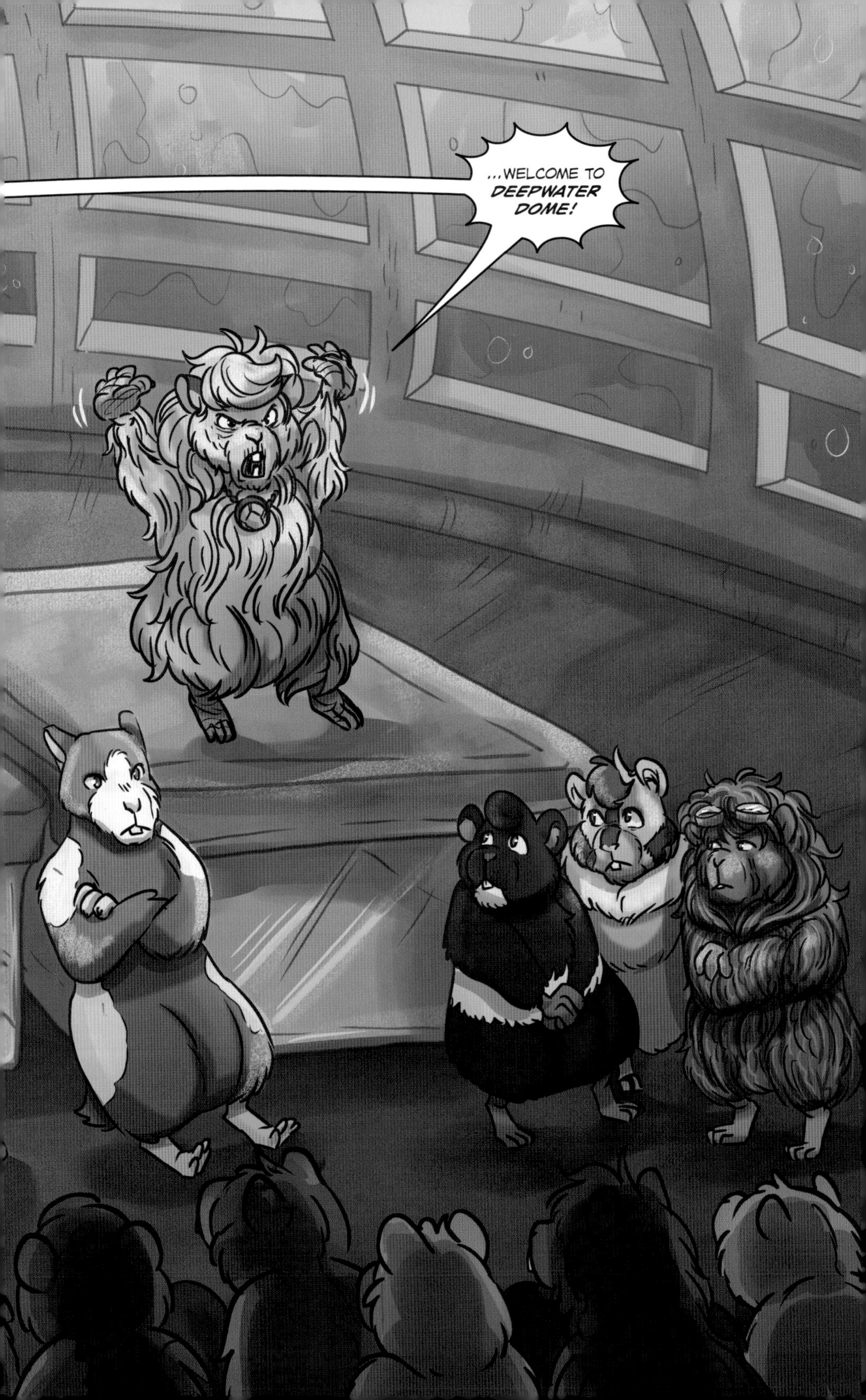
...WELCOME TO
DEEPWATER DOME!

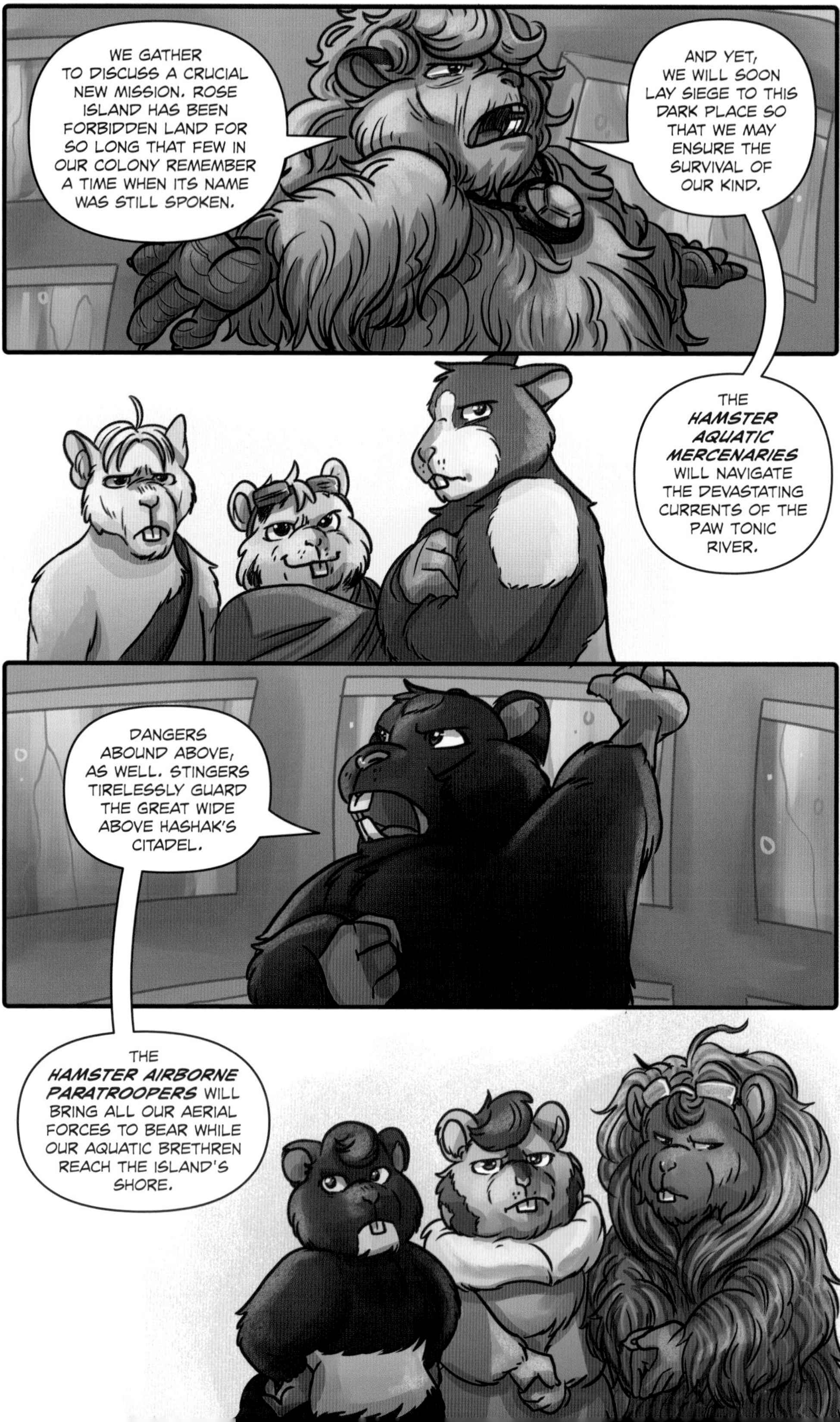
WE GATHER TO DISCUSS A CRUCIAL NEW MISSION. ROSE ISLAND HAS BEEN FORBIDDEN LAND FOR SO LONG THAT FEW IN OUR COLONY REMEMBER A TIME WHEN ITS NAME WAS STILL SPOKEN.
AND YET, WE WILL SOON LAY SIEGE TO THIS DARK PLACE SO THAT WE MAY ENSURE THE SURVIVAL OF OUR KIND.
THE *HAMSTER AQUATIC MERCENARIES* WILL NAVIGATE THE DEVASTATING CURRENTS OF THE PAW TONIC RIVER.
DANGERS ABOUND ABOVE, AS WELL. STINGERS TIRELESSLY GUARD THE GREAT WIDE ABOVE HASHAK'S CITADEL.
THE *HAMSTER AIRBORNE PARATROOPERS* WILL BRING ALL OUR AERIAL FORCES TO BEAR WHILE OUR AQUATIC BRETHREN REACH THE ISLAND'S SHORE.

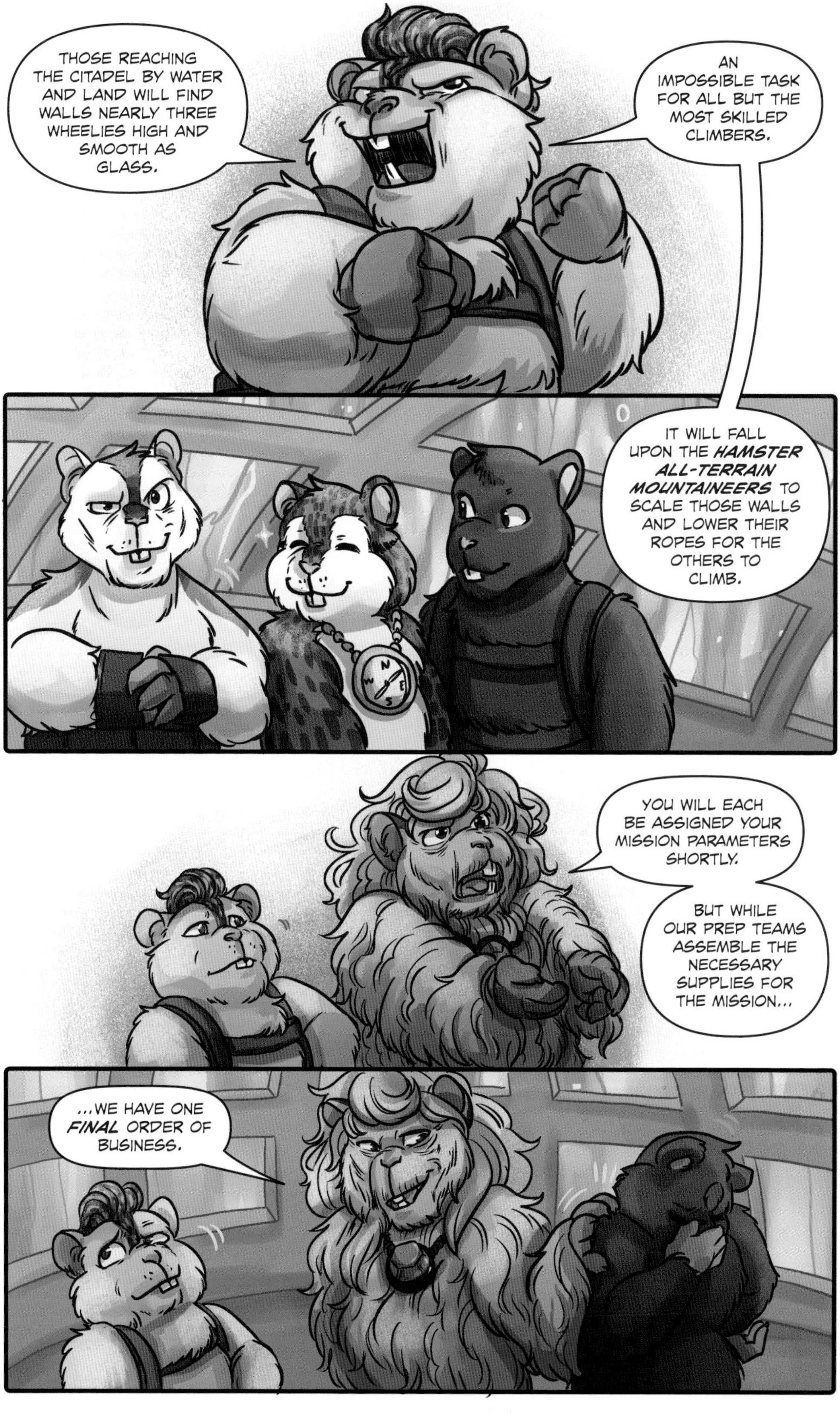
THOSE REACHING THE CITADEL BY WATER AND LAND WILL FIND WALLS NEARLY THREE WHEELIES HIGH AND SMOOTH AS GLASS.
AN IMPOSSIBLE TASK FOR ALL BUT THE MOST SKILLED CLIMBERS.
IT WILL FALL UPON THE *HAMSTER ALL-TERRAIN MOUNTAINEERS* TO SCALE THOSE WALLS AND LOWER THEIR ROPES FOR THE OTHERS TO CLIMB.
YOU WILL EACH BE ASSIGNED YOUR MISSION PARAMETERS SHORTLY.
BUT WHILE OUR PREP TEAMS ASSEMBLE THE NECESSARY SUPPLIES FOR THE MISSION...
...WE HAVE ONE *FINAL* ORDER OF BUSINESS.

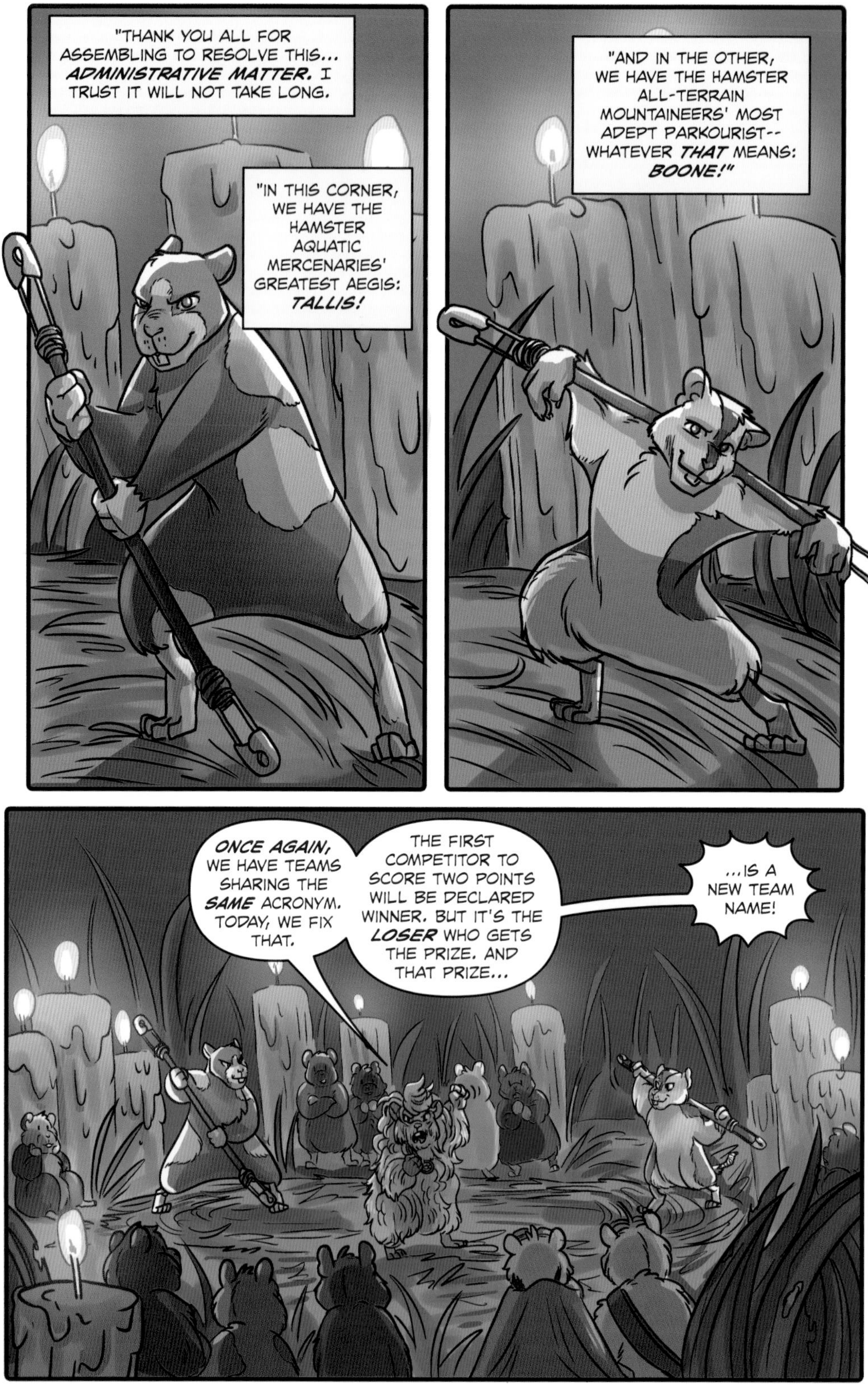
"THANK YOU ALL FOR ASSEMBLING TO RESOLVE THIS... ***ADMINISTRATIVE MATTER.*** I TRUST IT WILL NOT TAKE LONG.
"IN THIS CORNER, WE HAVE THE HAMSTER AQUATIC MERCENARIES' GREATEST AEGIS: ***TALLIS!***
"AND IN THE OTHER, WE HAVE THE HAMSTER ALL-TERRAIN MOUNTAINEERS' MOST ADEPT PARKOURIST-- WHATEVER ***THAT*** MEANS: ***BOONE!"***
ONCE AGAIN, WE HAVE TEAMS SHARING THE ***SAME*** ACRONYM. TODAY, WE FIX THAT.
THE FIRST COMPETITOR TO SCORE TWO POINTS WILL BE DECLARED WINNER. BUT IT'S THE ***LOSER*** WHO GETS THE PRIZE. AND THAT PRIZE...
...IS A NEW TEAM NAME!

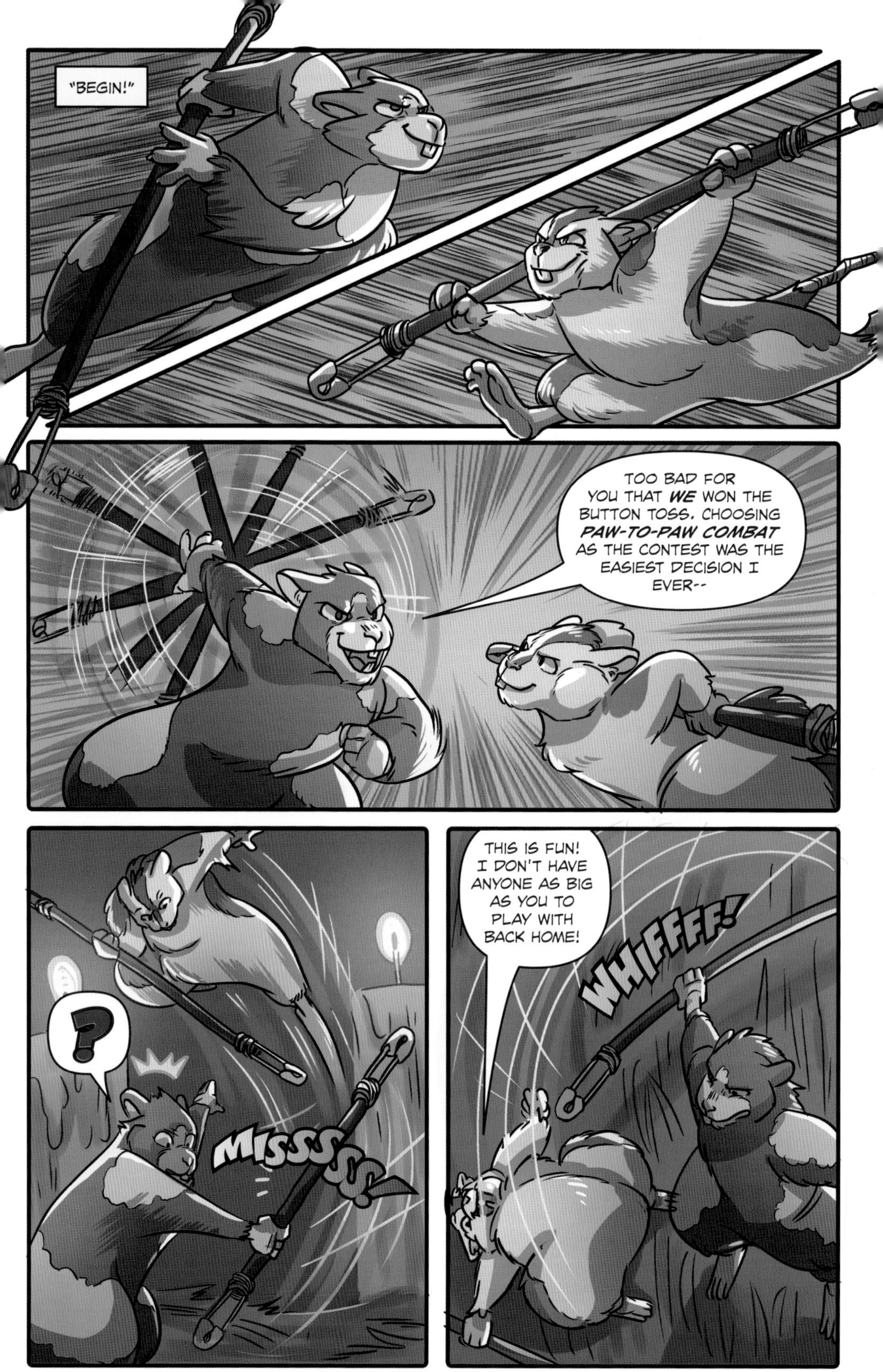
"BEGIN!"
TOO BAD FOR YOU THAT WE WON THE BUTTON TOSS. CHOOSING PAW-TO-PAW COMBAT AS THE CONTEST WAS THE EASIEST DECISION I EVER--
?
MISSSSS
THIS IS FUN! I DON'T HAVE ANYONE AS BIG AS YOU TO PLAY WITH BACK HOME!
WHIFFFF!

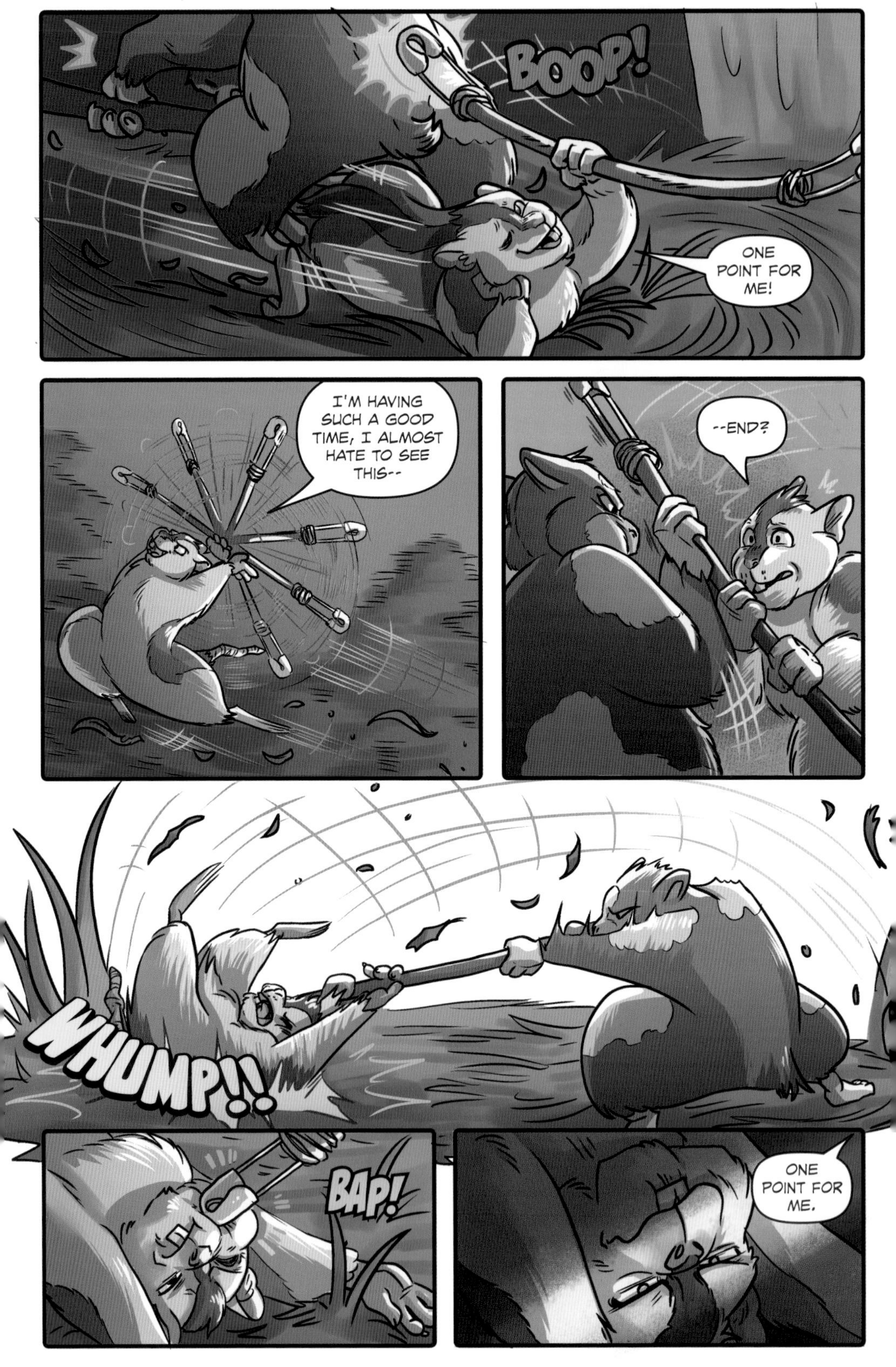
BOOP!
ONE POINT FOR ME!
I'M HAVING SUCH A GOOD TIME, I ALMOST HATE TO SEE THIS--
--END?
WHUMP!!
BAP!
ONE POINT FOR ME.

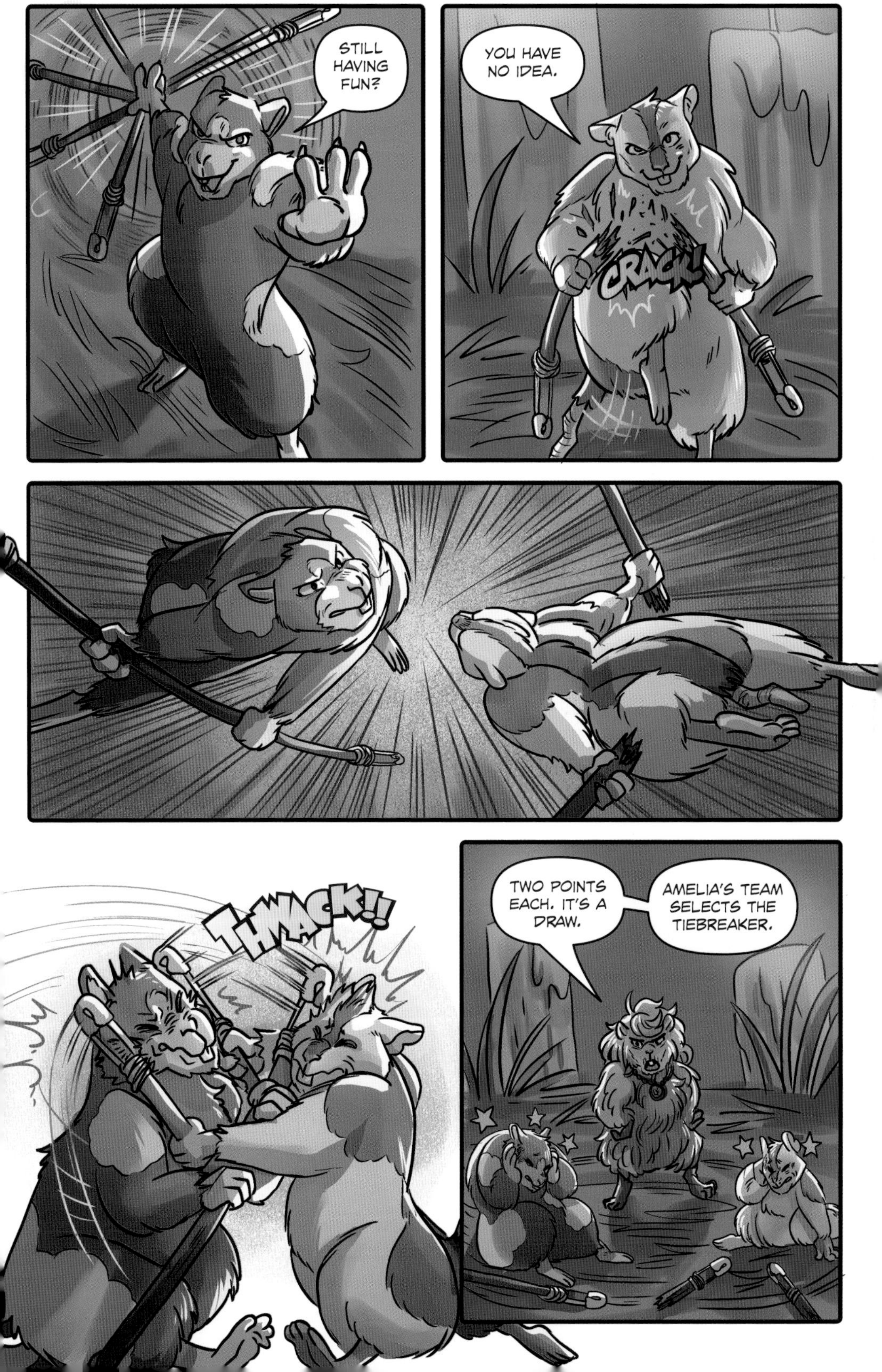
STILL HAVING FUN?
YOU HAVE NO IDEA.
CRACK!
THWACK!!
TWO POINTS EACH. IT'S A DRAW.
AMELIA'S TEAM SELECTS THE TIEBREAKER.

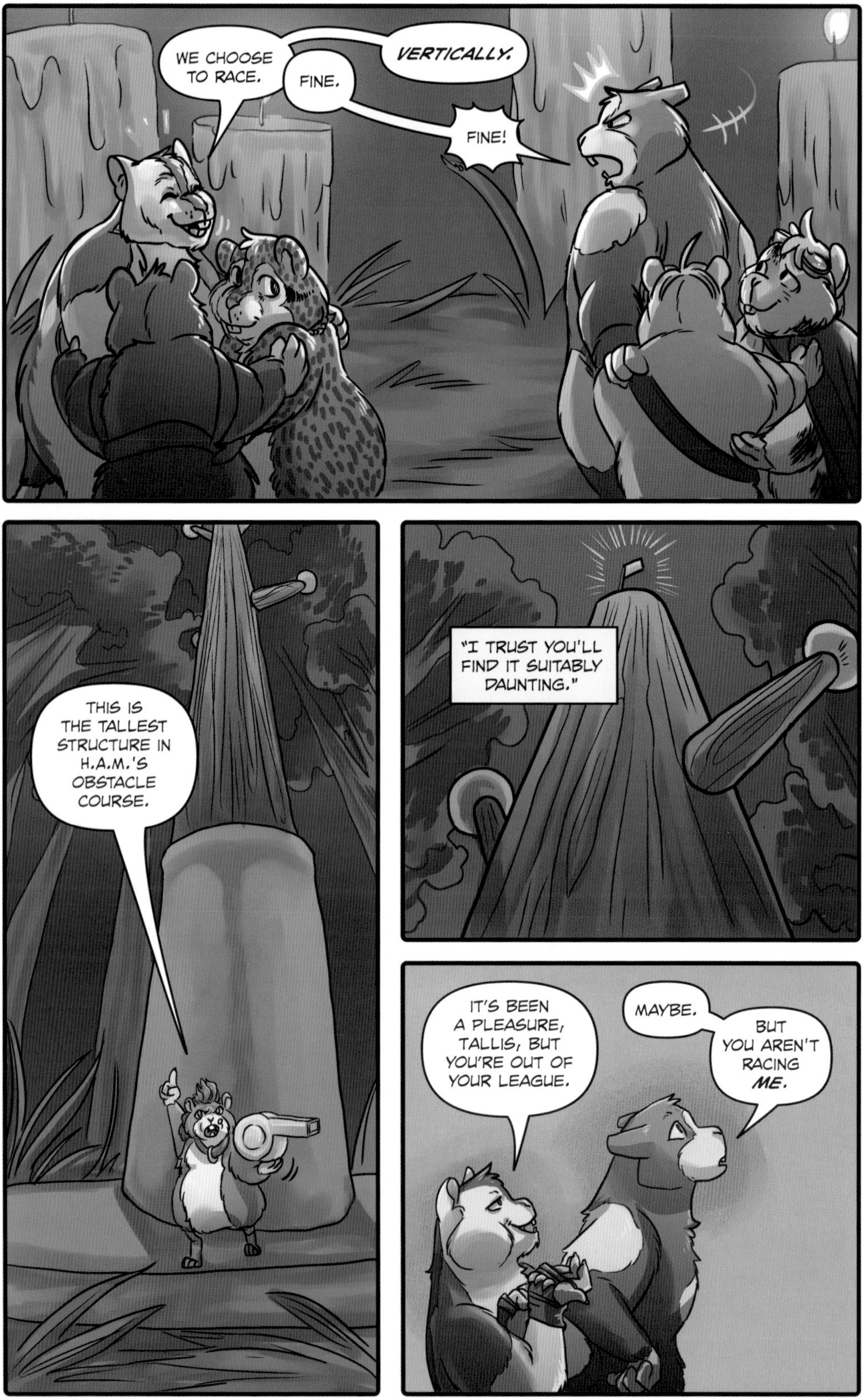
WE CHOOSE TO RACE.
VERTICALLY.
FINE.
FINE!
THIS IS THE TALLEST STRUCTURE IN H.A.M.'S OBSTACLE COURSE.
"I TRUST YOU'LL FIND IT SUITABLY DAUNTING."
IT'S BEEN A PLEASURE, TALLIS, BUT YOU'RE OUT OF YOUR LEAGUE.
MAYBE.
BUT YOU AREN'T RACING *ME.*

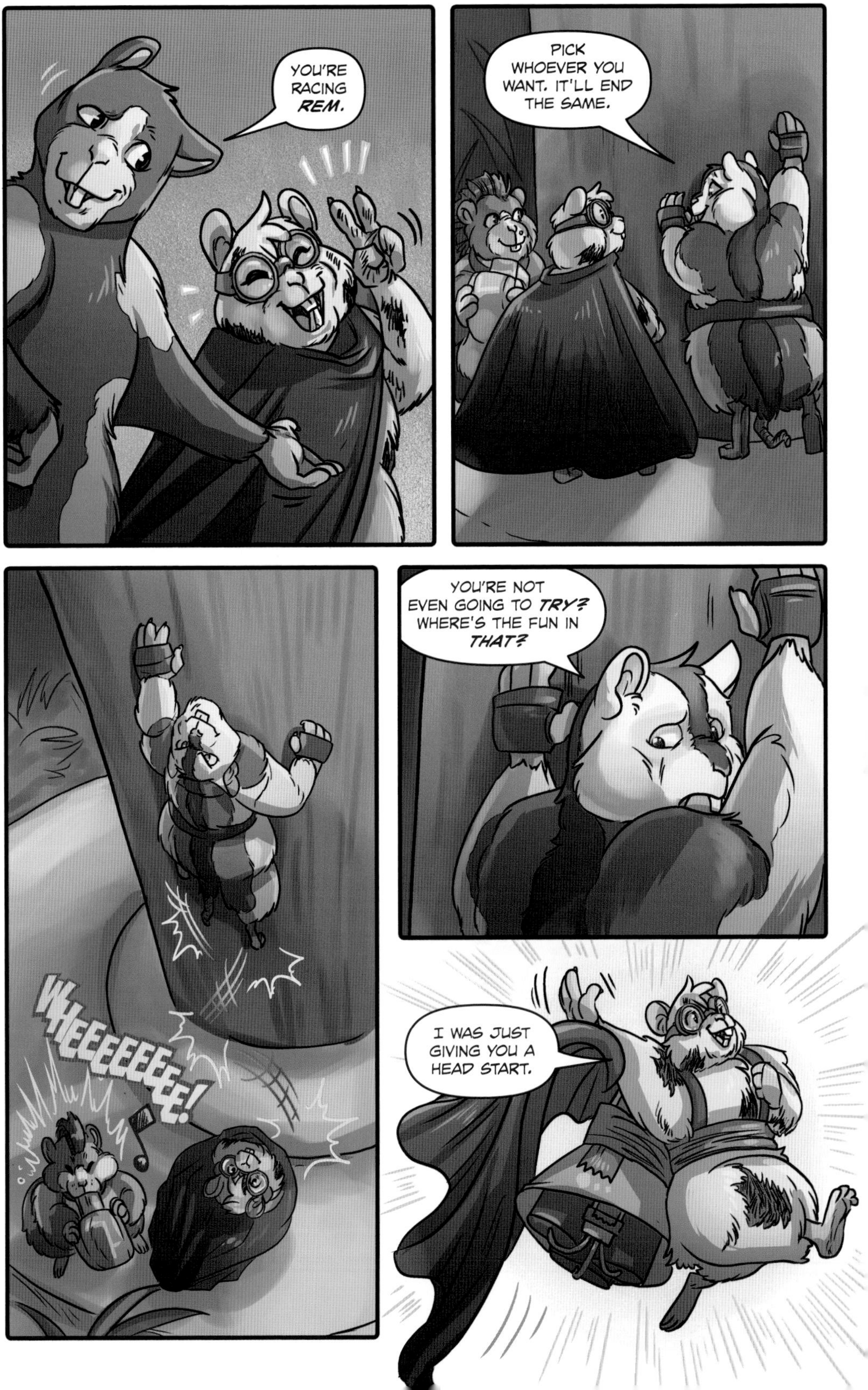
YOU'RE RACING REM.
PICK WHOEVER YOU WANT. IT'LL END THE SAME.
WHEEEEEEEEE!
YOU'RE NOT EVEN GOING TO TRY? WHERE'S THE FUN IN THAT?
I WAS JUST GIVING YOU A HEAD START.

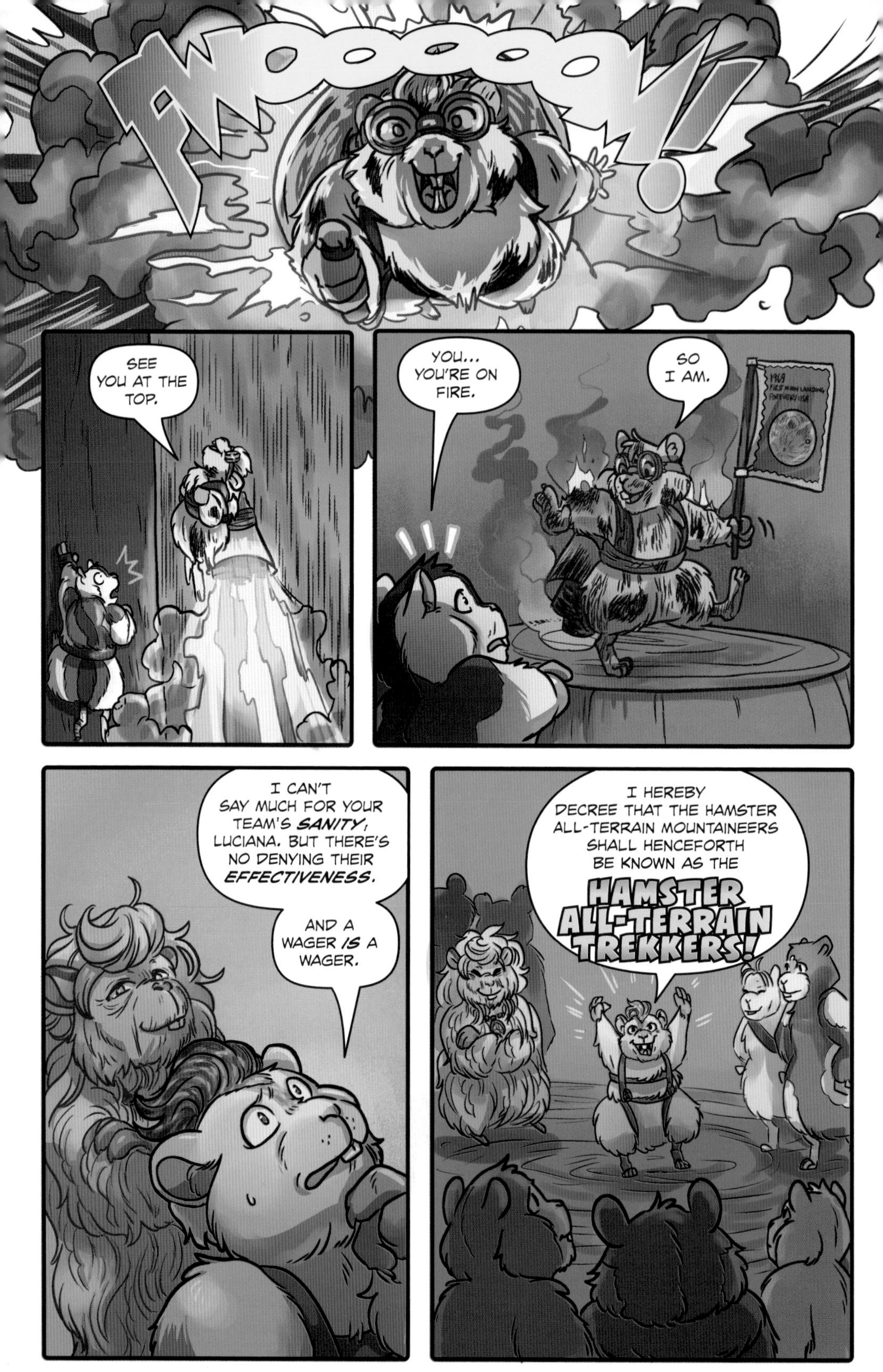
FWOOOOM!
SEE YOU AT THE TOP.
YOU... YOU'RE ON FIRE.
SO I AM.
1969 FIRST MAN LANDING
I CAN'T SAY MUCH FOR YOUR TEAM'S SANITY, LUCIANA. BUT THERE'S NO DENYING THEIR EFFECTIVENESS.
AND A WAGER IS A WAGER.
I HEREBY DECREE THAT THE HAMSTER ALL-TERRAIN MOUNTAINEERS SHALL HENCEFORTH BE KNOWN AS THE
HAMSTER ALL-TERRAIN TREKKERS!

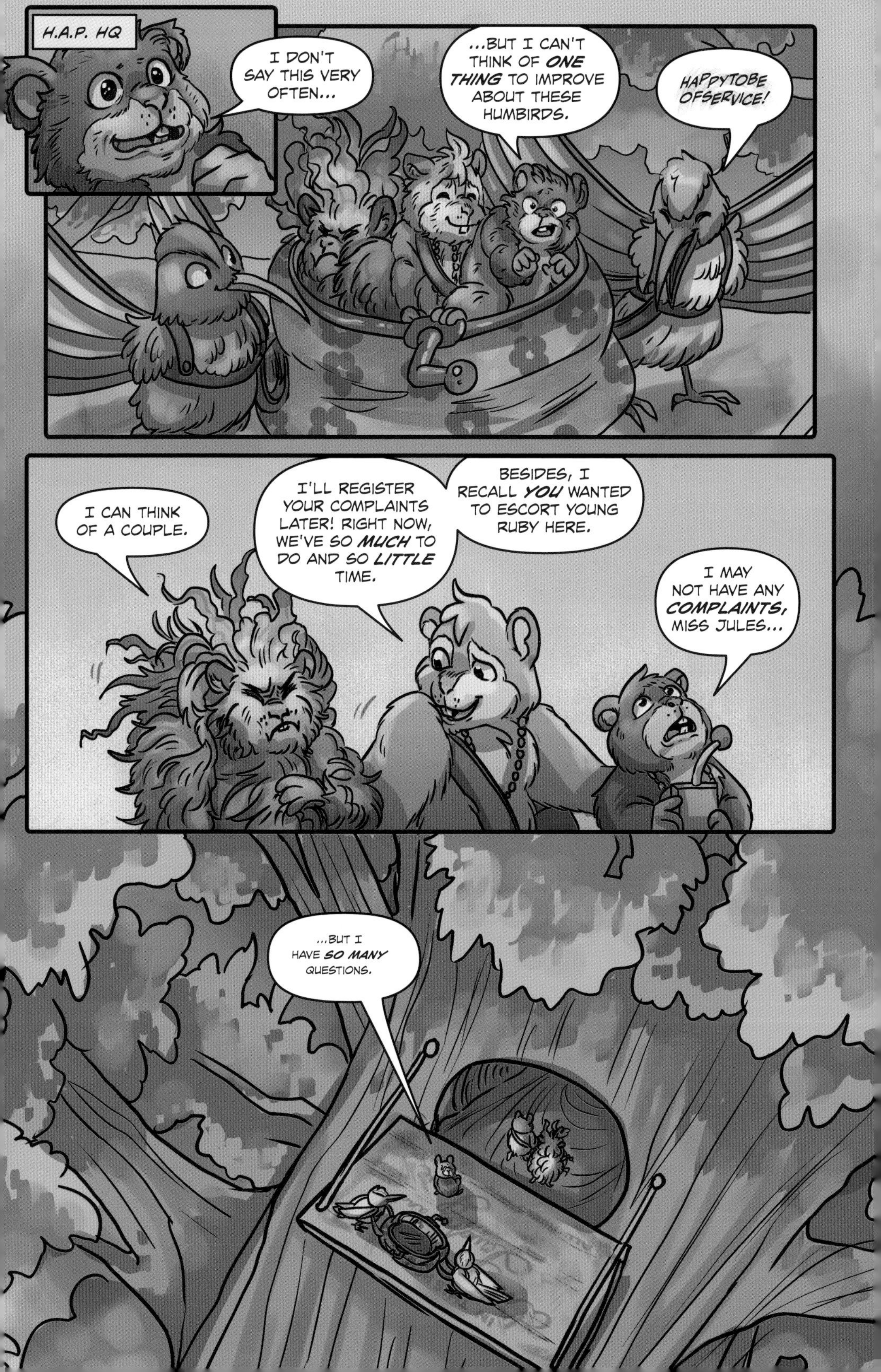
H.A.P. HQ
I DON'T SAY THIS VERY OFTEN...
...BUT I CAN'T THINK OF ONE THING TO IMPROVE ABOUT THESE HUMBIRDS.
HAPPYTOBE OFSERVICE!
I CAN THINK OF A COUPLE.
I'LL REGISTER YOUR COMPLAINTS LATER! RIGHT NOW, WE'VE SO MUCH TO DO AND SO LITTLE TIME.
BESIDES, I RECALL YOU WANTED TO ESCORT YOUNG RUBY HERE.
I MAY NOT HAVE ANY COMPLAINTS, MISS JULES...
...BUT I HAVE SO MANY QUESTIONS.

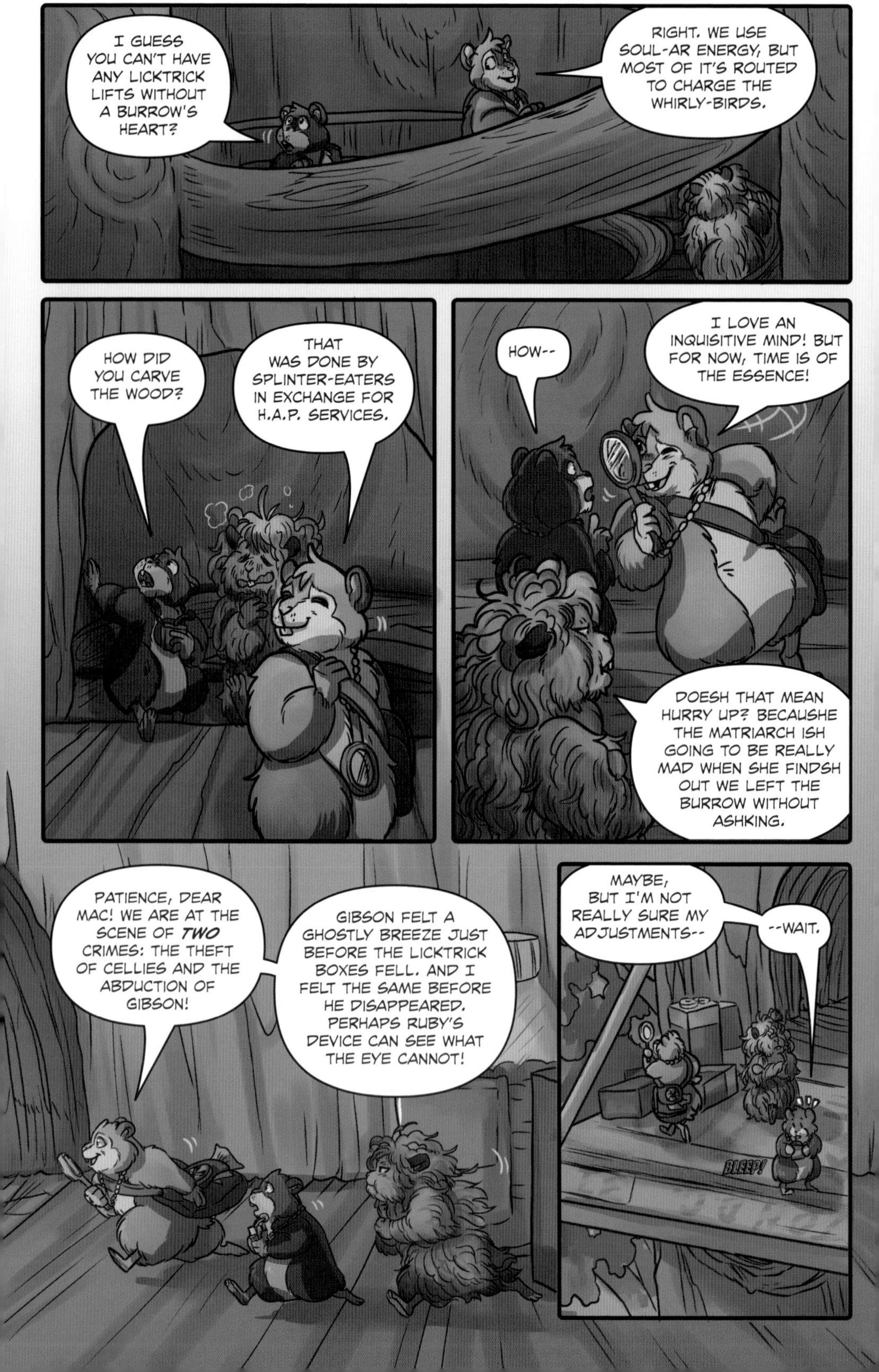
I GUESS YOU CAN'T HAVE ANY LICKTRICK LIFTS WITHOUT A BURROW'S HEART?
RIGHT. WE USE SOUL-AR ENERGY, BUT MOST OF IT'S ROUTED TO CHARGE THE WHIRLY-BIRDS.
HOW DID YOU CARVE THE WOOD?
THAT WAS DONE BY SPLINTER-EATERS IN EXCHANGE FOR H.A.P. SERVICES.
HOW--
I LOVE AN INQUISITIVE MIND! BUT FOR NOW, TIME IS OF THE ESSENCE!
DOESH THAT MEAN HURRY UP? BECAUSHE THE MATRIARCH ISH GOING TO BE REALLY MAD WHEN SHE FINDSH OUT WE LEFT THE BURROW WITHOUT ASHKING.
PATIENCE, DEAR MAC! WE ARE AT THE SCENE OF *TWO* CRIMES: THE THEFT OF CELLIES AND THE ABDUCTION OF GIBSON!
GIBSON FELT A GHOSTLY BREEZE JUST BEFORE THE LICKTRICK BOXES FELL. AND I FELT THE SAME BEFORE HE DISAPPEARED. PERHAPS RUBY'S DEVICE CAN SEE WHAT THE EYE CANNOT!
MAYBE, BUT I'M NOT REALLY SURE MY ADJUSTMENTS--
--WAIT.
BLEEP!

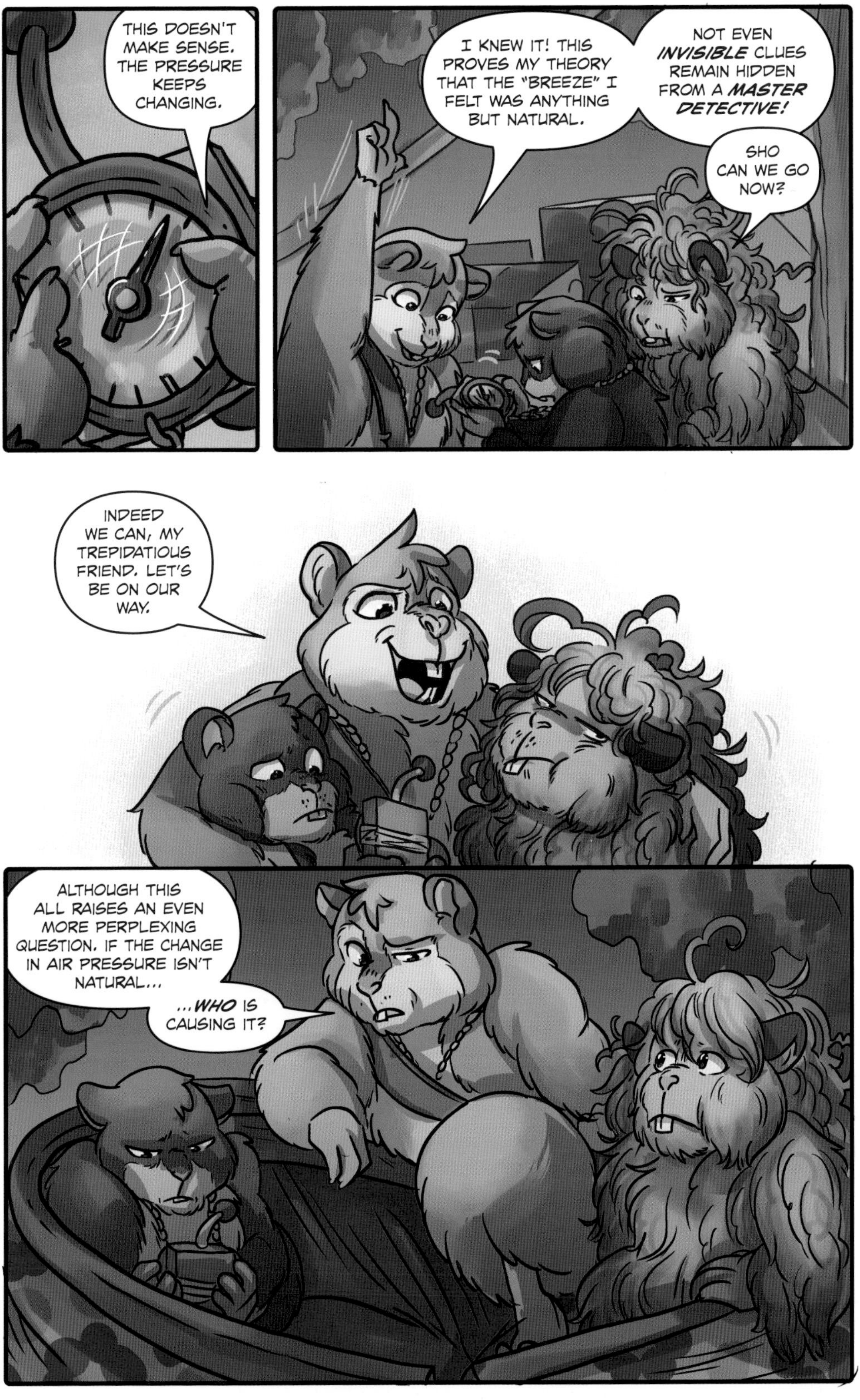
THIS DOESN'T MAKE SENSE. THE PRESSURE KEEPS CHANGING.
I KNEW IT! THIS PROVES MY THEORY THAT THE "BREEZE" I FELT WAS ANYTHING BUT NATURAL.
NOT EVEN INVISIBLE CLUES REMAIN HIDDEN FROM A MASTER DETECTIVE!
SHO CAN WE GO NOW?
INDEED WE CAN, MY TREPIDATIOUS FRIEND. LET'S BE ON OUR WAY.
ALTHOUGH THIS ALL RAISES AN EVEN MORE PERPLEXING QUESTION. IF THE CHANGE IN AIR PRESSURE ISN'T NATURAL...
...WHO IS CAUSING IT?

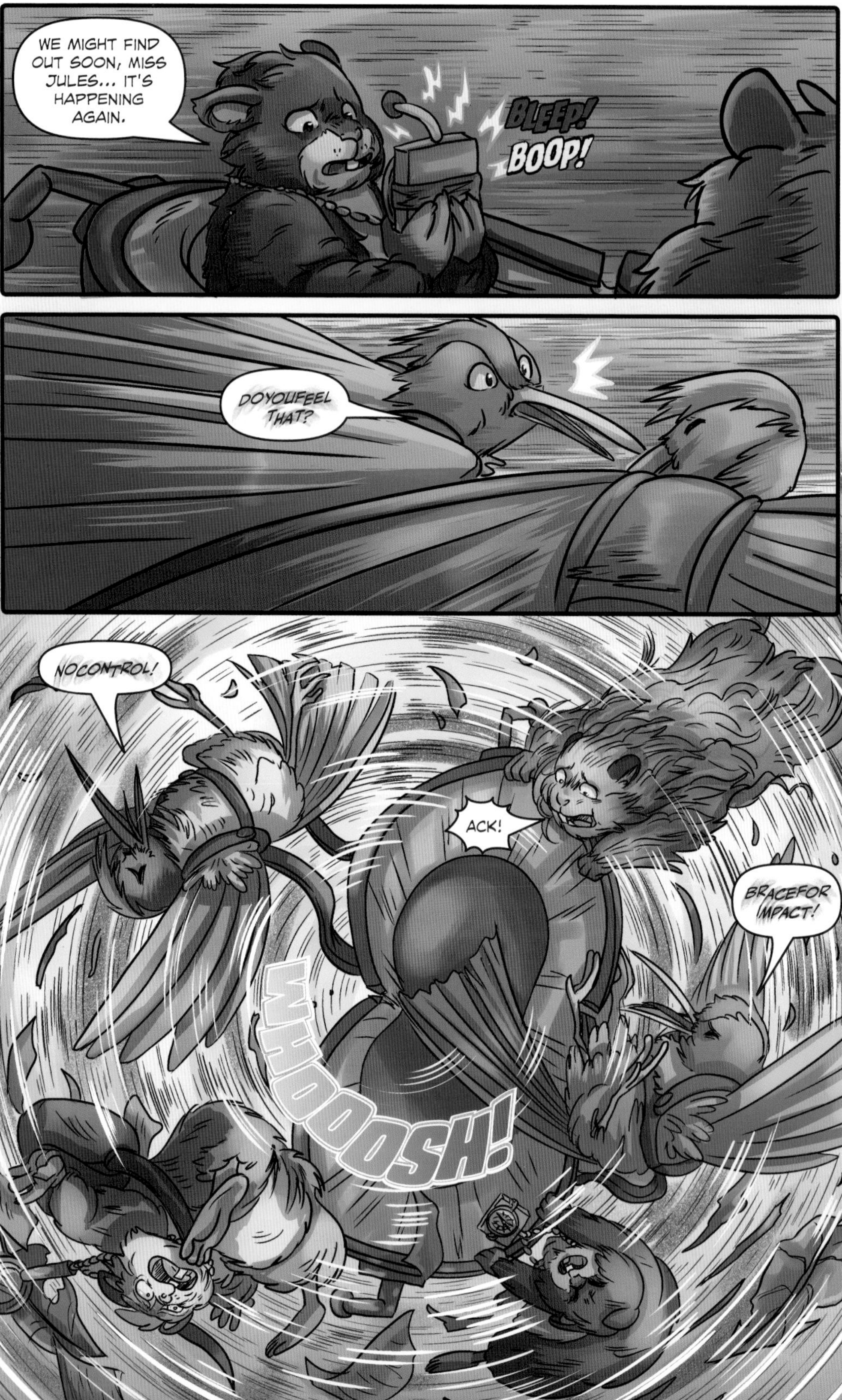
WE MIGHT FIND OUT SOON, MISS JULES... IT'S HAPPENING AGAIN.
BLEEP!
BOOP!
DOYOUFEEL THAT?
NOCONTROL!
ACK!
BRACEFOR IMPACT!
WHOOOSH!

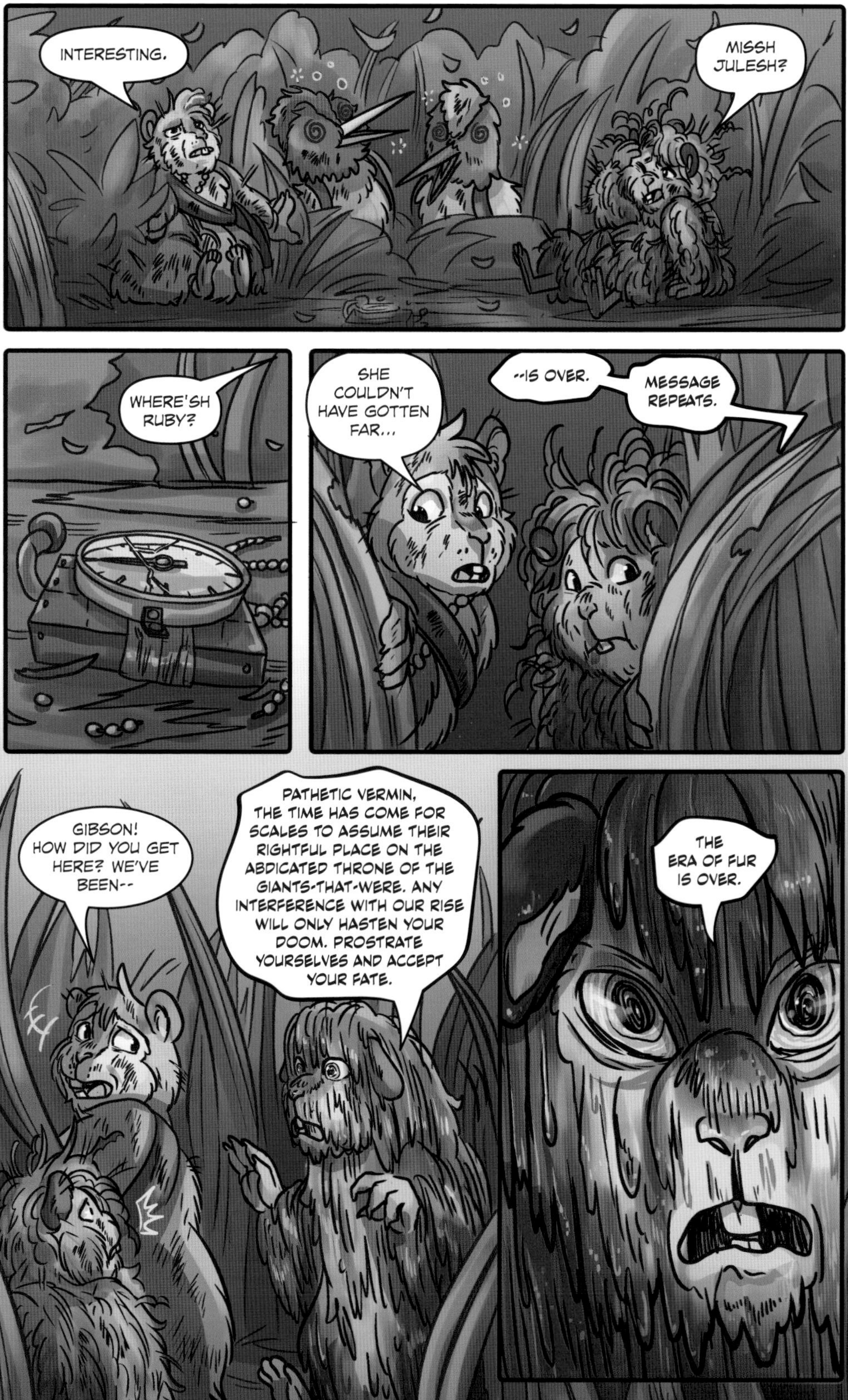
INTERESTING.
MISSH JULESH?
WHERE'SH RUBY?
SHE COULDN'T HAVE GOTTEN FAR...
--IS OVER.
MESSAGE REPEATS.
GIBSON! HOW DID YOU GET HERE? WE'VE BEEN--
PATHETIC VERMIN, THE TIME HAS COME FOR SCALES TO ASSUME THEIR RIGHTFUL PLACE ON THE ABDICATED THRONE OF THE GIANTS-THAT-WERE. ANY INTERFERENCE WITH OUR RISE WILL ONLY HASTEN YOUR DOOM. PROSTRATE YOURSELVES AND ACCEPT YOUR FATE.
THE ERA OF FUR IS OVER.

Amelia

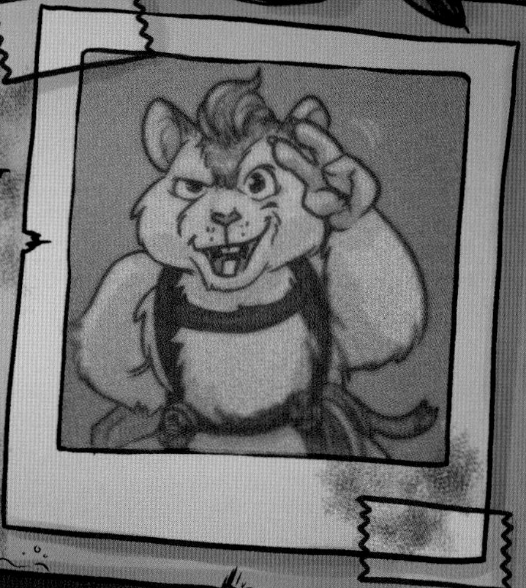

Appearance: Roborovski (Phodopus roborovskii)
Title: H.A.T. High Chair
Behavioral Patterns: Upbeat, confident in all situations. Unique ability to see potential in the underutilized. Leads through encouragement and an "all hamsters are equal" mentality. When questioned re: this approach, she simply responded, "When the rope breaks, we all fall together."

Notes: H.A.T.'s belief that the Giants now live in the "Deep Well" is even more ridiculous than H.A.M.'s theory about a "Wet City."

Boone

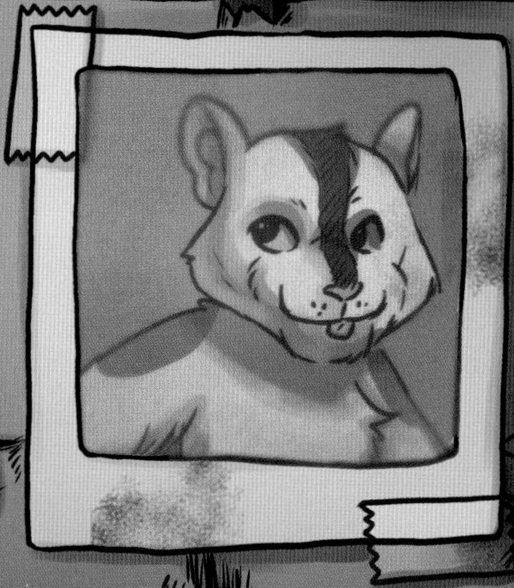

Appearance: Chinese Dwarf (Cricetulus griseus)
Title: H.A.T. Parkourist
Behavioral Patterns: Loves a challenge. An extraordinary combatant, they are supremely confident, occasionally to their detriment.

Enthusiast of slick-surface climbing. Capable of scaling sheer surfaces by finding cracks and crevices that seem invisible to the untrained eye.

Notes: Growing rivalry with Tallis will likely motivate both hamsters.

Cook

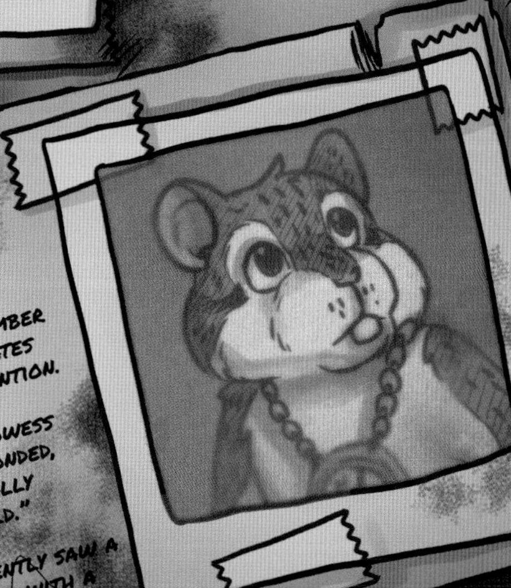

Appearance: Roborovski (Phodopus roborovskii)
Title: H.A.T. Abseiler
Behavioral Patterns: A gifted climber who rarely speaks and demonstrates no desire to be the focus of attention.

Upon being asked if Boone's prowess overshadowed his own, he responded, "Each loop of the cord is equally important for the knot to hold."

Notes: Insistence that he recently saw a three-pawed hamster arguing with a lily-leaper merits consideration that he may need a long rest before returning to the field.

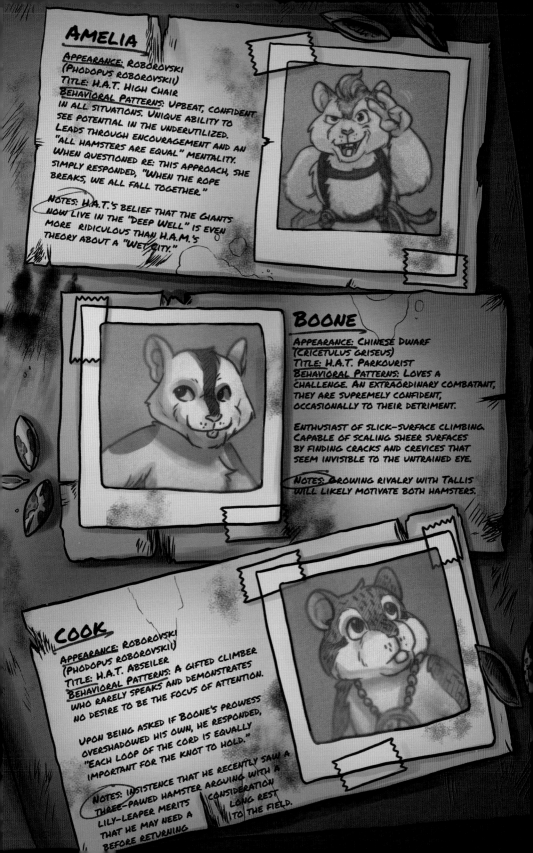

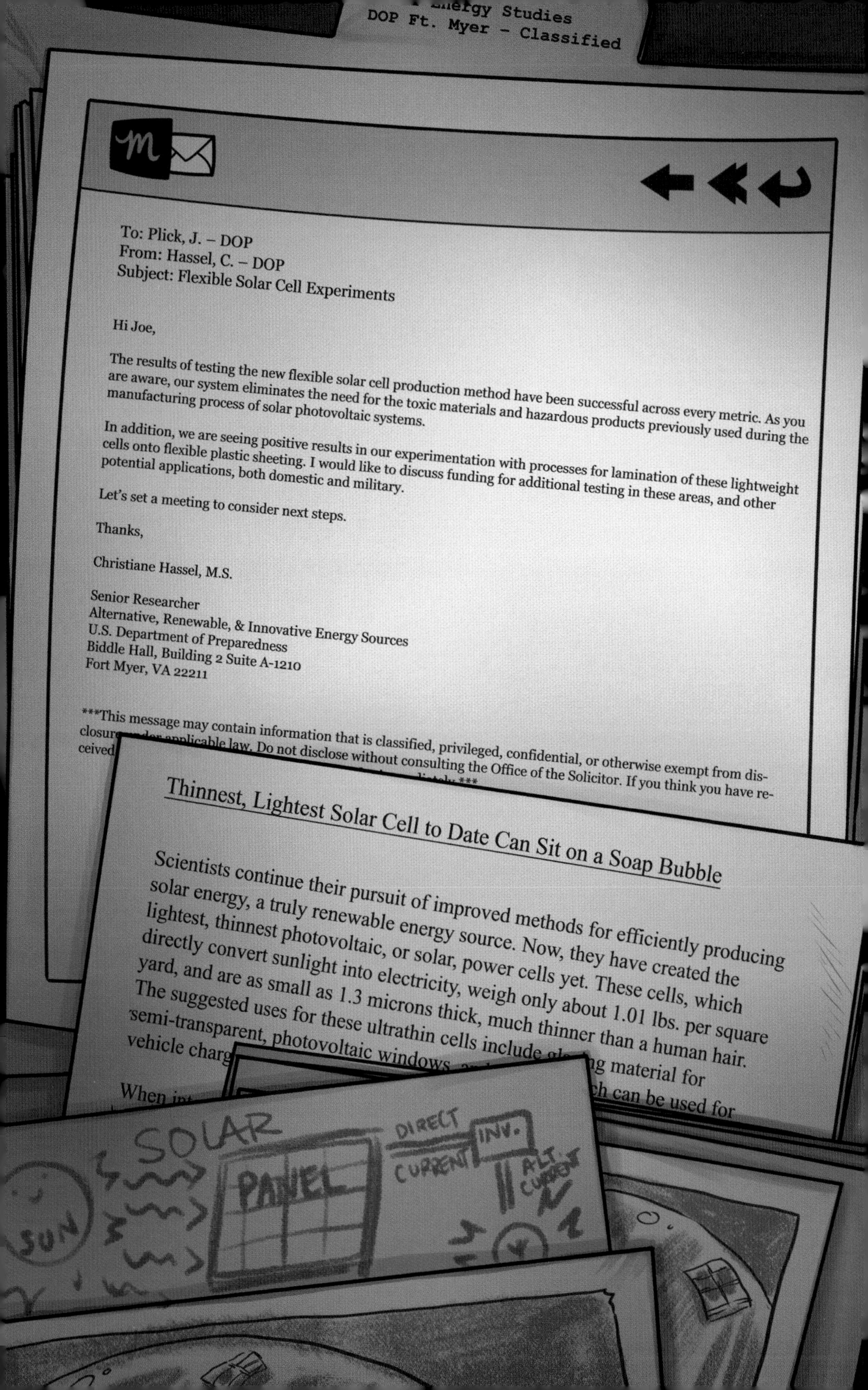
nergy Studies
DOP Ft. Myer - Classified
To: Plick, J. – DOP
From: Hassel, C. – DOP
Subject: Flexible Solar Cell Experiments
Hi Joe,
The results of testing the new flexible solar cell production method have been successful across every metric. As you are aware, our system eliminates the need for the toxic materials and hazardous products previously used during the manufacturing process of solar photovoltaic systems.
In addition, we are seeing positive results in our experimentation with processes for lamination of these lightweight cells onto flexible plastic sheeting. I would like to discuss funding for additional testing in these areas, and other potential applications, both domestic and military.
Let's set a meeting to consider next steps.
Thanks,
Christiane Hassel, M.S.
Senior Researcher
Alternative, Renewable, & Innovative Energy Sources
U.S. Department of Preparedness
Biddle Hall, Building 2 Suite A-1210
Fort Myer, VA 22211
***This message may contain information that is classified, privileged, confidential, or otherwise exempt from dis-
Do not disclose without consulting the Office of the Solicitor. If you think you have re-
Thinnest, Lightest Solar Cell to Date Can Sit on a Soap Bubble
Scientists continue their pursuit of improved methods for efficiently producing solar energy, a truly renewable energy source. Now, they have created the lightest, thinnest photovoltaic, or solar, power cells yet. These cells, which directly convert sunlight into electricity, weigh only about 1.01 lbs. per square yard, and are as small as 1.3 microns thick, much thinner than a human hair. The suggested uses for these ultrathin cells include
semi-transparent, photovoltaic windows
material for
vehicle charg
When
ch can be used for
SOLAR
PANEL
DIRECT CURRENT
INV.
ALT. CURRENT
SUN

CHAPTER FOUR

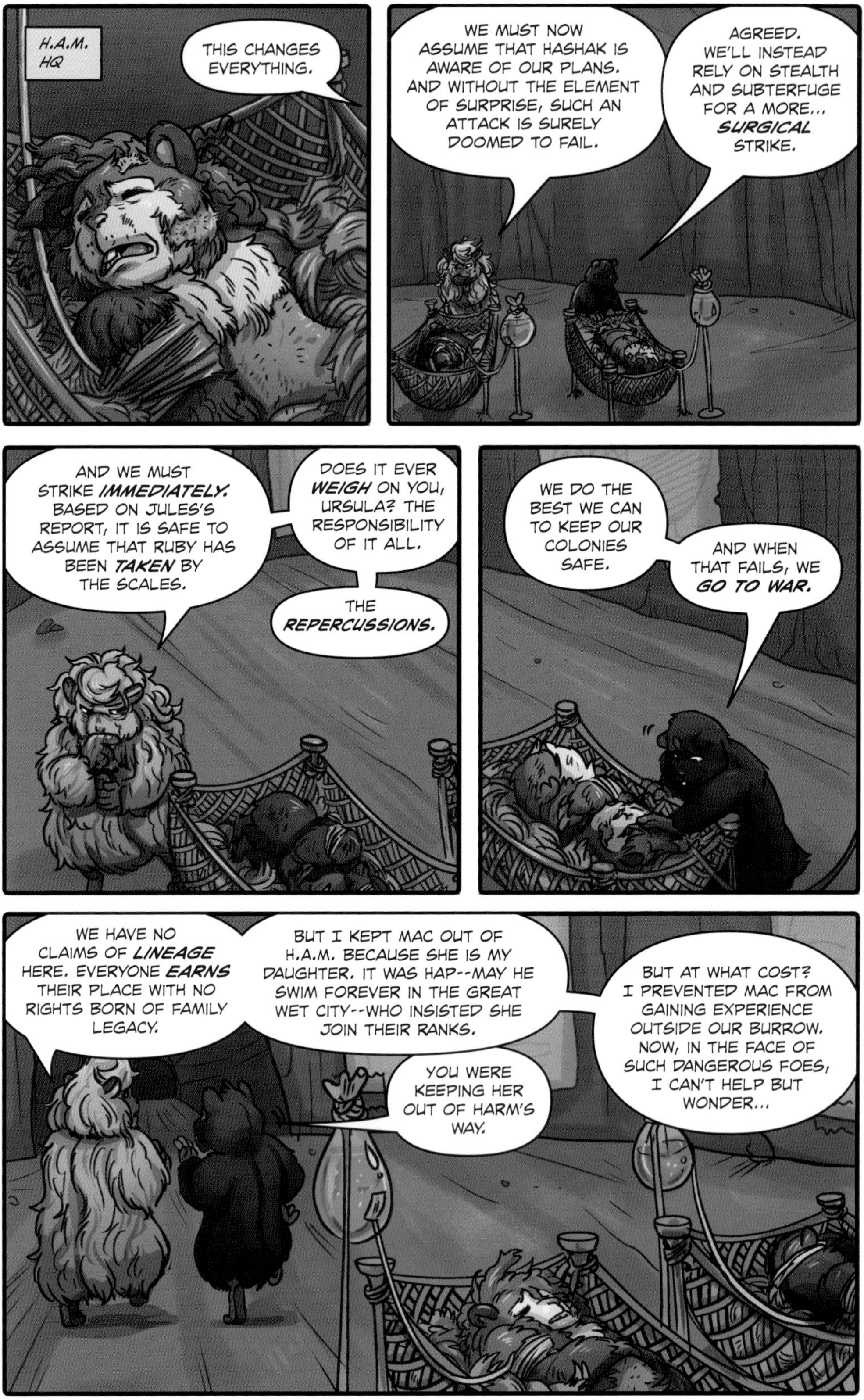
H.A.M. HQ
THIS CHANGES EVERYTHING.
WE MUST NOW ASSUME THAT HASHAK IS AWARE OF OUR PLANS. AND WITHOUT THE ELEMENT OF SURPRISE, SUCH AN ATTACK IS SURELY DOOMED TO FAIL.
AGREED. WE'LL INSTEAD RELY ON STEALTH AND SUBTERFUGE FOR A MORE... *SURGICAL* STRIKE.
AND WE MUST STRIKE *IMMEDIATELY.* BASED ON JULES'S REPORT, IT IS SAFE TO ASSUME THAT RUBY HAS BEEN *TAKEN* BY THE SCALES.
DOES IT EVER *WEIGH* ON YOU, URSULA? THE RESPONSIBILITY OF IT ALL.
THE *REPERCUSSIONS.*
WE DO THE BEST WE CAN TO KEEP OUR COLONIES SAFE.
AND WHEN THAT FAILS, WE ***GO TO WAR.***
WE HAVE NO CLAIMS OF *LINEAGE* HERE. EVERYONE *EARNS* THEIR PLACE WITH NO RIGHTS BORN OF FAMILY LEGACY.
BUT I KEPT MAC OUT OF H.A.M. BECAUSE SHE IS MY DAUGHTER. IT WAS HAP--MAY HE SWIM FOREVER IN THE GREAT WET CITY--WHO INSISTED SHE JOIN THEIR RANKS.
YOU WERE KEEPING HER OUT OF HARM'S WAY.
BUT AT WHAT COST? I PREVENTED MAC FROM GAINING EXPERIENCE OUTSIDE OUR BURROW. NOW, IN THE FACE OF SUCH DANGEROUS FOES, I CAN'T HELP BUT WONDER...

"...WILL SHE BE STRONG ENOUGH?"

I KNOW THAT LOOK.

OH? AND WHAT LOOK IS THAT?

THE "WILL I BE COMING HOME *IN* MY SHIP, OR ARE *PIECES* OF MY *SHIP* COMING HOME IN MY *POCKET?*" LOOK.

WE'VE *BOTH* HAD SOME EXPERIENCE WITH THE LATTER, I SUPPOSE.

INDEED. AND IF I UNDERSTAND THE NEW MISSION PARAMETERS, I'M LIKELY TO HAVE IT AGAIN.

GOOD TO SEE YOU, IVES.

YOU TOO, NEIL.

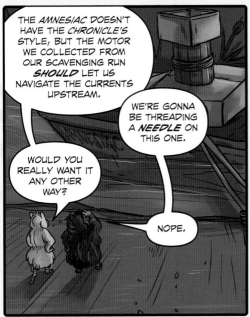

THE *AMNESIAC* DOESN'T HAVE THE *CHRONICLE'S* STYLE, BUT THE MOTOR WE COLLECTED FROM OUR SCAVENGING RUN *SHOULD* LET US NAVIGATE THE CURRENTS UPSTREAM.

WE'RE GONNA BE THREADING A *NEEDLE* ON THIS ONE.

WOULD YOU REALLY WANT IT ANY OTHER WAY?

NOPE.

MY BROTHER USED TO SAY A *SAILOR* LOOKS ACROSS THE WATER AND CALCULATES THE DISTANCE HOME. BUT A *CAPTAIN* KNOWS THE WATER *IS* HOME.

WHERE'S YOUR BROTHER NOW?

HOME.

YOU WOULD HAVE LIKED HIM. HE HAD GREAT FUR.

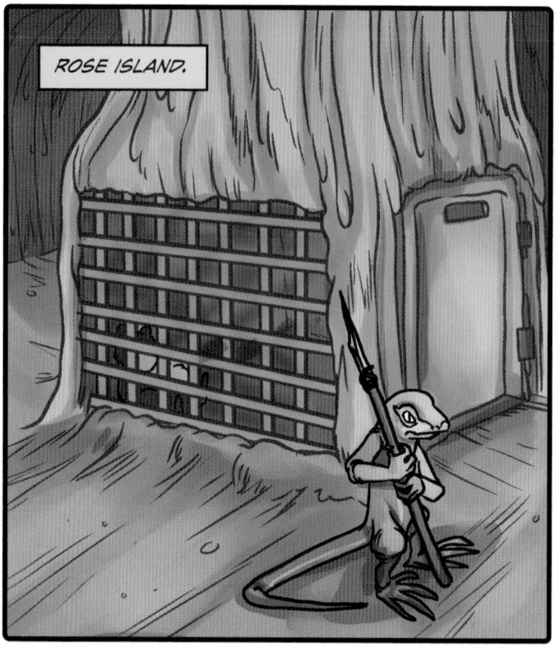
ROSE ISLAND.

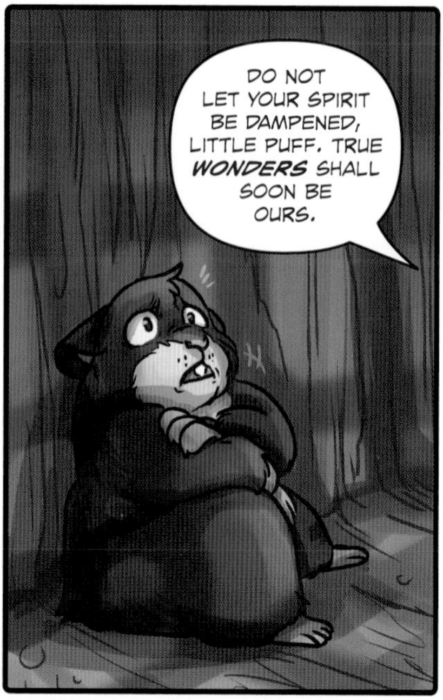
DO NOT LET YOUR SPIRIT BE DAMPENED, LITTLE PUFF. TRUE WONDERS SHALL SOON BE OURS.

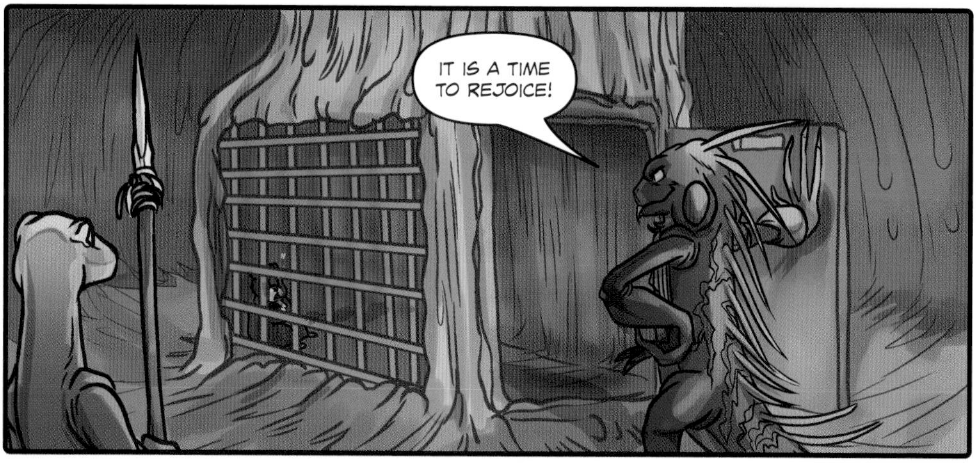
IT IS A TIME TO REJOICE!

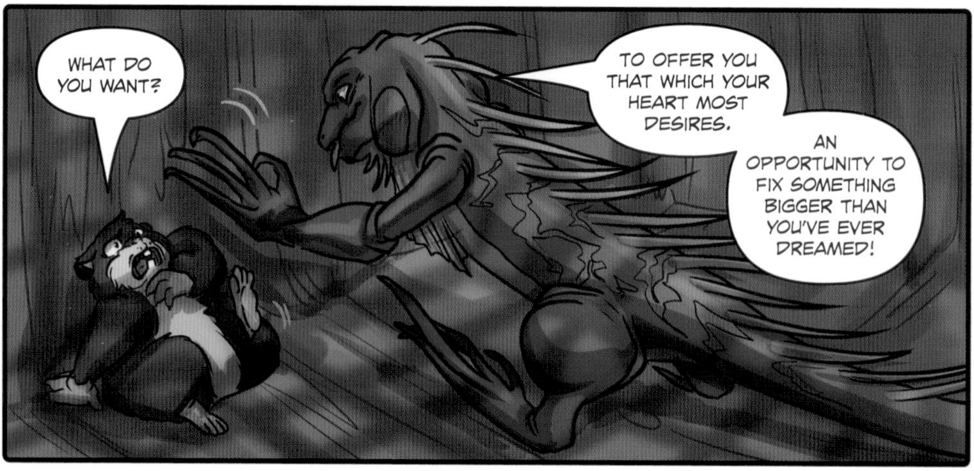
WHAT DO YOU WANT?
TO OFFER YOU THAT WHICH YOUR HEART MOST DESIRES.
AN OPPORTUNITY TO FIX SOMETHING BIGGER THAN YOU'VE EVER DREAMED!

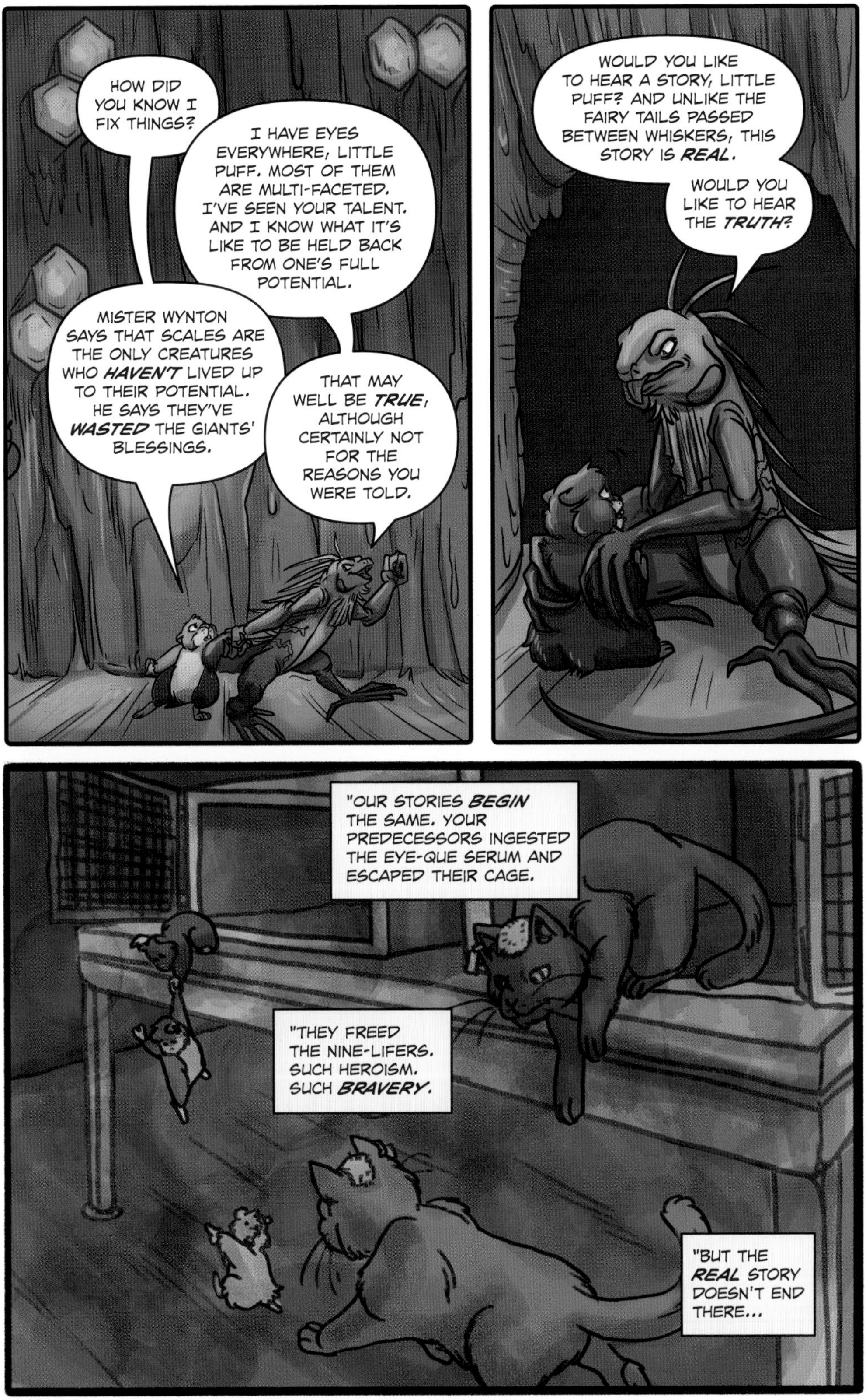
HOW DID YOU KNOW I FIX THINGS?
I HAVE EYES EVERYWHERE, LITTLE PUFF. MOST OF THEM ARE MULTI-FACETED. I'VE SEEN YOUR TALENT. AND I KNOW WHAT IT'S LIKE TO BE HELD BACK FROM ONE'S FULL POTENTIAL.
MISTER WYNTON SAYS THAT SCALES ARE THE ONLY CREATURES WHO HAVEN'T LIVED UP TO THEIR POTENTIAL. HE SAYS THEY'VE WASTED THE GIANTS' BLESSINGS.
THAT MAY WELL BE TRUE, ALTHOUGH CERTAINLY NOT FOR THE REASONS YOU WERE TOLD.
WOULD YOU LIKE TO HEAR A STORY, LITTLE PUFF? AND UNLIKE THE FAIRY TAILS PASSED BETWEEN WHISKERS, THIS STORY IS REAL.
WOULD YOU LIKE TO HEAR THE TRUTH?
"OUR STORIES BEGIN THE SAME. YOUR PREDECESSORS INGESTED THE EYE-QUE SERUM AND ESCAPED THEIR CAGE.
"THEY FREED THE NINE-LIFERS. SUCH HEROISM. SUCH BRAVERY.
"BUT THE REAL STORY DOESN'T END THERE...

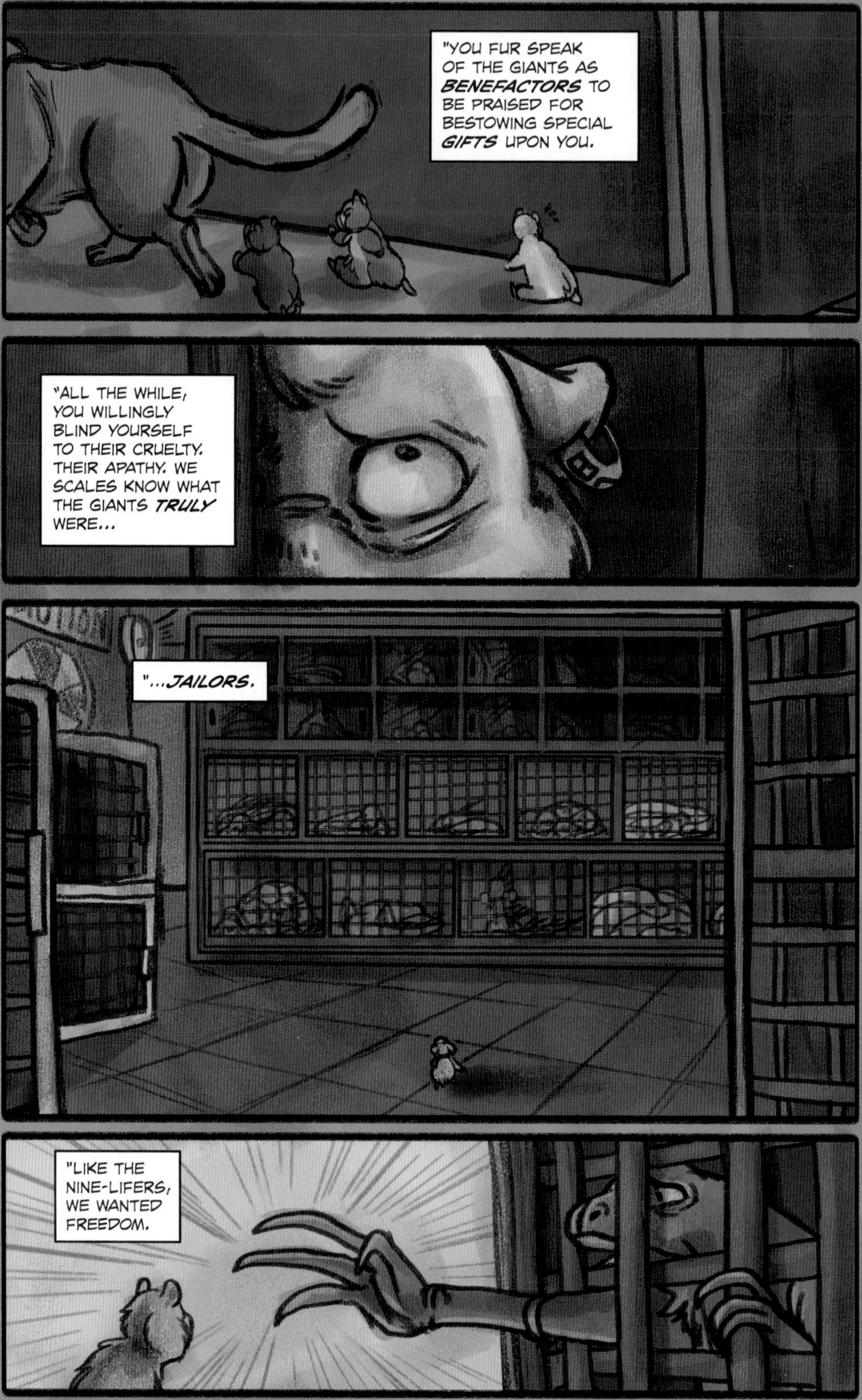
"YOU FUR SPEAK OF THE GIANTS AS BENEFACTORS TO BE PRAISED FOR BESTOWING SPECIAL GIFTS UPON YOU.
"ALL THE WHILE, YOU WILLINGLY BLIND YOURSELF TO THEIR CRUELTY. THEIR APATHY. WE SCALES KNOW WHAT THE GIANTS TRULY WERE...
"...JAILORS.
"LIKE THE NINE-LIFERS, WE WANTED FREEDOM.

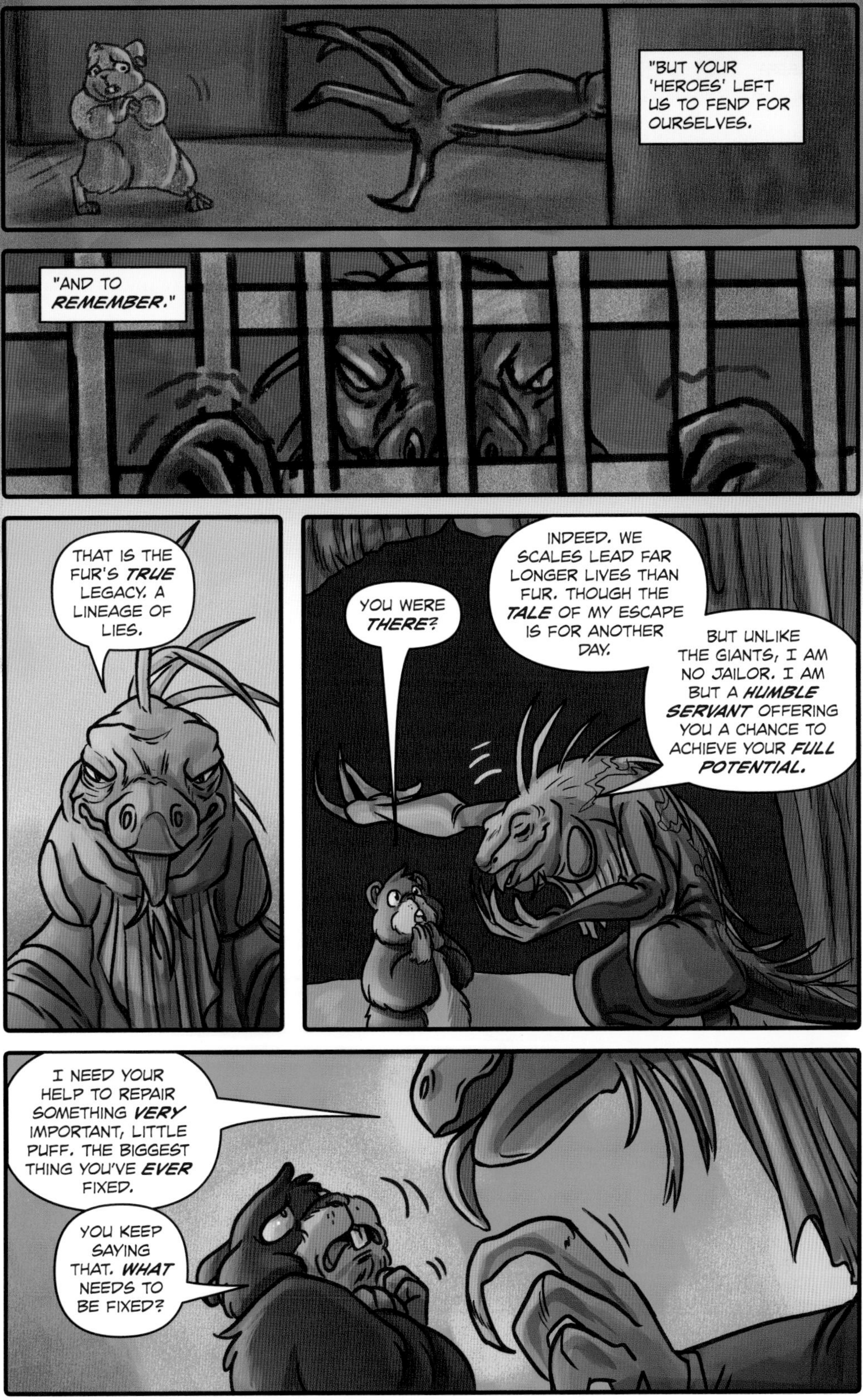
"BUT YOUR 'HEROES' LEFT US TO FEND FOR OURSELVES.
"AND TO REMEMBER."
THAT IS THE FUR'S TRUE LEGACY. A LINEAGE OF LIES.
YOU WERE THERE?
INDEED. WE SCALES LEAD FAR LONGER LIVES THAN FUR. THOUGH THE TALE OF MY ESCAPE IS FOR ANOTHER DAY.
BUT UNLIKE THE GIANTS, I AM NO JAILOR. I AM BUT A HUMBLE SERVANT OFFERING YOU A CHANCE TO ACHIEVE YOUR FULL POTENTIAL.
I NEED YOUR HELP TO REPAIR SOMETHING VERY IMPORTANT, LITTLE PUFF. THE BIGGEST THING YOU'VE EVER FIXED.
YOU KEEP SAYING THAT. WHAT NEEDS TO BE FIXED?

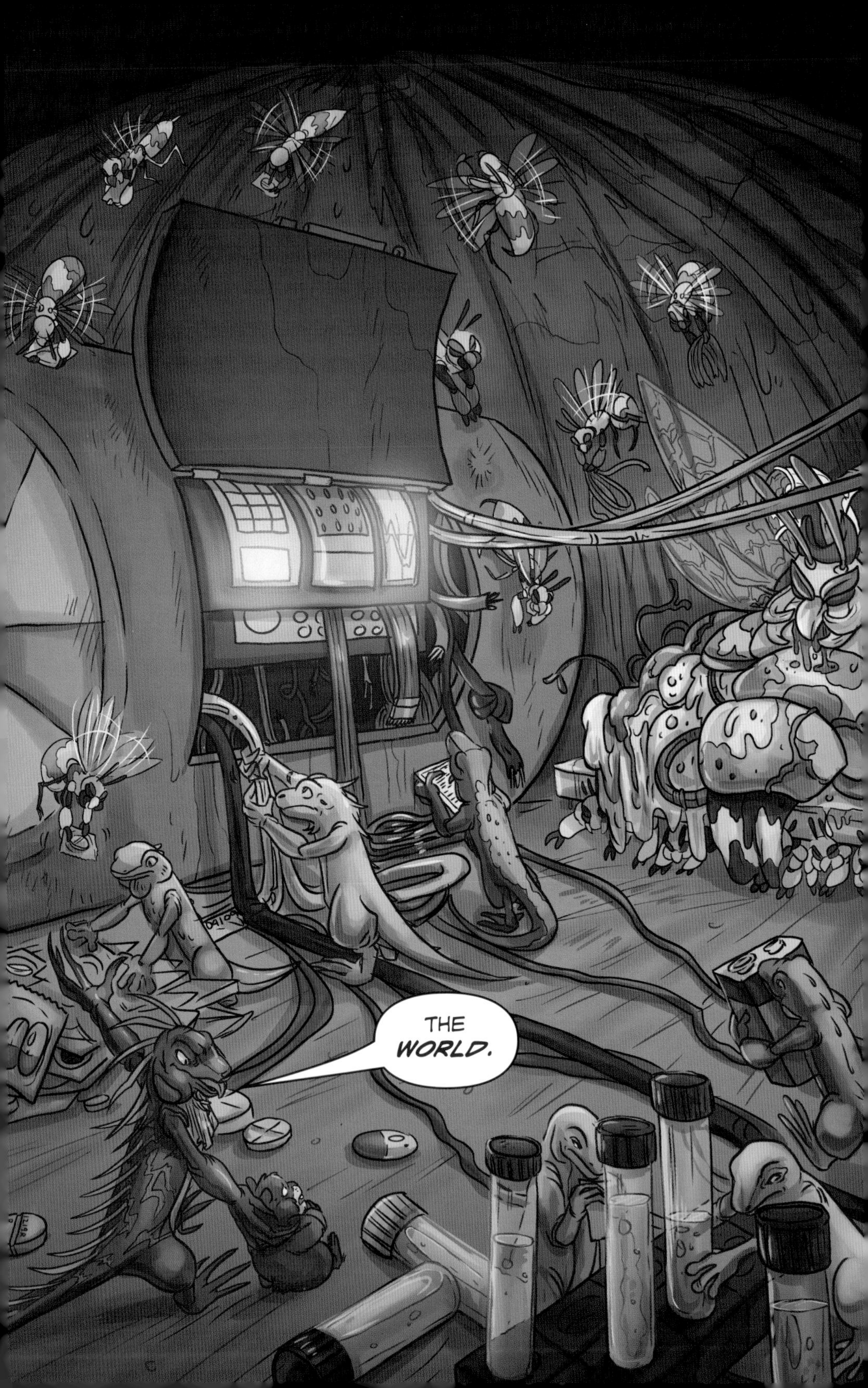
THE *WORLD.*

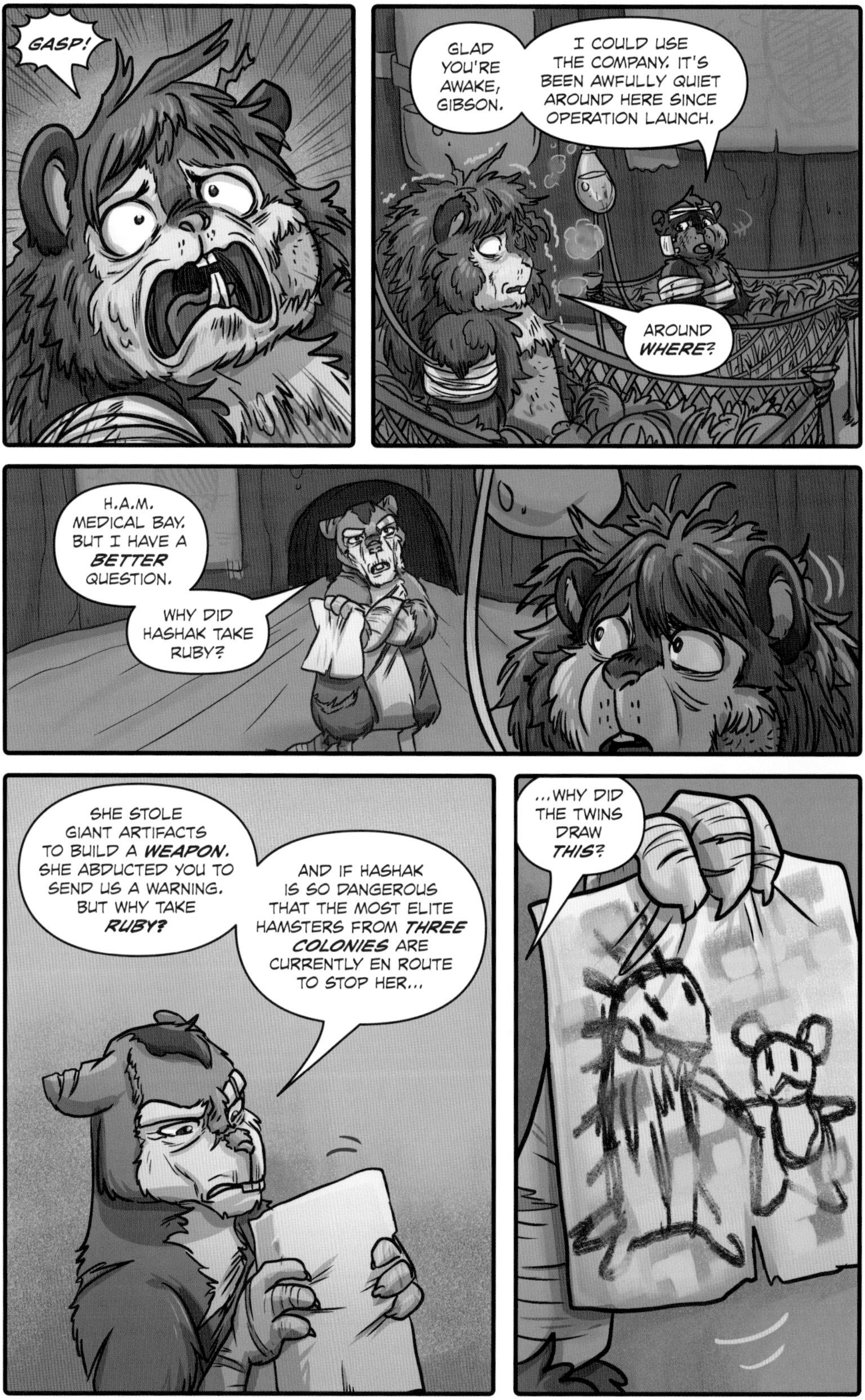
GASP!
GLAD YOU'RE AWAKE, GIBSON.
I COULD USE THE COMPANY. IT'S BEEN AWFULLY QUIET AROUND HERE SINCE OPERATION LAUNCH.
AROUND WHERE?
H.A.M. MEDICAL BAY. BUT I HAVE A BETTER QUESTION.
WHY DID HASHAK TAKE RUBY?
SHE STOLE GIANT ARTIFACTS TO BUILD A WEAPON. SHE ABDUCTED YOU TO SEND US A WARNING. BUT WHY TAKE RUBY?
AND IF HASHAK IS SO DANGEROUS THAT THE MOST ELITE HAMSTERS FROM THREE COLONIES ARE CURRENTLY EN ROUTE TO STOP HER...
...WHY DID THE TWINS DRAW THIS?

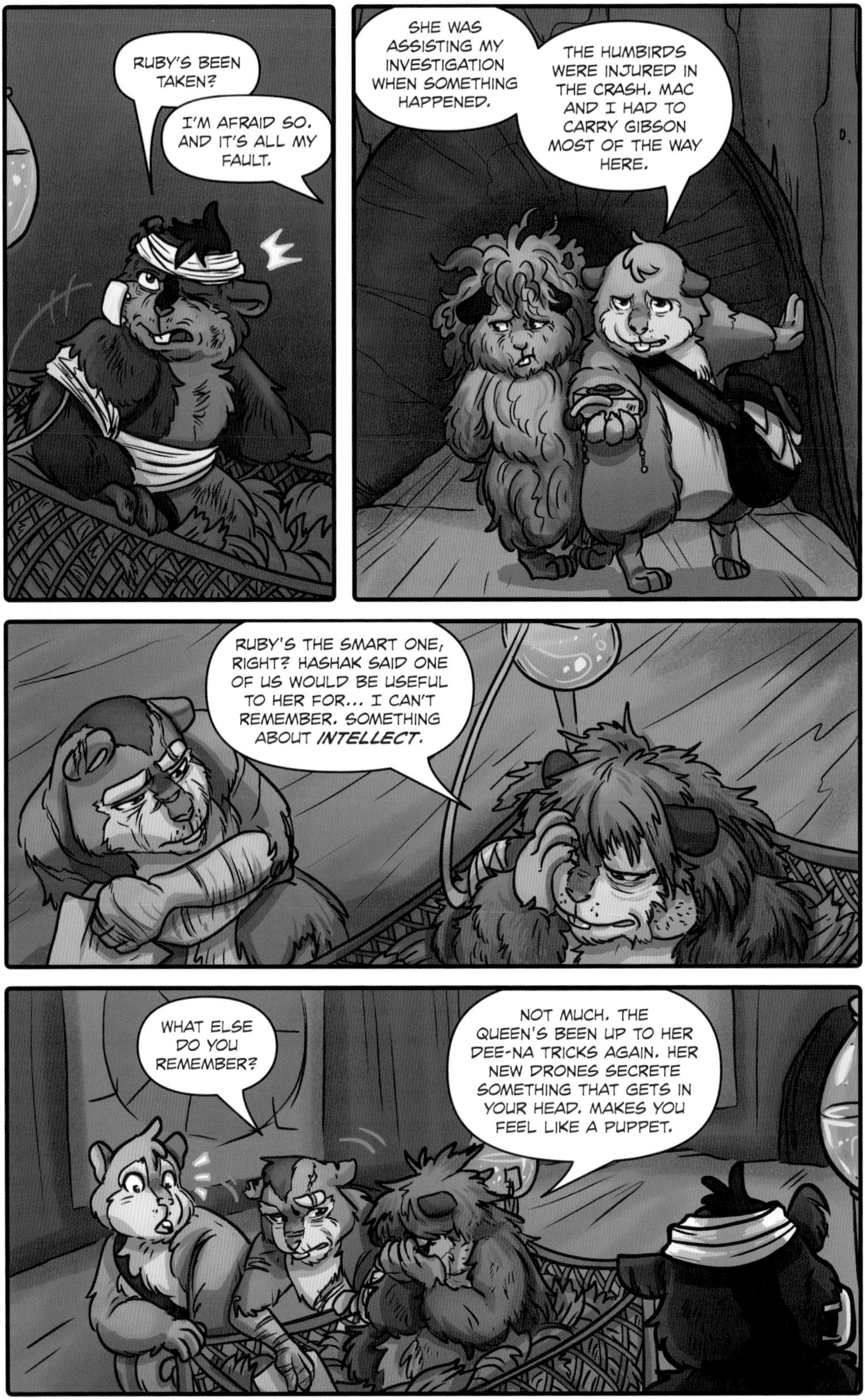
RUBY'S BEEN TAKEN?
I'M AFRAID SO. AND IT'S ALL MY FAULT.
SHE WAS ASSISTING MY INVESTIGATION WHEN SOMETHING HAPPENED.
THE HUMBIRDS WERE INJURED IN THE CRASH. MAC AND I HAD TO CARRY GIBSON MOST OF THE WAY HERE.
RUBY'S THE SMART ONE, RIGHT? HASHAK SAID ONE OF US WOULD BE USEFUL TO HER FOR... I CAN'T REMEMBER. SOMETHING ABOUT *INTELLECT*.
WHAT ELSE DO YOU REMEMBER?
NOT MUCH. THE QUEEN'S BEEN UP TO HER DEE-NA TRICKS AGAIN. HER NEW DRONES SECRETE SOMETHING THAT GETS IN YOUR HEAD. MAKES YOU FEEL LIKE A PUPPET.

WYNTON, WHAT'S THAT?

SOMETHING OUR TWINS DREW WITH FARSIGHT. IT'S RUBY AND HASHAK, LOOKING RATHER COZY.

I CAN SEE *THAT*. I MEAN, WHAT'S ALL THIS COLORING *AROUND* THEM?

NOTHING, AS FAR AS WE CAN TELL. THEY'VE BEEN DRAWING IT FOR WEEKS.

I CAN'T BELIEVE I OVERLOOKED IT FOR SO LONG. THE CLUES WERE ALL THERE!

MAC! COME HITHER, MY GOOD LASS!

WHAT DO--

--HEY!

I'VE SEEN THAT COLOR PATTERN BEFORE.

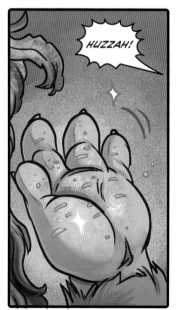

HUZZAH!

FIRST, AT THE DOCKS WHERE THE CELLIES WERE STOLEN AND GIBSON WAS TAKEN. NOW AT THE CRASH WHERE RUBY DISAPPEARED. WE'VE ALWAYS BELIEVED THEY WERE *HARMLESS*.

IT APPEARS WE WERE *WRONG*.

WRONG ABOUT *WHAT*?

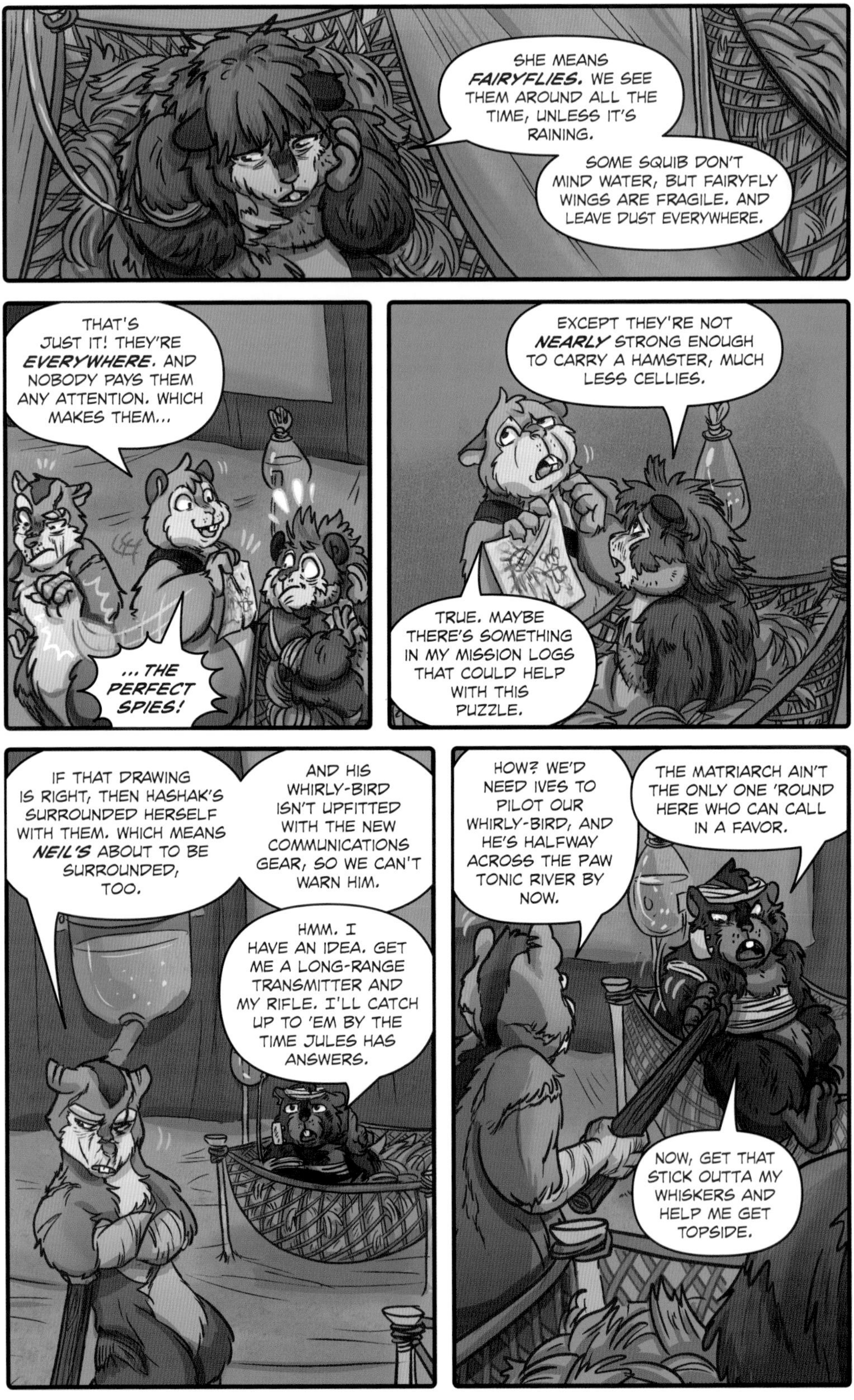
SHE MEANS FAIRYFLIES. WE SEE THEM AROUND ALL THE TIME, UNLESS IT'S RAINING.
SOME SQUIB DON'T MIND WATER, BUT FAIRYFLY WINGS ARE FRAGILE. AND LEAVE DUST EVERYWHERE.
THAT'S JUST IT! THEY'RE EVERYWHERE. AND NOBODY PAYS THEM ANY ATTENTION. WHICH MAKES THEM...
...THE PERFECT SPIES!
EXCEPT THEY'RE NOT NEARLY STRONG ENOUGH TO CARRY A HAMSTER, MUCH LESS CELLIES.
TRUE. MAYBE THERE'S SOMETHING IN MY MISSION LOGS THAT COULD HELP WITH THIS PUZZLE.
IF THAT DRAWING IS RIGHT, THEN HASHAK'S SURROUNDED HERSELF WITH THEM. WHICH MEANS NEIL'S ABOUT TO BE SURROUNDED, TOO.
AND HIS WHIRLY-BIRD ISN'T UPFITTED WITH THE NEW COMMUNICATIONS GEAR, SO WE CAN'T WARN HIM.
HMM. I HAVE AN IDEA. GET ME A LONG-RANGE TRANSMITTER AND MY RIFLE. I'LL CATCH UP TO 'EM BY THE TIME JULES HAS ANSWERS.
HOW? WE'D NEED IVES TO PILOT OUR WHIRLY-BIRD, AND HE'S HALFWAY ACROSS THE PAW TONIC RIVER BY NOW.
THE MATRIARCH AIN'T THE ONLY ONE 'ROUND HERE WHO CAN CALL IN A FAVOR.
NOW, GET THAT STICK OUTTA MY WHISKERS AND HELP ME GET TOPSIDE.

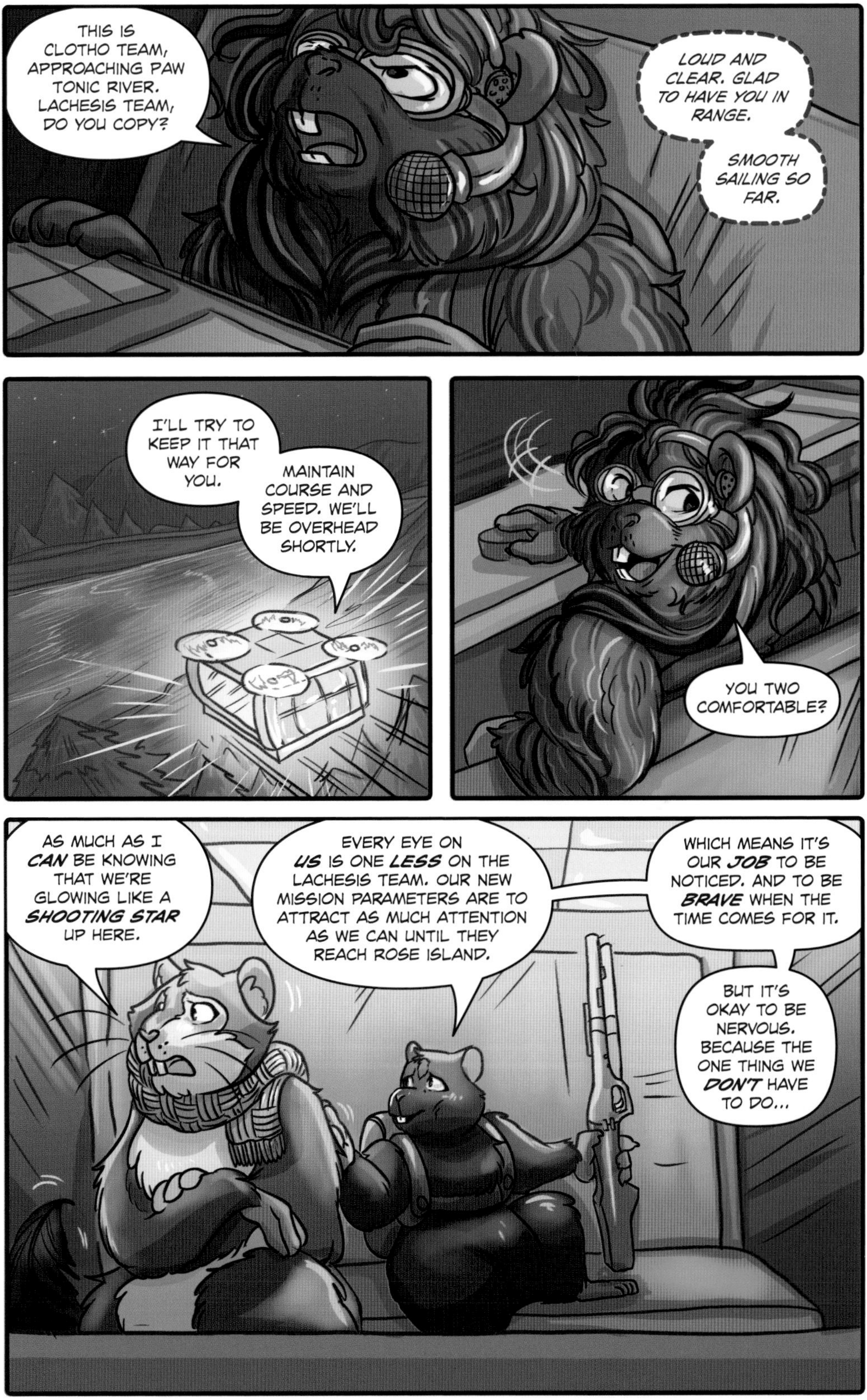
THIS IS CLOTHO TEAM, APPROACHING PAW TONIC RIVER. LACHESIS TEAM, DO YOU COPY?
LOUD AND CLEAR. GLAD TO HAVE YOU IN RANGE.
SMOOTH SAILING SO FAR.
I'LL TRY TO KEEP IT THAT WAY FOR YOU.
MAINTAIN COURSE AND SPEED. WE'LL BE OVERHEAD SHORTLY.
YOU TWO COMFORTABLE?
AS MUCH AS I ***CAN*** BE KNOWING THAT WE'RE GLOWING LIKE A ***SHOOTING STAR*** UP HERE.
EVERY EYE ON ***US*** IS ONE ***LESS*** ON THE LACHESIS TEAM. OUR NEW MISSION PARAMETERS ARE TO ATTRACT AS MUCH ATTENTION AS WE CAN UNTIL THEY REACH ROSE ISLAND.
WHICH MEANS IT'S OUR ***JOB*** TO BE NOTICED. AND TO BE ***BRAVE*** WHEN THE TIME COMES FOR IT.
BUT IT'S OKAY TO BE NERVOUS. BECAUSE THE ONE THING WE ***DON'T*** HAVE TO DO...

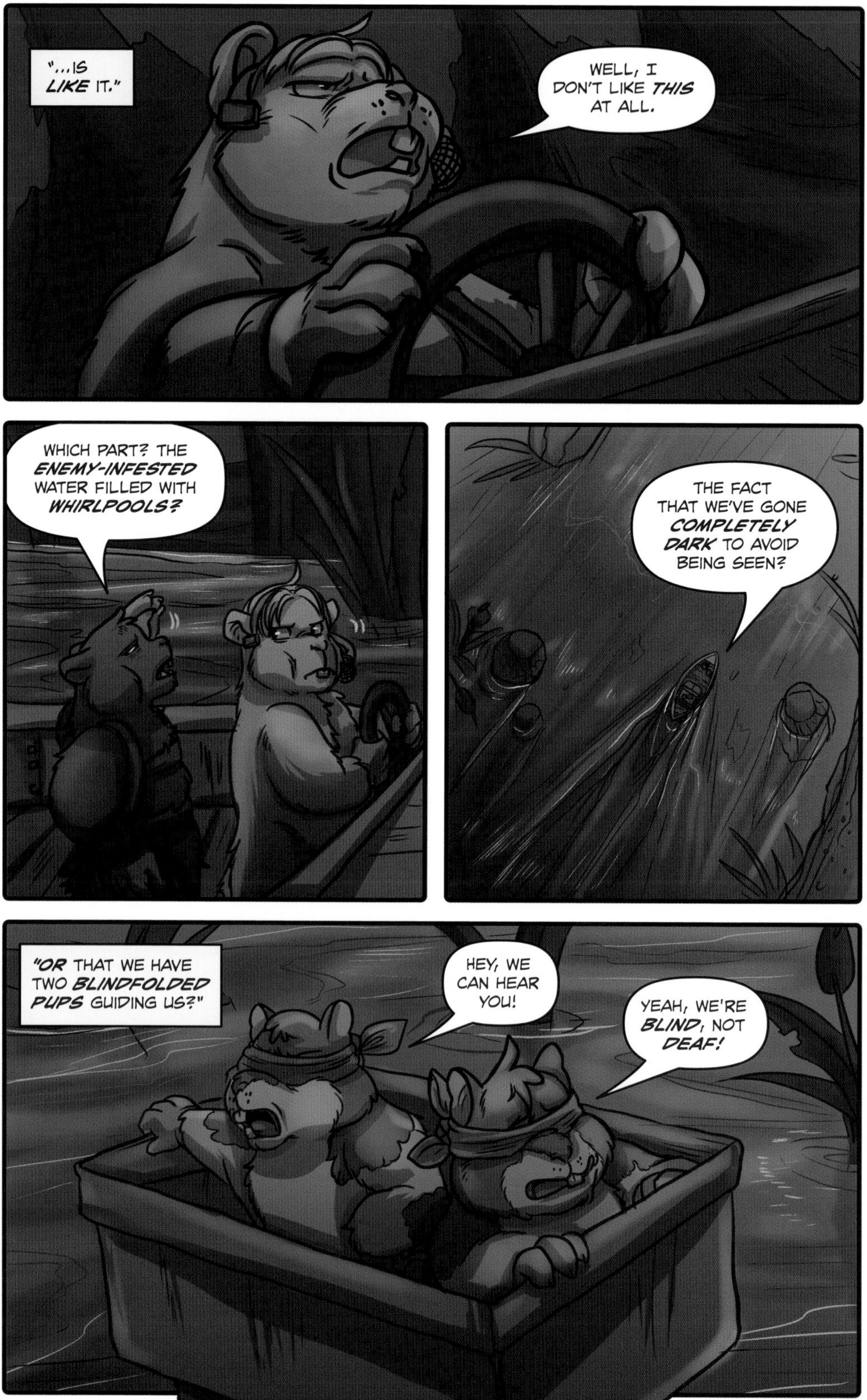
"...IS *LIKE* IT."
WELL, I DON'T LIKE *THIS* AT ALL.
WHICH PART? THE *ENEMY-INFESTED* WATER FILLED WITH *WHIRLPOOLS?*
THE FACT THAT WE'VE GONE *COMPLETELY DARK* TO AVOID BEING SEEN?
"OR THAT WE HAVE TWO *BLINDFOLDED PUPS* GUIDING US?"
HEY, WE CAN HEAR YOU!
YEAH, WE'RE *BLIND*, NOT *DEAF!*

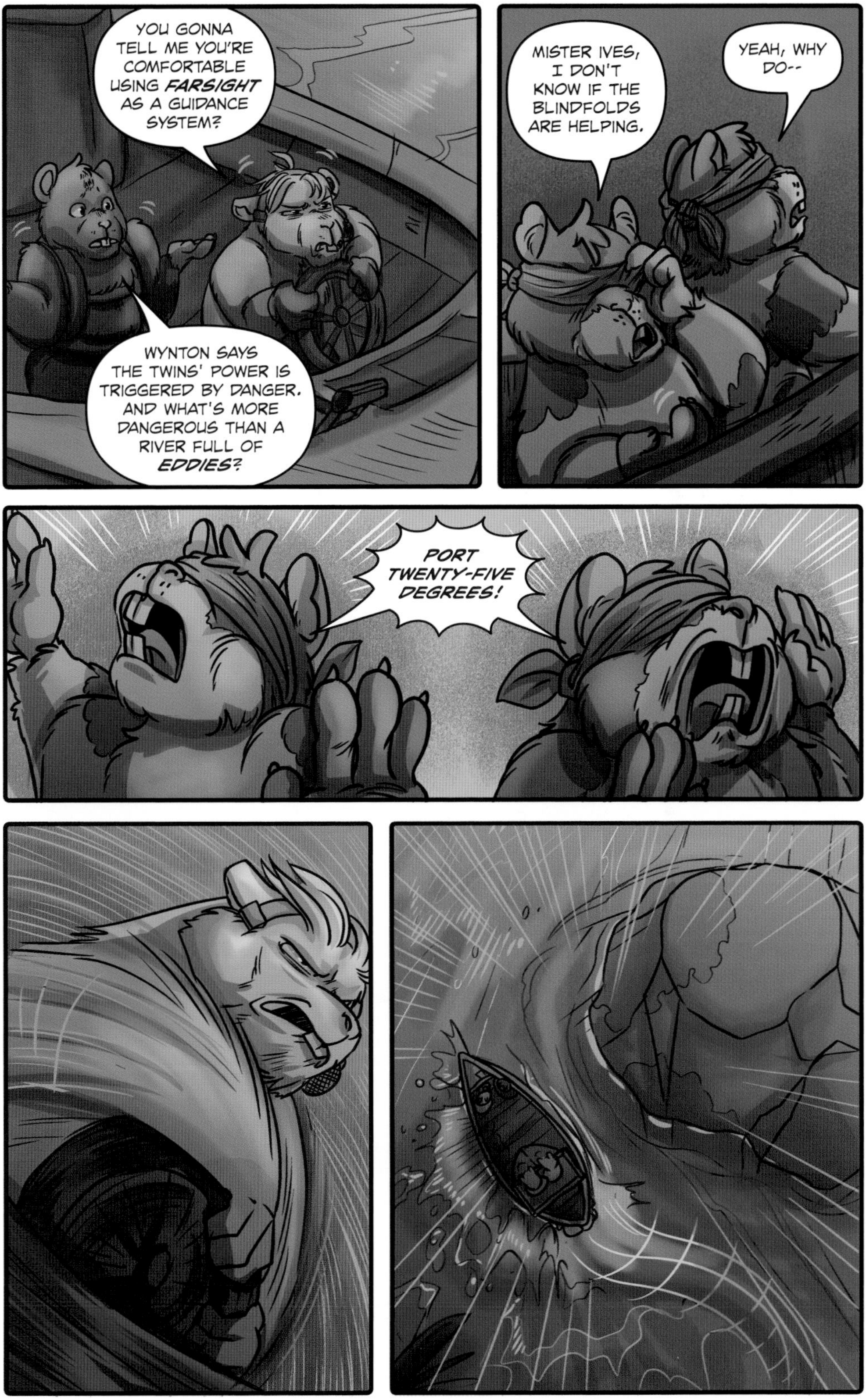
YOU GONNA TELL ME YOU'RE COMFORTABLE USING *FARSIGHT* AS A GUIDANCE SYSTEM?
WYNTON SAYS THE TWINS' POWER IS TRIGGERED BY DANGER. AND WHAT'S MORE DANGEROUS THAN A RIVER FULL OF *EDDIES*?
MISTER IVES, I DON'T KNOW IF THE BLINDFOLDS ARE HELPING.
YEAH, WHY DO--
PORT TWENTY-FIVE DEGREES!

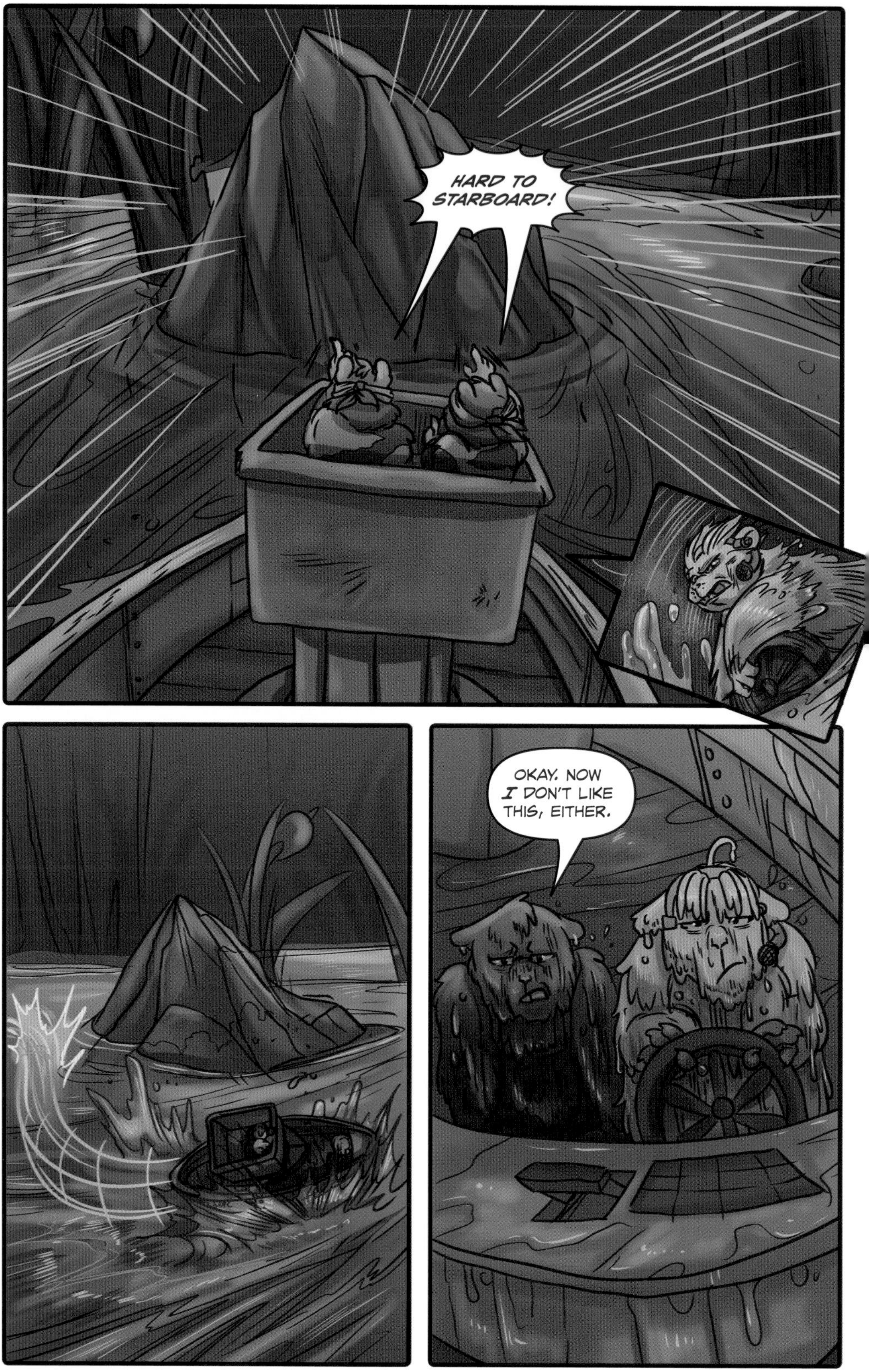
HARD TO STARBOARD!
OKAY. NOW I DON'T LIKE THIS, EITHER.

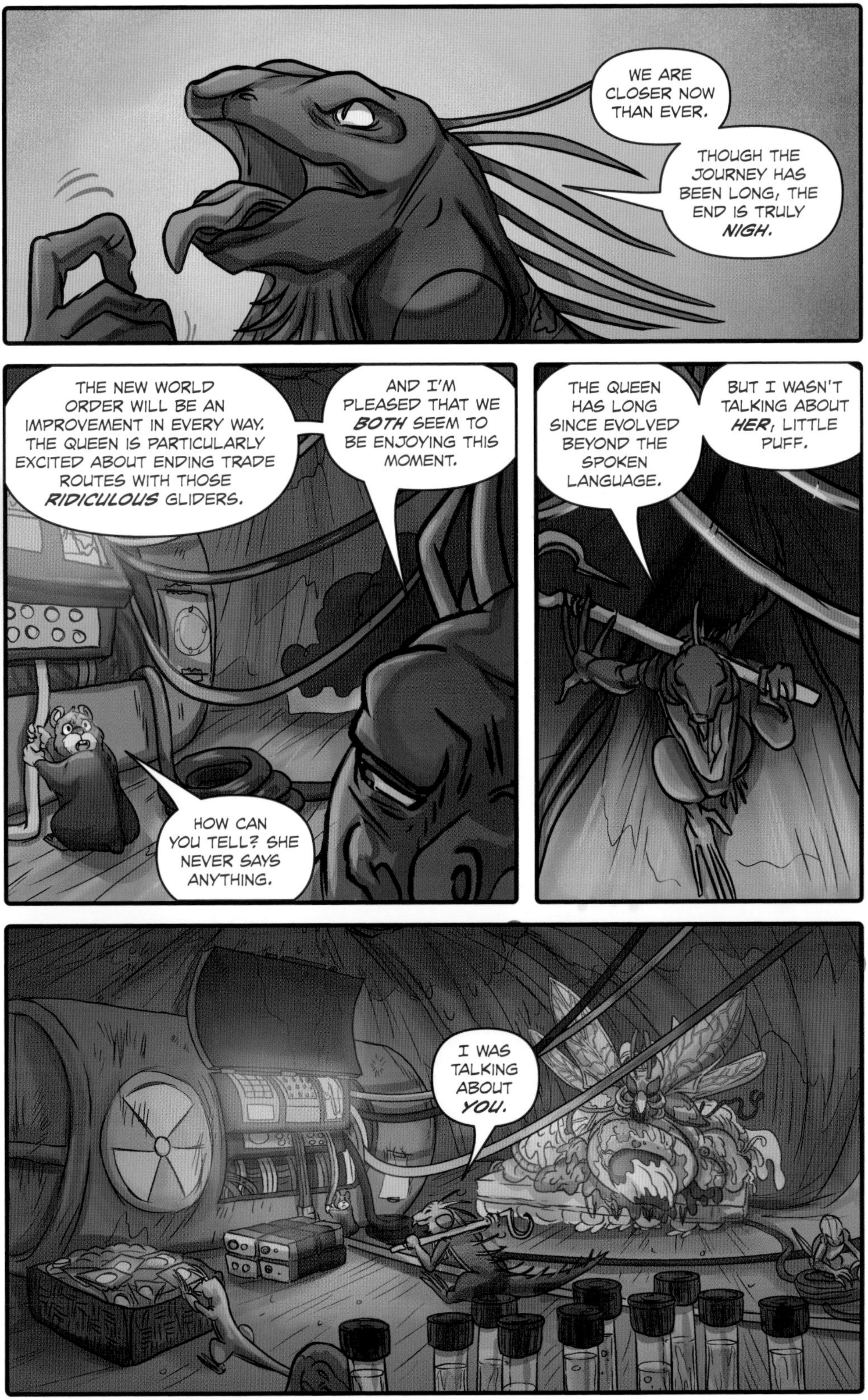
WE ARE CLOSER NOW THAN EVER.
THOUGH THE JOURNEY HAS BEEN LONG, THE END IS TRULY *NIGH*.
THE NEW WORLD ORDER WILL BE AN IMPROVEMENT IN EVERY WAY. THE QUEEN IS PARTICULARLY EXCITED ABOUT ENDING TRADE ROUTES WITH THOSE *RIDICULOUS* GLIDERS.
AND I'M PLEASED THAT WE *BOTH* SEEM TO BE ENJOYING THIS MOMENT.
HOW CAN YOU TELL? SHE NEVER SAYS ANYTHING.
THE QUEEN HAS LONG SINCE EVOLVED BEYOND THE SPOKEN LANGUAGE.
BUT I WASN'T TALKING ABOUT *HER*, LITTLE PUFF.
I WAS TALKING ABOUT *YOU*.

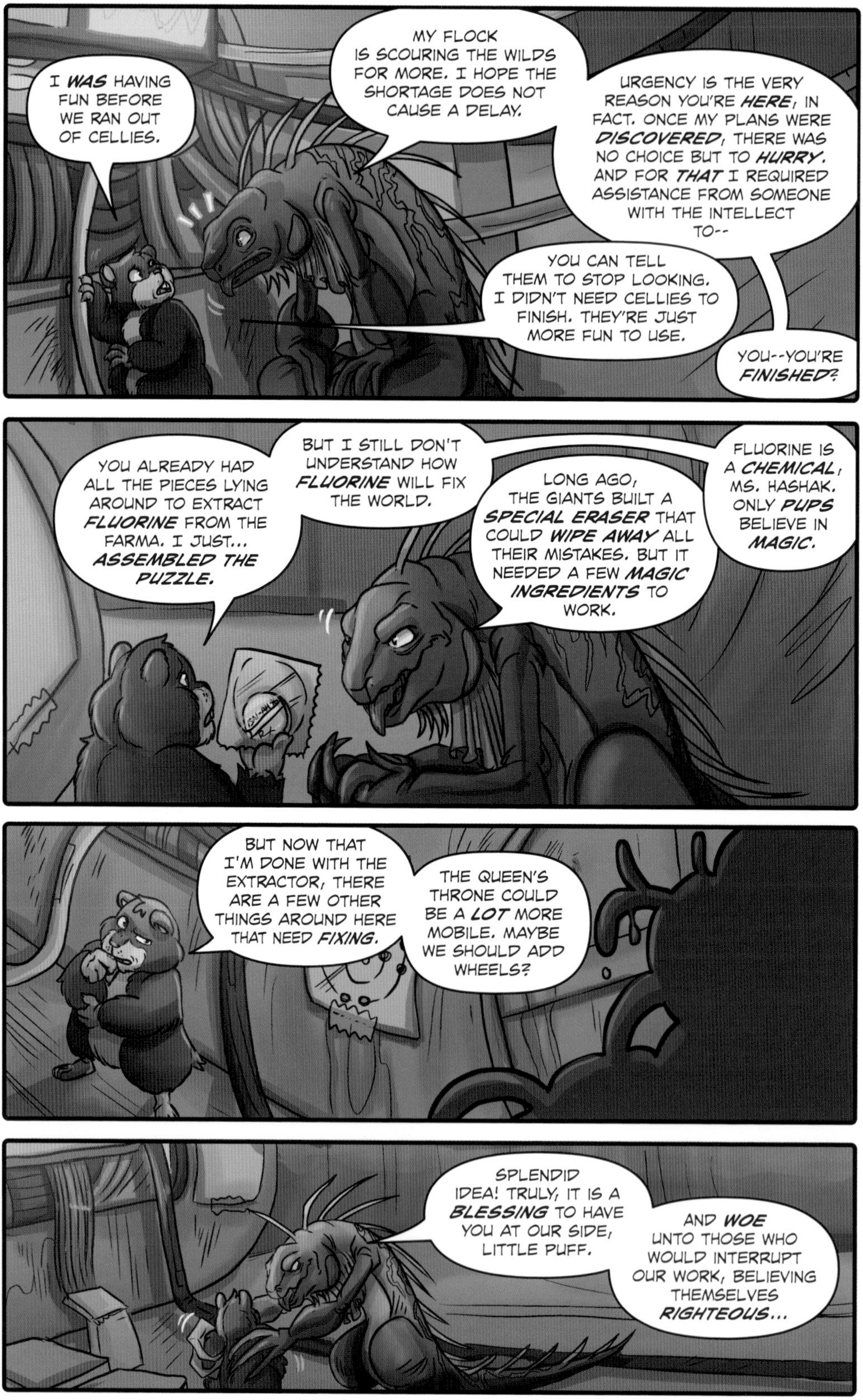
I WAS HAVING FUN BEFORE WE RAN OUT OF CELLIES.
MY FLOCK IS SCOURING THE WILDS FOR MORE. I HOPE THE SHORTAGE DOES NOT CAUSE A DELAY.
URGENCY IS THE VERY REASON YOU'RE HERE, IN FACT. ONCE MY PLANS WERE DISCOVERED, THERE WAS NO CHOICE BUT TO HURRY. AND FOR THAT I REQUIRED ASSISTANCE FROM SOMEONE WITH THE INTELLECT TO--
YOU CAN TELL THEM TO STOP LOOKING. I DIDN'T NEED CELLIES TO FINISH. THEY'RE JUST MORE FUN TO USE.
YOU--YOU'RE FINISHED?
YOU ALREADY HAD ALL THE PIECES LYING AROUND TO EXTRACT FLUORINE FROM THE FARMA. I JUST... ASSEMBLED THE PUZZLE.
BUT I STILL DON'T UNDERSTAND HOW FLUORINE WILL FIX THE WORLD.
LONG AGO, THE GIANTS BUILT A SPECIAL ERASER THAT COULD WIPE AWAY ALL THEIR MISTAKES. BUT IT NEEDED A FEW MAGIC INGREDIENTS TO WORK.
FLUORINE IS A CHEMICAL, MS. HASHAK. ONLY PUPS BELIEVE IN MAGIC.
BUT NOW THAT I'M DONE WITH THE EXTRACTOR, THERE ARE A FEW OTHER THINGS AROUND HERE THAT NEED FIXING.
THE QUEEN'S THRONE COULD BE A LOT MORE MOBILE. MAYBE WE SHOULD ADD WHEELS?
SPLENDID IDEA! TRULY, IT IS A BLESSING TO HAVE YOU AT OUR SIDE, LITTLE PUFF.
AND WOE UNTO THOSE WHO WOULD INTERRUPT OUR WORK, BELIEVING THEMSELVES RIGHTEOUS...

"...FOR THEY SHALL RECEIVE AN AWAKENING MOST *DIRE*."

WHRRRRRRR

HEY, I DON'T KNOW HOW THE OTHER TEAMS ARE DOING. BUT IF *OUR* JOB IS TO BE A DISTRACTION...

"...WE'VE SUCCEEDED."

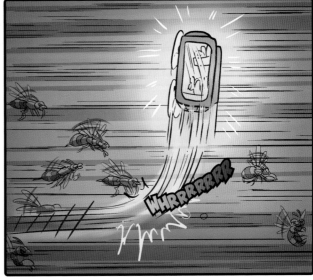

WHRRRRRRR

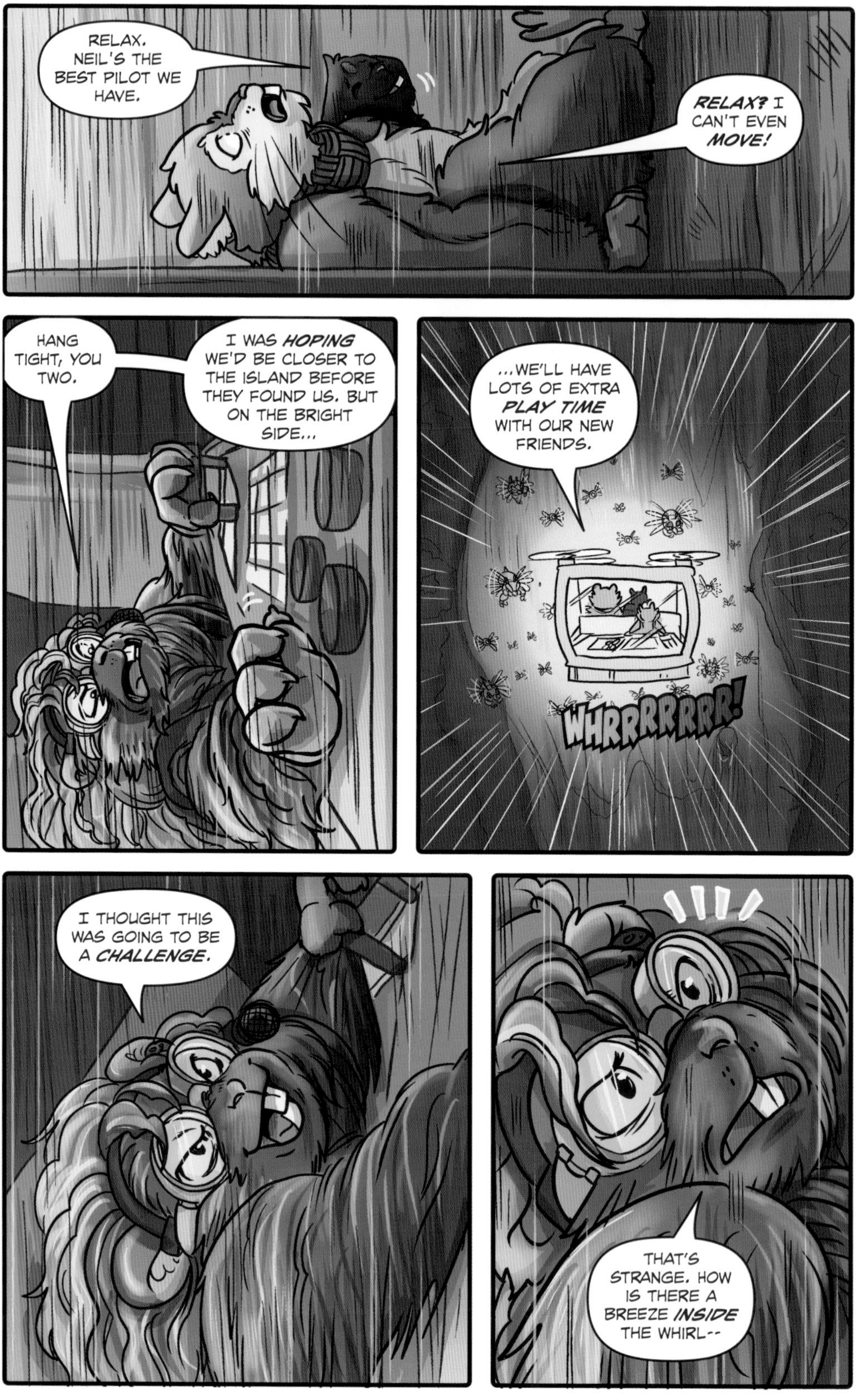
RELAX. NEIL'S THE BEST PILOT WE HAVE.
RELAX? I CAN'T EVEN MOVE!
HANG TIGHT, YOU TWO.
I WAS HOPING WE'D BE CLOSER TO THE ISLAND BEFORE THEY FOUND US. BUT ON THE BRIGHT SIDE...
...WE'LL HAVE LOTS OF EXTRA PLAY TIME WITH OUR NEW FRIENDS.
WHRRRRRRR!
I THOUGHT THIS WAS GOING TO BE A CHALLENGE.
THAT'S STRANGE. HOW IS THERE A BREEZE INSIDE THE WHIRL--

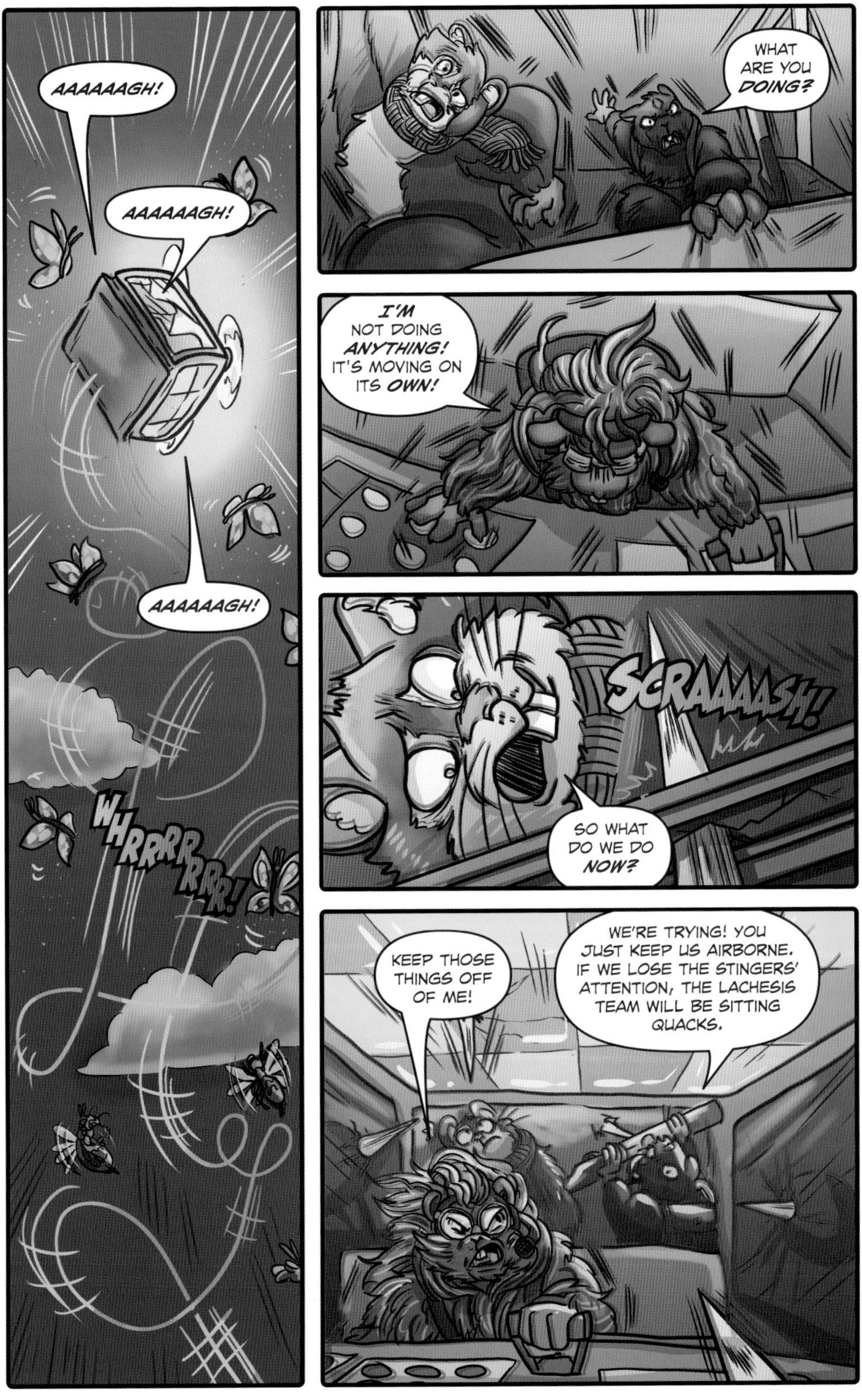
AAAAAAGH!
AAAAAAGH!
AAAAAAGH!
WHRRRRRRRR!
WHAT ARE YOU DOING?
I'M NOT DOING ANYTHING! IT'S MOVING ON ITS OWN!
SCRAAAASH!
SO WHAT DO WE DO NOW?
KEEP THOSE THINGS OFF OF ME!
WE'RE TRYING! YOU JUST KEEP US AIRBORNE. IF WE LOSE THE STINGERS' ATTENTION, THE LACHESIS TEAM WILL BE SITTING QUACKS.

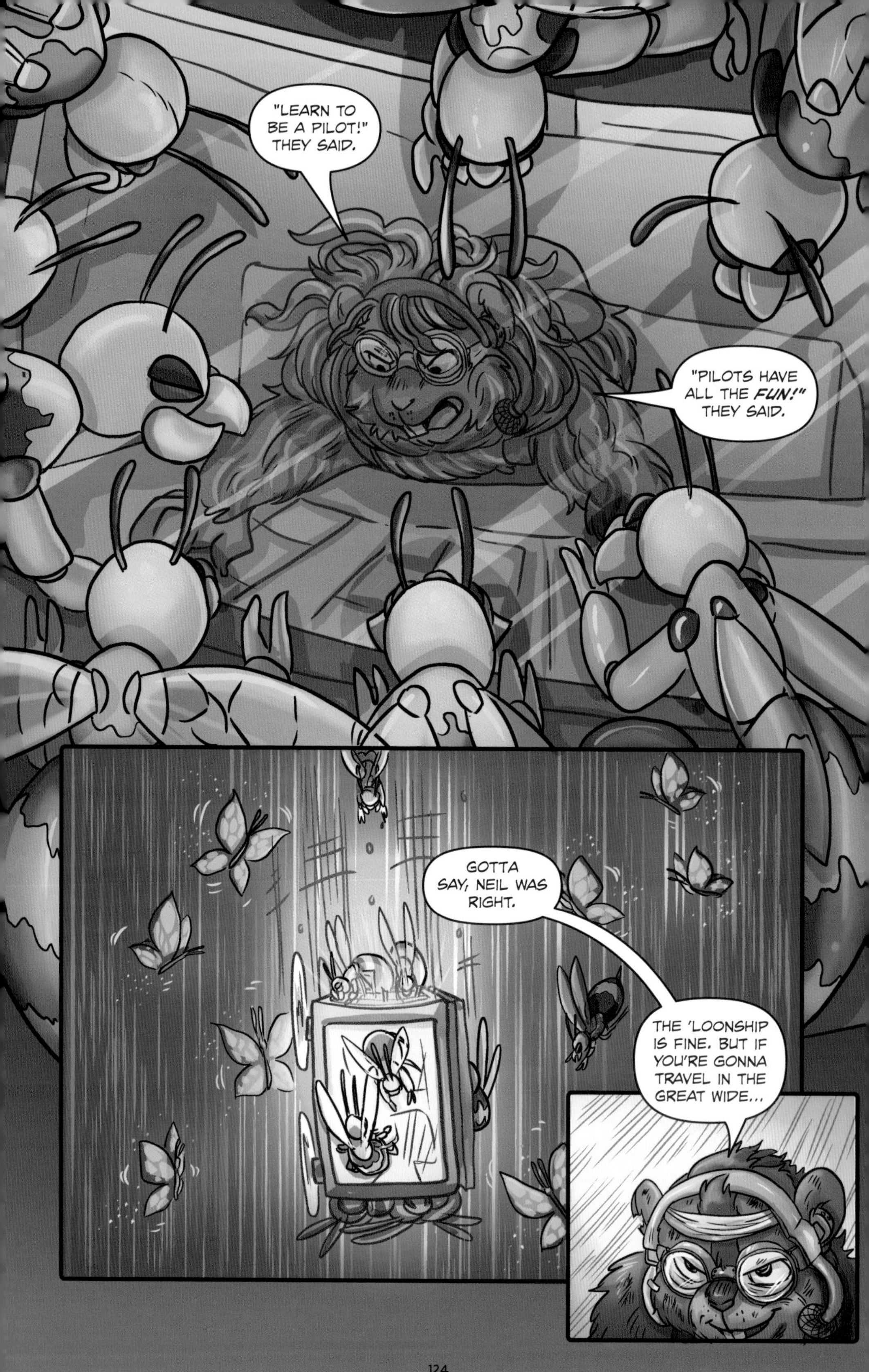
"LEARN TO BE A PILOT!" THEY SAID.
"PILOTS HAVE ALL THE *FUN!*" THEY SAID.
GOTTA SAY, NEIL WAS RIGHT.
THE 'LOONSHIP IS FINE. BUT IF YOU'RE GONNA TRAVEL IN THE GREAT WIDE...

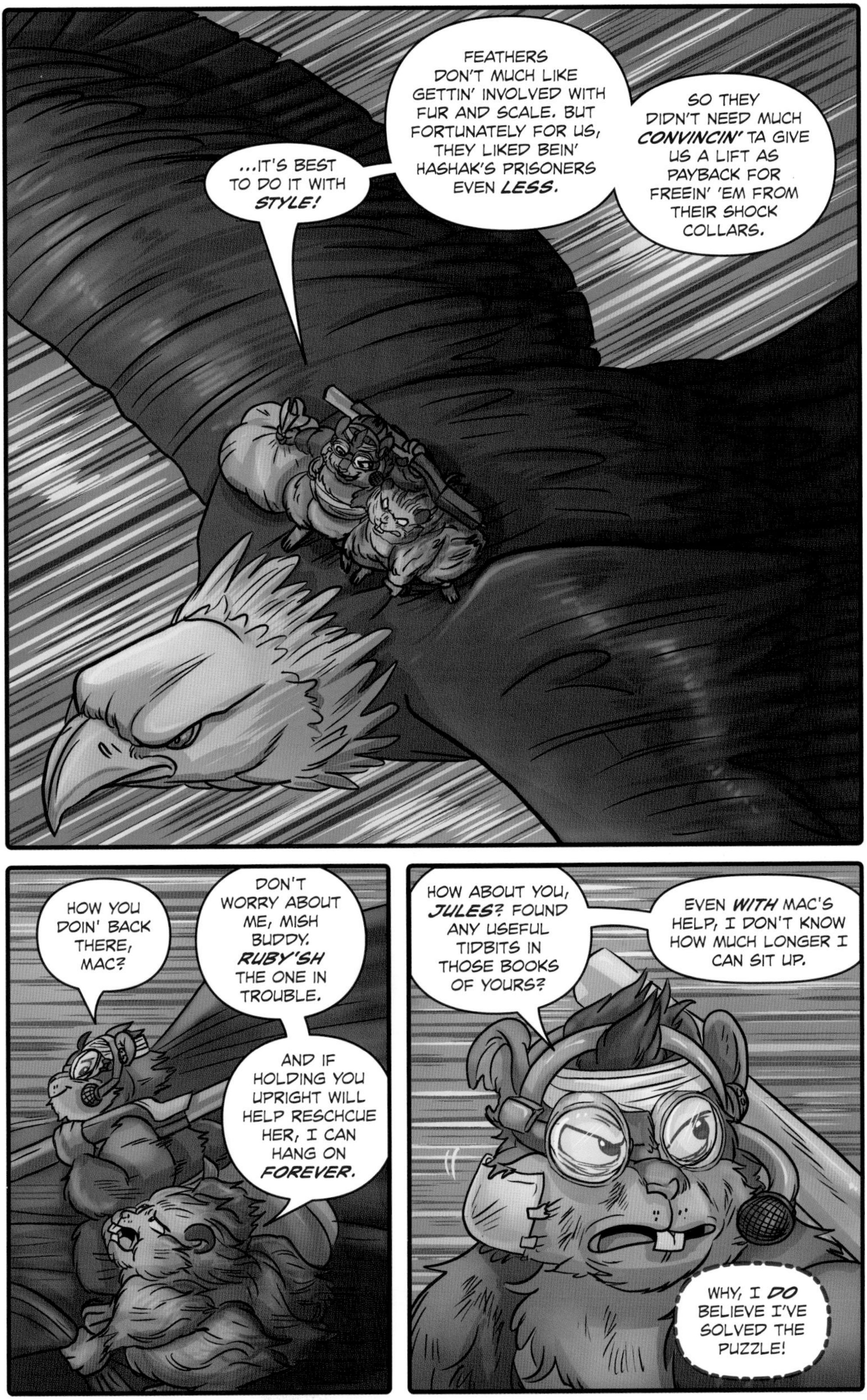
...IT'S BEST TO DO IT WITH STYLE!
FEATHERS DON'T MUCH LIKE GETTIN' INVOLVED WITH FUR AND SCALE. BUT FORTUNATELY FOR US, THEY LIKED BEIN' HASHAK'S PRISONERS EVEN LESS.
SO THEY DIDN'T NEED MUCH CONVINCIN' TA GIVE US A LIFT AS PAYBACK FOR FREEIN' 'EM FROM THEIR SHOCK COLLARS.
HOW YOU DOIN' BACK THERE, MAC?
DON'T WORRY ABOUT ME, MISH BUDDY. RUBY'SH THE ONE IN TROUBLE.
AND IF HOLDING YOU UPRIGHT WILL HELP RESCHCUE HER, I CAN HANG ON FOREVER.
HOW ABOUT YOU, JULES? FOUND ANY USEFUL TIDBITS IN THOSE BOOKS OF YOURS?
EVEN WITH MAC'S HELP, I DON'T KNOW HOW MUCH LONGER I CAN SIT UP.
WHY, I DO BELIEVE I'VE SOLVED THE PUZZLE!

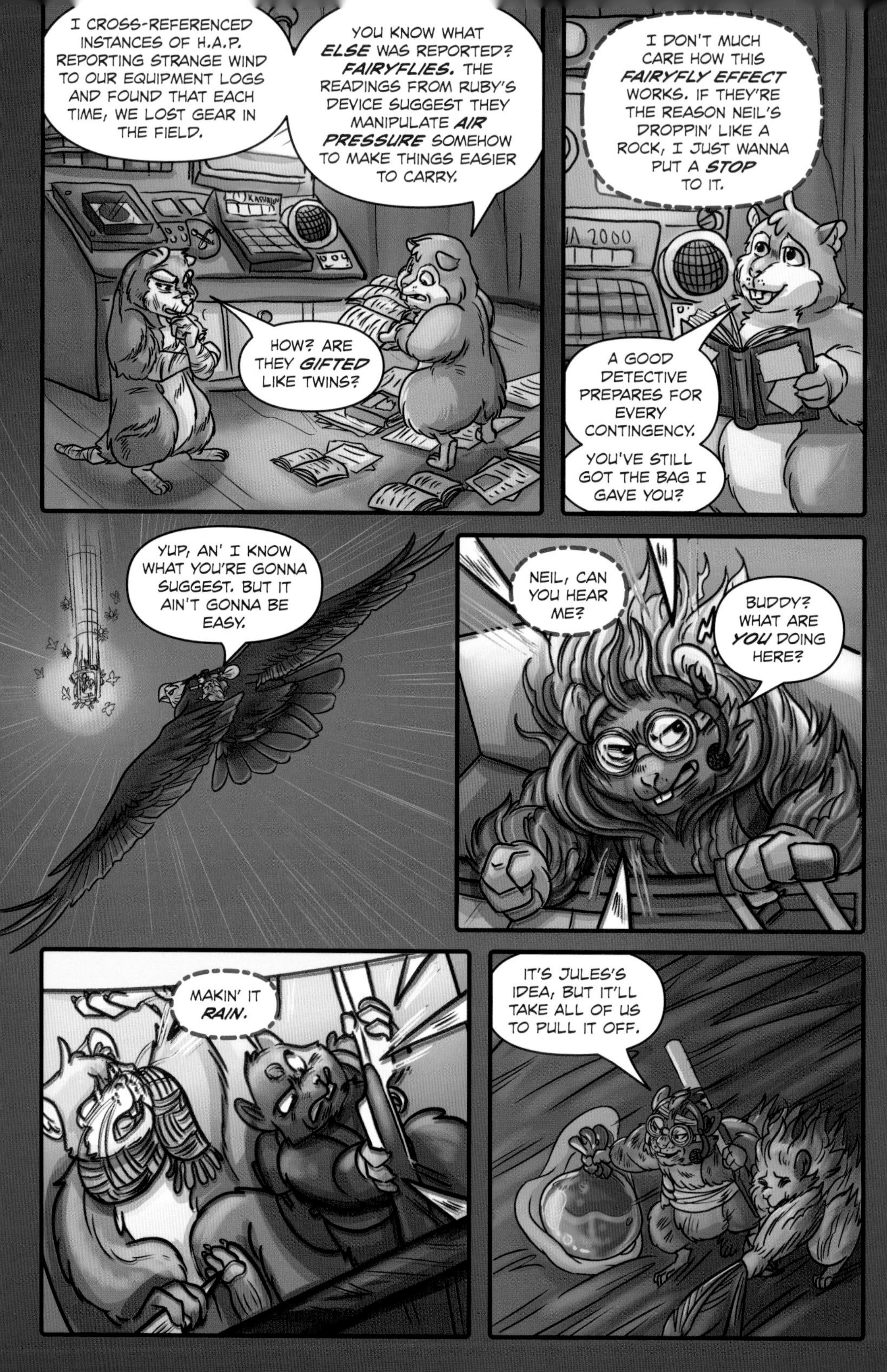
I CROSS-REFERENCED INSTANCES OF H.A.P. REPORTING STRANGE WIND TO OUR EQUIPMENT LOGS AND FOUND THAT EACH TIME, WE LOST GEAR IN THE FIELD.
YOU KNOW WHAT ELSE WAS REPORTED? FAIRYFLIES. THE READINGS FROM RUBY'S DEVICE SUGGEST THEY MANIPULATE AIR PRESSURE SOMEHOW TO MAKE THINGS EASIER TO CARRY.
HOW? ARE THEY GIFTED LIKE TWINS?
I DON'T MUCH CARE HOW THIS FAIRYFLY EFFECT WORKS. IF THEY'RE THE REASON NEIL'S DROPPIN' LIKE A ROCK, I JUST WANNA PUT A STOP TO IT.
A GOOD DETECTIVE PREPARES FOR EVERY CONTINGENCY.
YOU'VE STILL GOT THE BAG I GAVE YOU?
YUP, AN' I KNOW WHAT YOU'RE GONNA SUGGEST. BUT IT AIN'T GONNA BE EASY.
NEIL, CAN YOU HEAR ME?
BUDDY? WHAT ARE YOU DOING HERE?
MAKIN' IT RAIN.
IT'S JULES'S IDEA, BUT IT'LL TAKE ALL OF US TO PULL IT OFF.

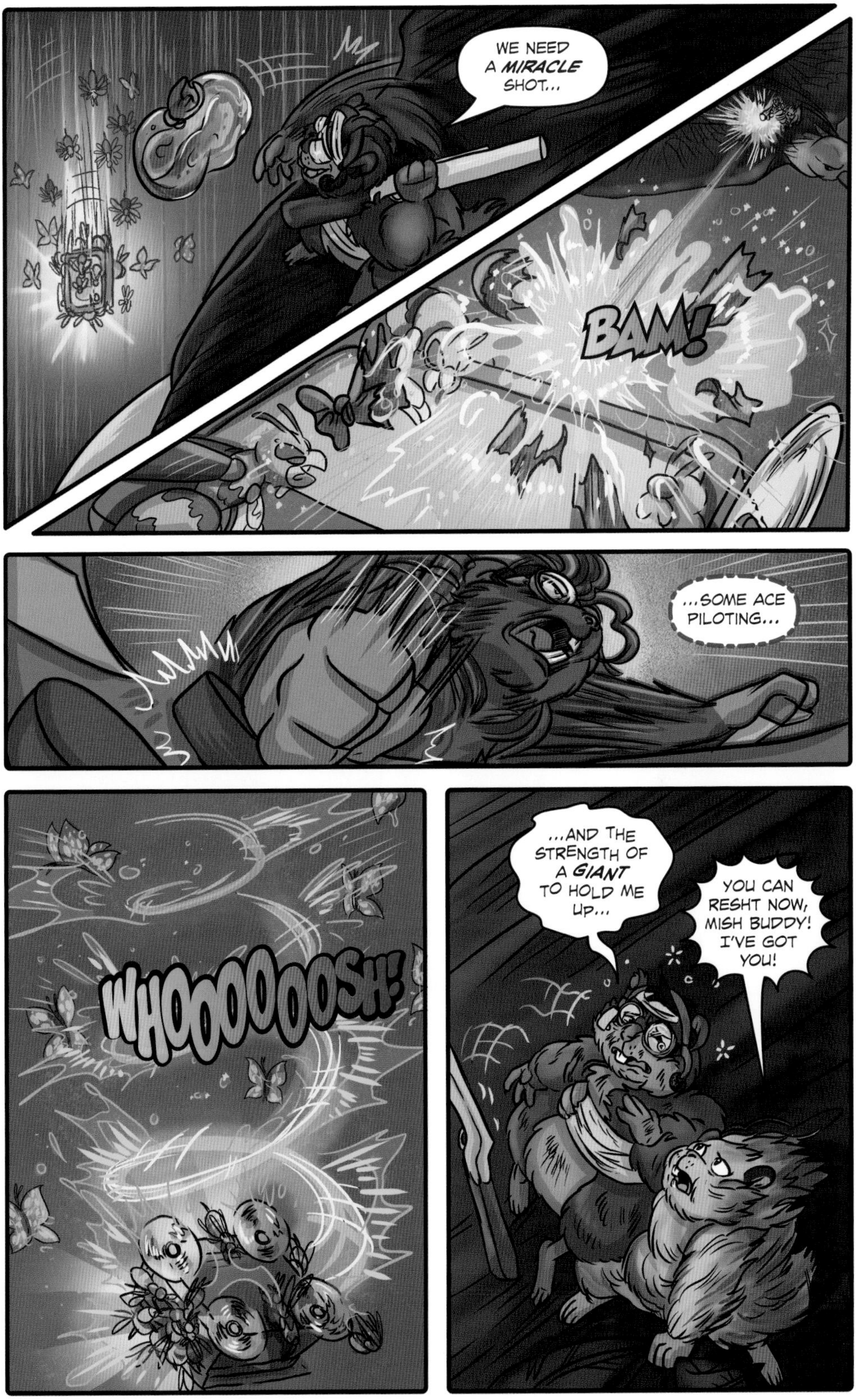
WE NEED A MIRACLE SHOT...
BAM!
...SOME ACE PILOTING...
WHOOOOOOOSH!
...AND THE STRENGTH OF A GIANT TO HOLD ME UP...
YOU CAN RESHT NOW, MISH BUDDY! I'VE GOT YOU!

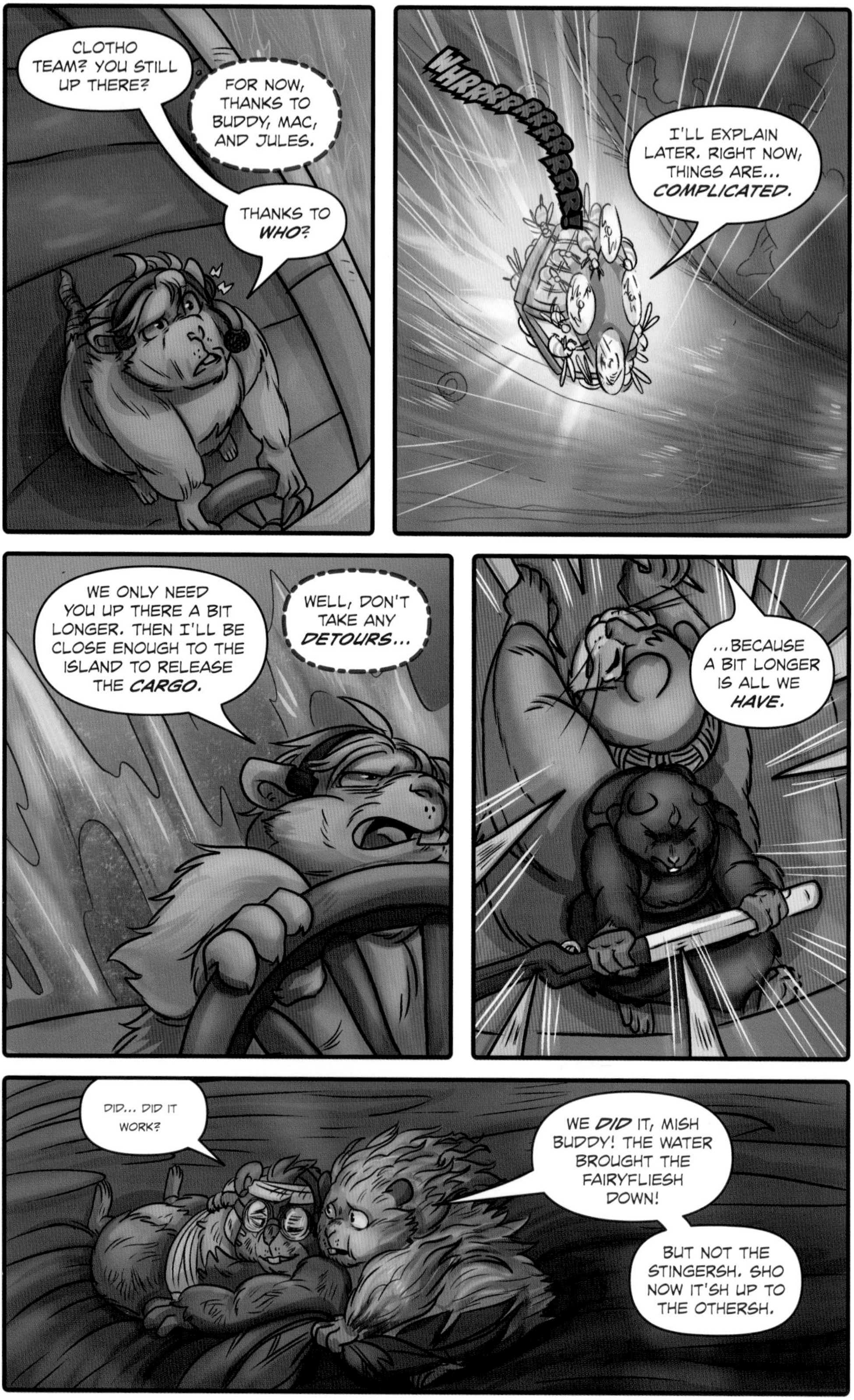
CLOTHO TEAM? YOU STILL UP THERE?
FOR NOW, THANKS TO BUDDY, MAC, AND JULES.
THANKS TO WHO?
WHRRRRRRRRRRR!
I'LL EXPLAIN LATER. RIGHT NOW, THINGS ARE... COMPLICATED.
WE ONLY NEED YOU UP THERE A BIT LONGER. THEN I'LL BE CLOSE ENOUGH TO THE ISLAND TO RELEASE THE CARGO.
WELL, DON'T TAKE ANY DETOURS...
...BECAUSE A BIT LONGER IS ALL WE HAVE.
DID... DID IT WORK?
WE DID IT, MISH BUDDY! THE WATER BROUGHT THE FAIRYFLIESH DOWN!
BUT NOT THE STINGERSH. SHO NOW IT'SH UP TO THE OTHERSH.

WEIRD. I DIDN'T NOTICE ANY CLOUDS EARLIER.

TORI? ANI? YOU SEEING ANYTHING UP THERE?

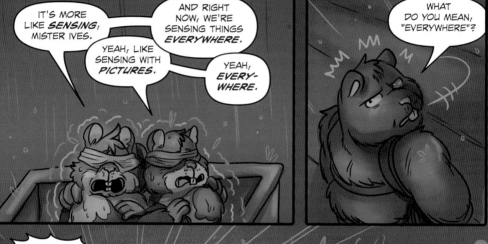

IT'S MORE LIKE *SENSING*, MISTER IVES.

AND RIGHT NOW, WE'RE SENSING THINGS *EVERYWHERE*.

YEAH, LIKE SENSING WITH *PICTURES*.

YEAH, *EVERY-WHERE*.

WHAT DO YOU MEAN, "EVERYWHERE"?

EVERYWHERE!!

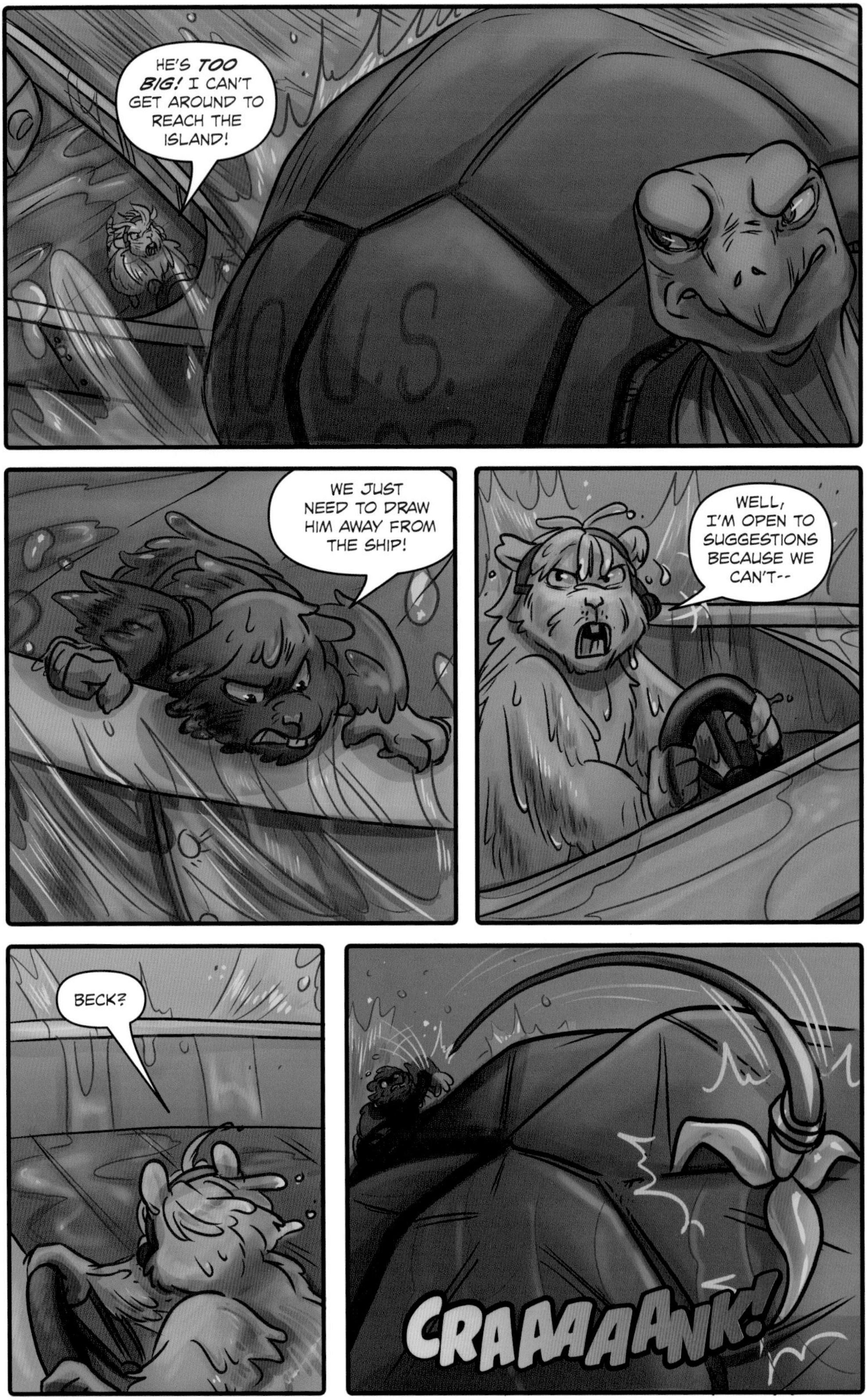
HE'S TOO BIG! I CAN'T GET AROUND TO REACH THE ISLAND!
WE JUST NEED TO DRAW HIM AWAY FROM THE SHIP!
WELL, I'M OPEN TO SUGGESTIONS BECAUSE WE CAN'T--
BECK?
CRAAAAANK!

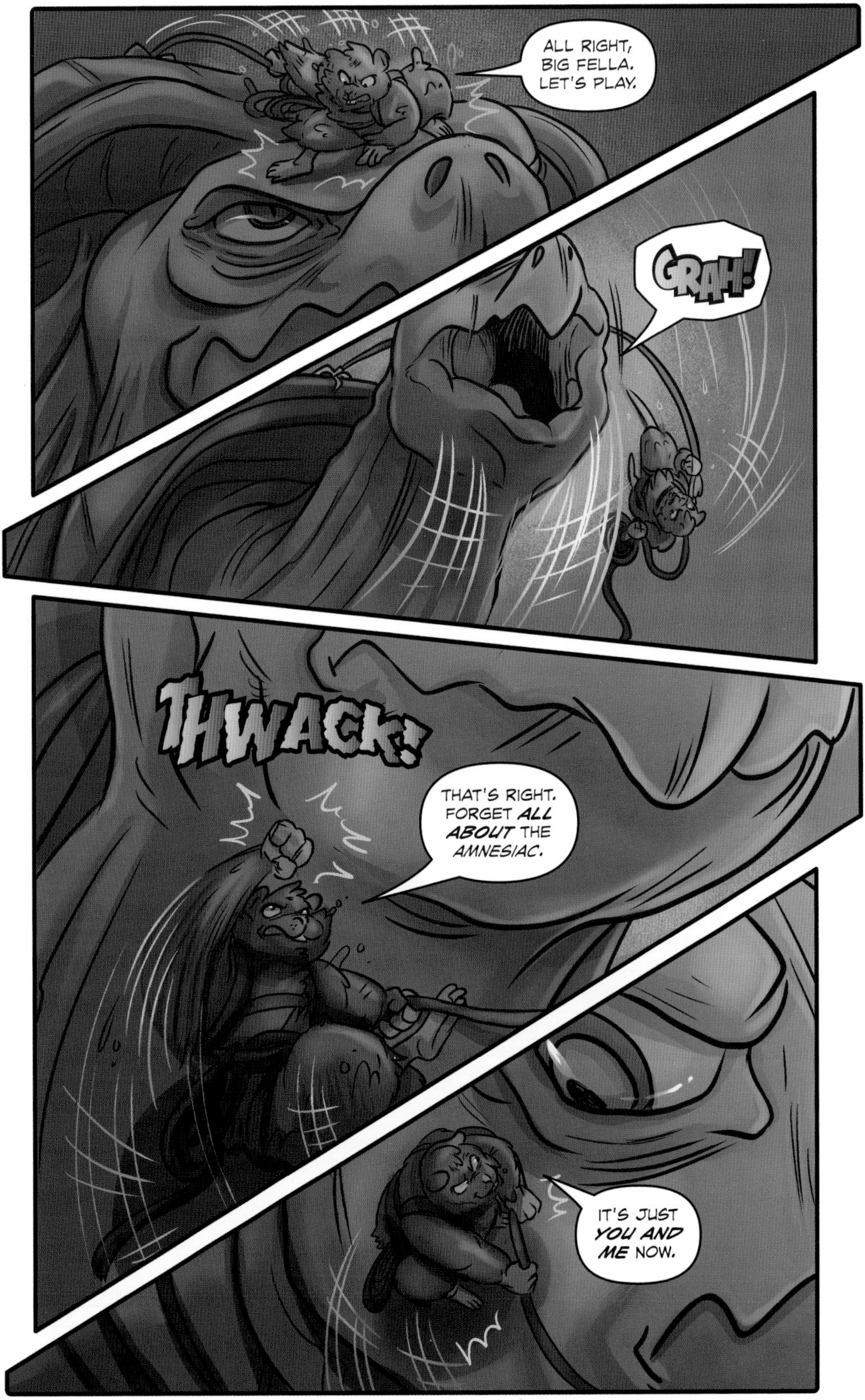
ALL RIGHT, BIG FELLA. LET'S PLAY.
GRAH!
THWACK!
THAT'S RIGHT. FORGET ALL ABOUT THE AMNESIAC.
IT'S JUST YOU AND ME NOW.

THIS IS FOR YOU, GUNTHER. I MISSED MY CHANCE TO BE A HERO BACK THEN.

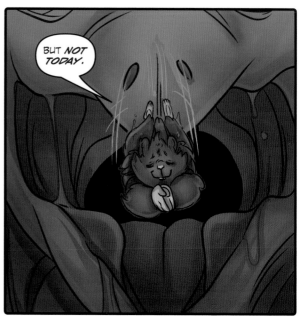

BUT *NOT TODAY.*

IT'S WORKING! BECK'S LEADING THE HARDBACK OUT OF THE WAY. THIS IS OUR CHANCE!

NEIL, IF YOU CAN HEAR ME, I'M RELEASING THE CARGO, SO I NEED EVERY HEAD TURNED TOWARDS THE GREAT WIDE. *RIGHT. NOW.*

CLICK!

NEIL?

KA-BOOOOOOOOOON!

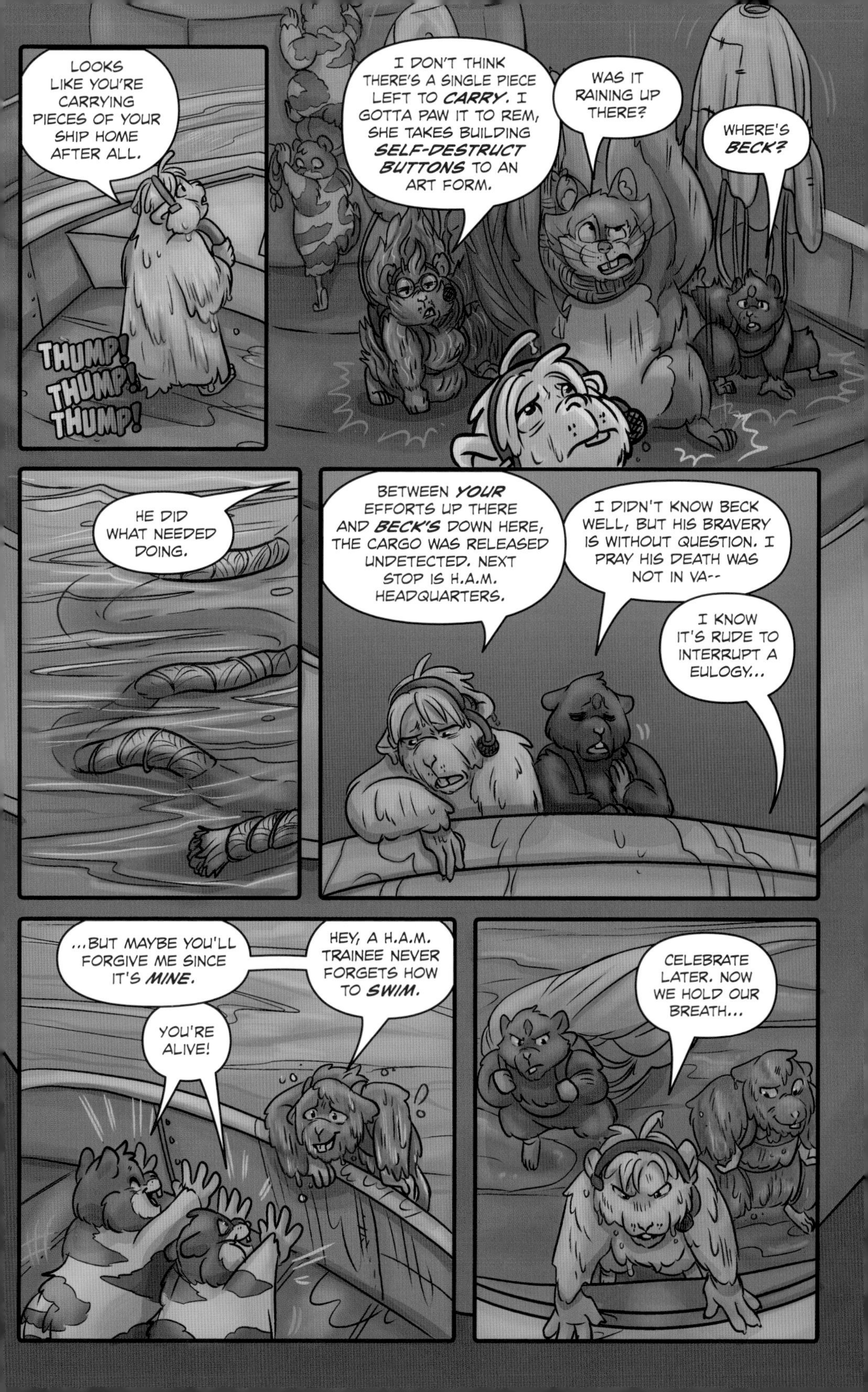

LOOKS LIKE YOU'RE CARRYING PIECES OF YOUR SHIP HOME AFTER ALL.
THUMP! THUMP! THUMP!
I DON'T THINK THERE'S A SINGLE PIECE LEFT TO CARRY. I GOTTA PAW IT TO REM, SHE TAKES BUILDING SELF-DESTRUCT BUTTONS TO AN ART FORM.
WAS IT RAINING UP THERE?
WHERE'S BECK?
HE DID WHAT NEEDED DOING.
BETWEEN YOUR EFFORTS UP THERE AND BECK'S DOWN HERE, THE CARGO WAS RELEASED UNDETECTED. NEXT STOP IS H.A.M. HEADQUARTERS.
I DIDN'T KNOW BECK WELL, BUT HIS BRAVERY IS WITHOUT QUESTION. I PRAY HIS DEATH WAS NOT IN VA--
I KNOW IT'S RUDE TO INTERRUPT A EULOGY...
...BUT MAYBE YOU'LL FORGIVE ME SINCE IT'S MINE.
HEY, A H.A.M. TRAINEE NEVER FORGETS HOW TO SWIM.
YOU'RE ALIVE!
CELEBRATE LATER. NOW WE HOLD OUR BREATH...

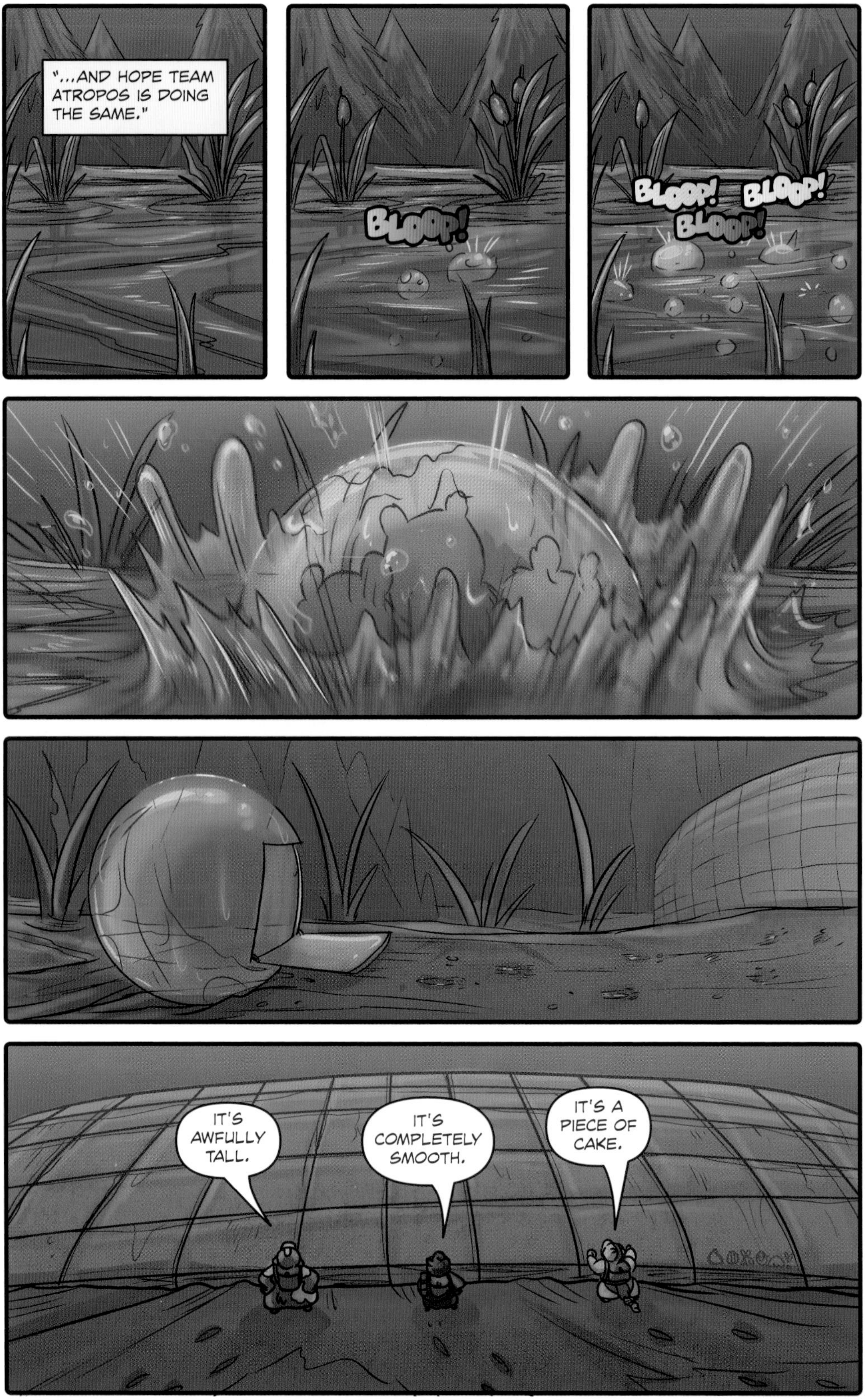
"...AND HOPE TEAM ATROPOS IS DOING THE SAME."
BLOOP!
BLOOP!
BLOOP!
BLOOP!
IT'S AWFULLY TALL.
IT'S COMPLETELY SMOOTH.
IT'S A PIECE OF CAKE.

NO MATTER *HOW* IMPOSSIBLE IT LOOKS TO THE NAKED EYE, THERE'S ALWAYS A WAY FORWARD. A WAY *UP*.

CLINK!

BUT WHOEVER SAID, "IT'S THE JOURNEY; AND NOT THE DESTINATION;" WASN'T TRYING TO AVOID AN ARMY OF SCALES.

SO, I'LL LEAVE A TRAIL OF ROPES FOR YOU TO FOLLOW. JUST KEEP CLIMBING *UP,* AND DON'T LOOK DOWN.

AND THE REAL REWARD DOESN'T COME FROM THE JOURNEY *OR* THE DESTINATION.

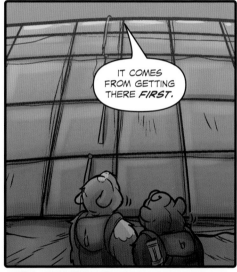

IT COMES FROM GETTING THERE *FIRST.*

ON THE OTHER PAW, THERE *IS* SUCH A THING AS GETTING A BIT *AHEAD OF YOURSELF.*

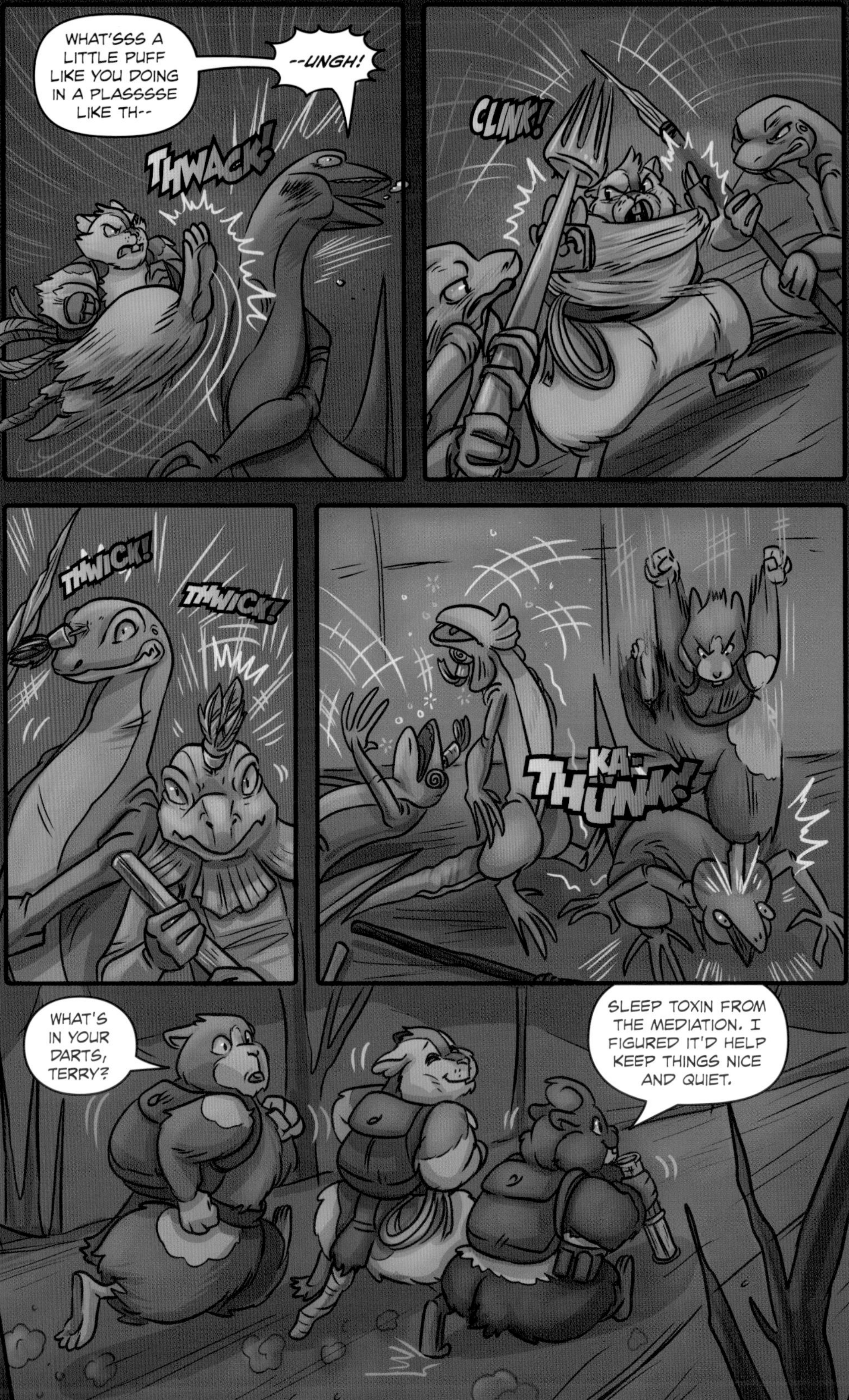
WHAT'SSS A LITTLE PUFF LIKE YOU DOING IN A PLASSSSE LIKE TH--
--UNGH!
THWACK!
CLINK!
THWICK!
THWICK!
KA-THUNK!
WHAT'S IN YOUR DARTS, TERRY?
SLEEP TOXIN FROM THE MEDIATION. I FIGURED IT'D HELP KEEP THINGS NICE AND QUIET.

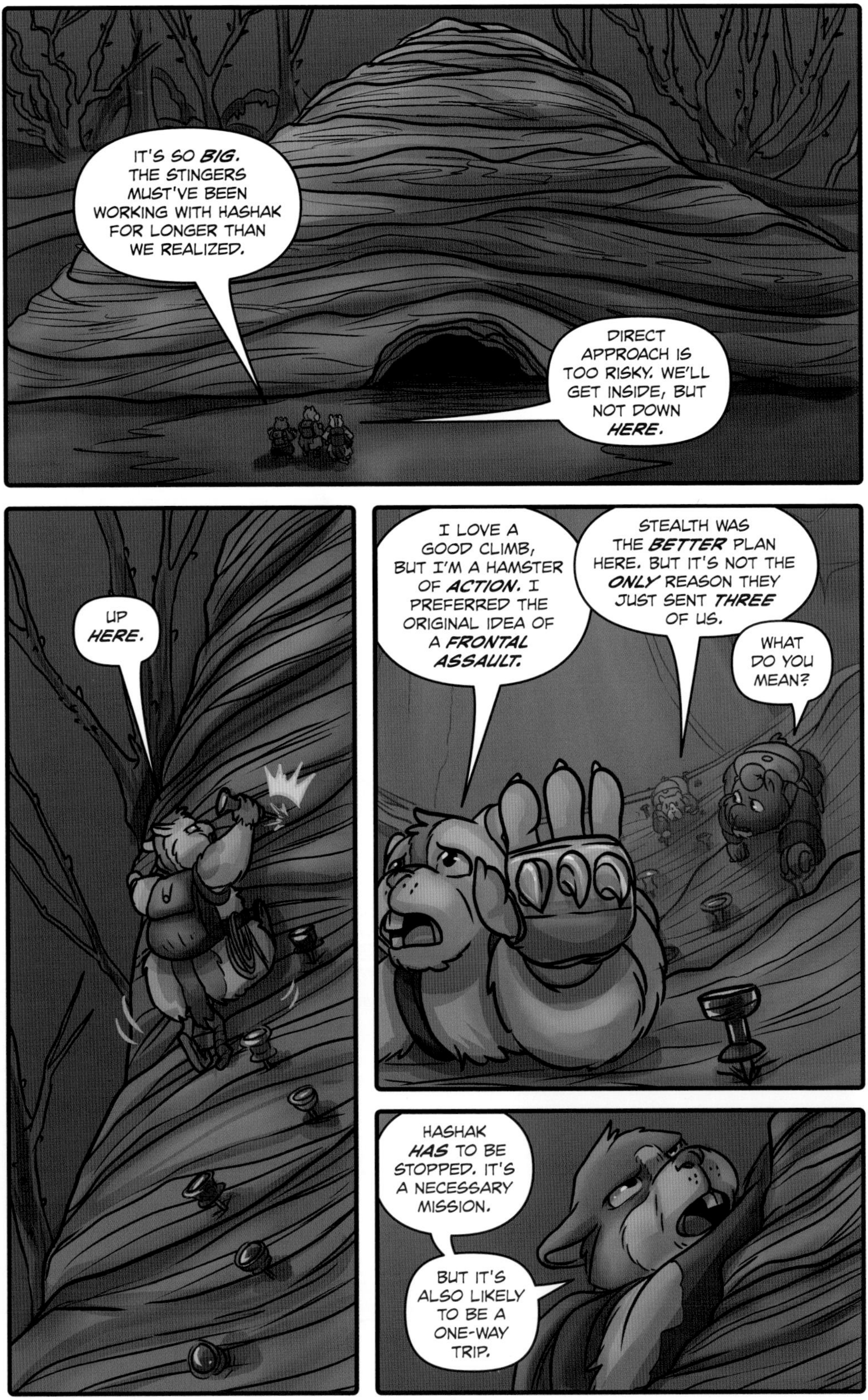

IT'S SO *BIG.* THE STINGERS MUST'VE BEEN WORKING WITH HASHAK FOR LONGER THAN WE REALIZED.
DIRECT APPROACH IS TOO RISKY. WE'LL GET INSIDE, BUT NOT DOWN *HERE.*
UP *HERE.*
I LOVE A GOOD CLIMB, BUT I'M A HAMSTER OF *ACTION.* I PREFERRED THE ORIGINAL IDEA OF A *FRONTAL ASSAULT.*
STEALTH WAS THE *BETTER* PLAN HERE. BUT IT'S NOT THE *ONLY* REASON THEY JUST SENT *THREE* OF US.
WHAT DO YOU MEAN?
HASHAK *HAS* TO BE STOPPED. IT'S A NECESSARY MISSION.
BUT IT'S ALSO LIKELY TO BE A ONE-WAY TRIP.

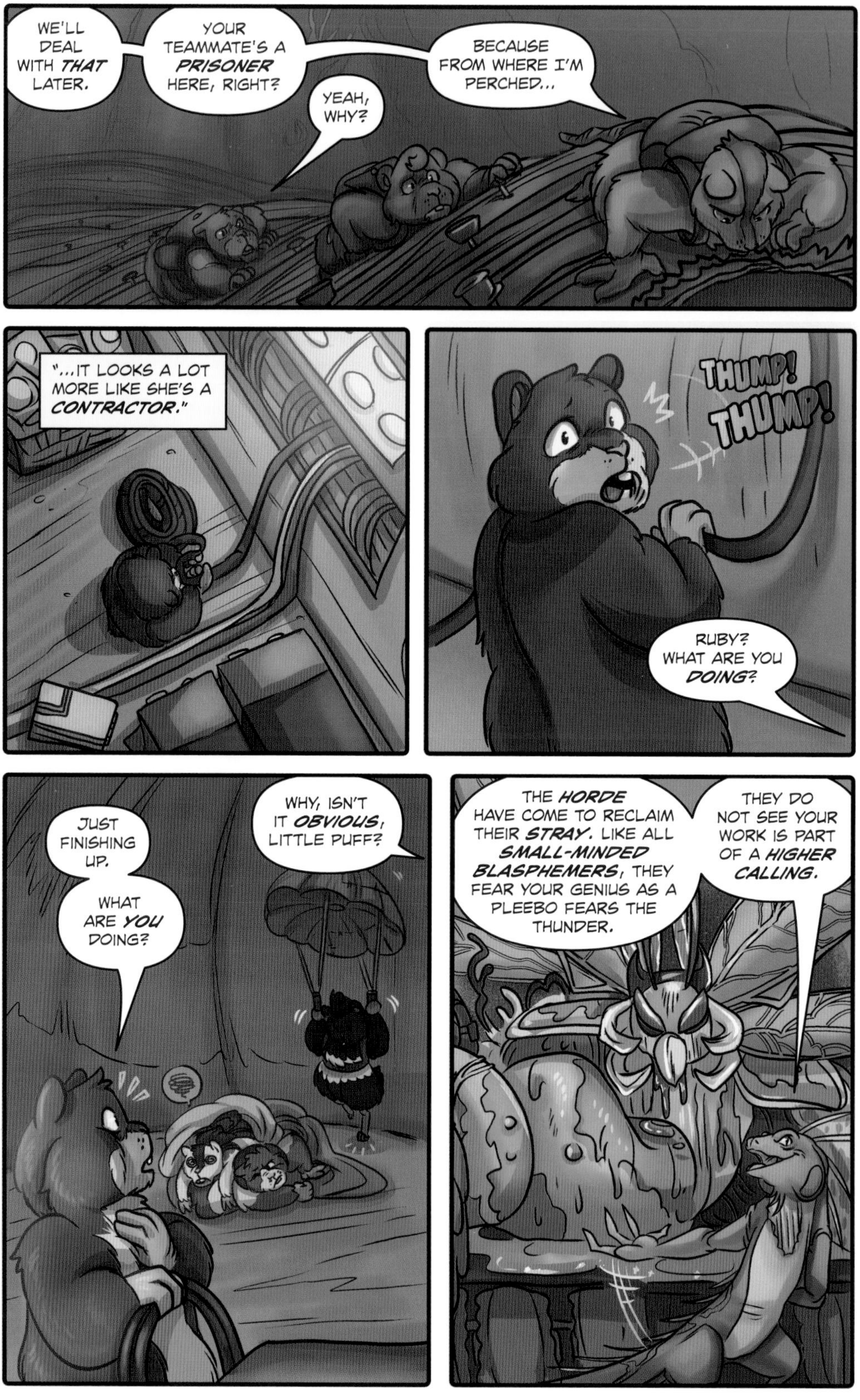
WE'LL DEAL WITH *THAT* LATER.
YOUR TEAMMATE'S A *PRISONER* HERE, RIGHT?
YEAH, WHY?
BECAUSE FROM WHERE I'M PERCHED...
"...IT LOOKS A LOT MORE LIKE SHE'S A *CONTRACTOR*."
THUMP! THUMP!
RUBY? WHAT ARE YOU *DOING*?
JUST FINISHING UP.
WHAT ARE *YOU* DOING?
WHY, ISN'T IT *OBVIOUS*, LITTLE PUFF?
THE *HORDE* HAVE COME TO RECLAIM THEIR *STRAY*. LIKE ALL *SMALL-MINDED BLASPHEMERS*, THEY FEAR YOUR GENIUS AS A PLEEBO FEARS THE THUNDER.
THEY DO NOT SEE YOUR WORK IS PART OF A *HIGHER CALLING*.

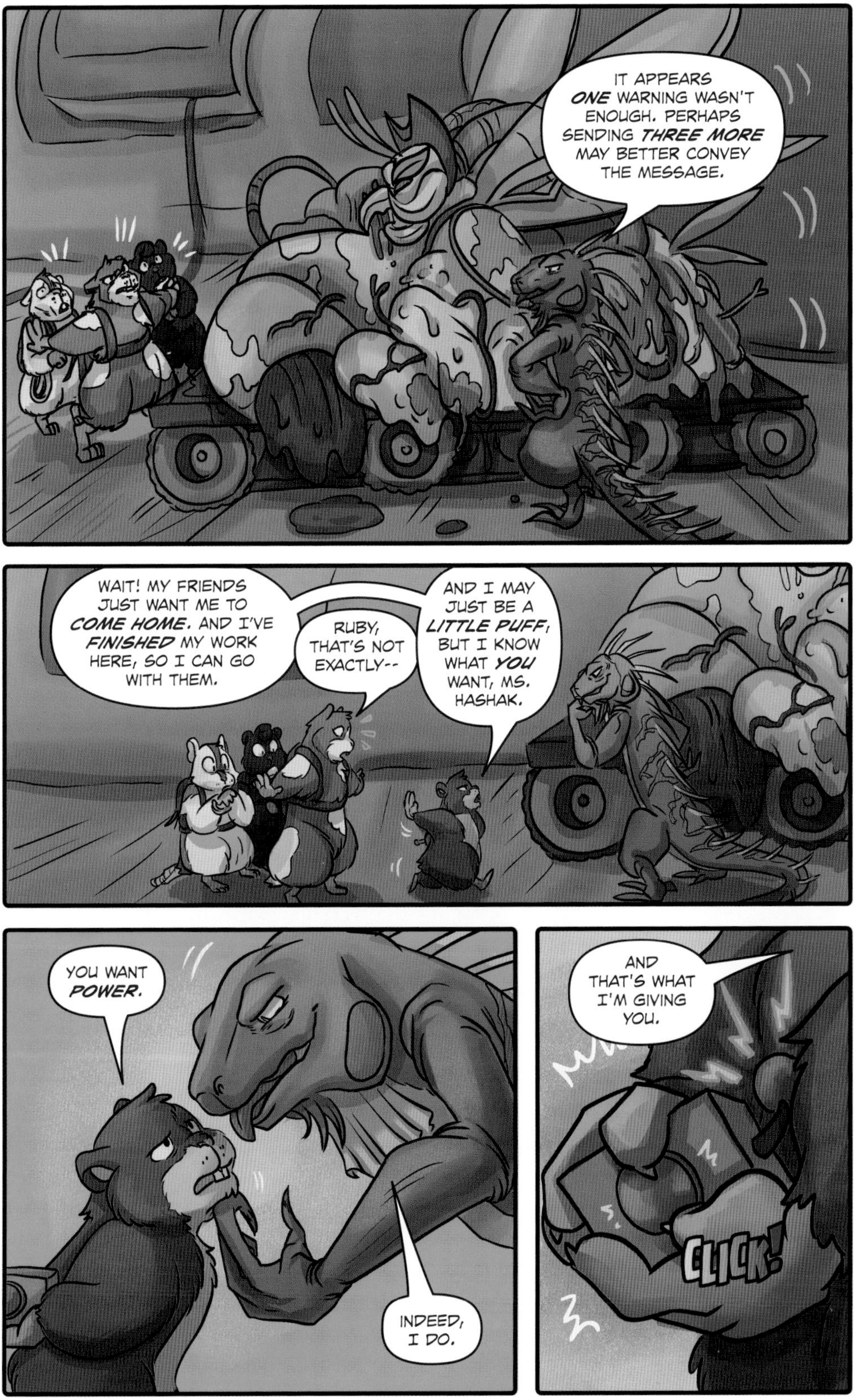
IT APPEARS ONE WARNING WASN'T ENOUGH. PERHAPS SENDING THREE MORE MAY BETTER CONVEY THE MESSAGE.
WAIT! MY FRIENDS JUST WANT ME TO COME HOME. AND I'VE FINISHED MY WORK HERE, SO I CAN GO WITH THEM.
RUBY, THAT'S NOT EXACTLY--
AND I MAY JUST BE A LITTLE PUFF, BUT I KNOW WHAT YOU WANT, MS. HASHAK.
YOU WANT POWER.
INDEED, I DO.
AND THAT'S WHAT I'M GIVING YOU.
CLICK!

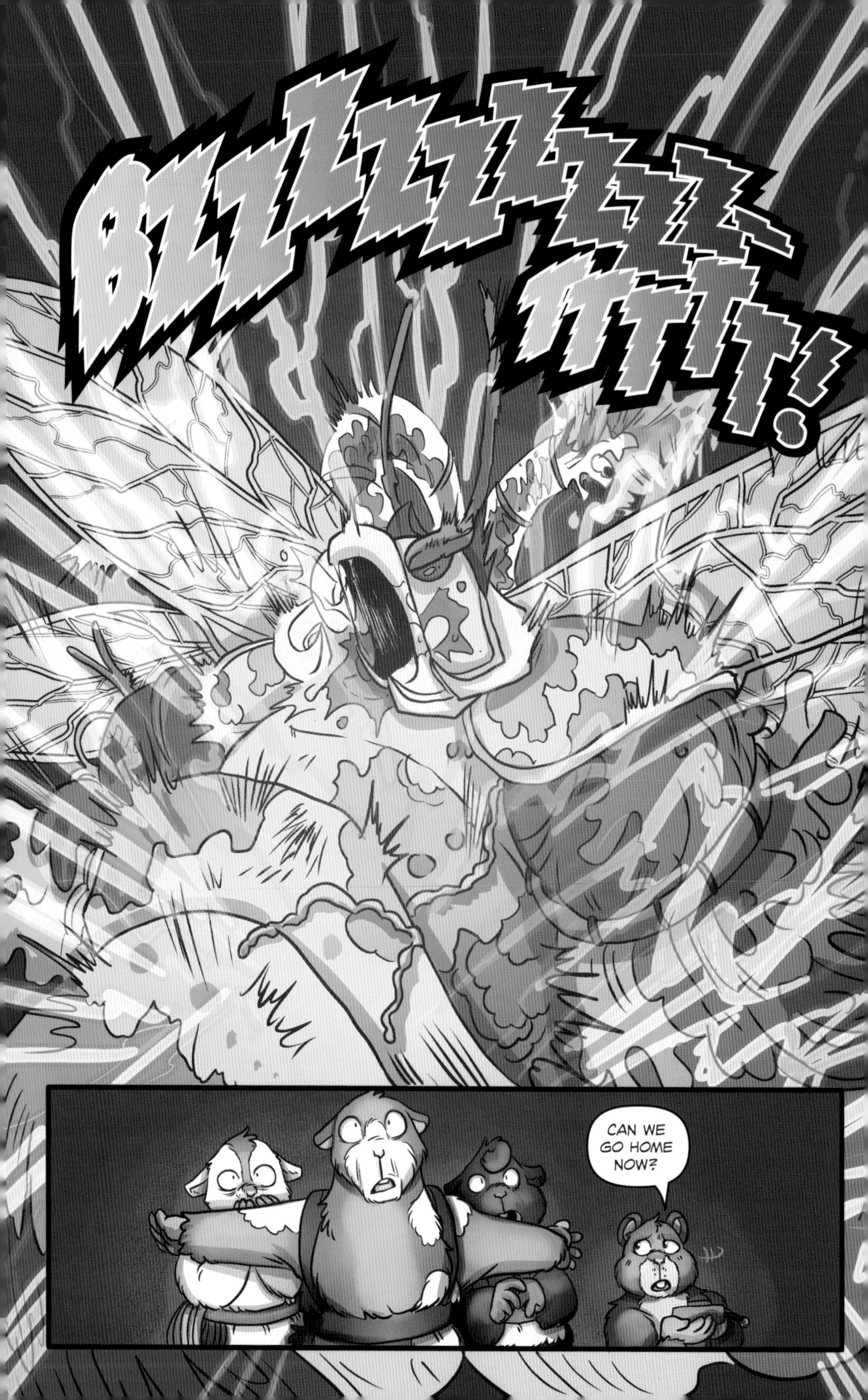
BZZZZZZZZ-ZTTTT!
CAN WE GO HOME NOW?

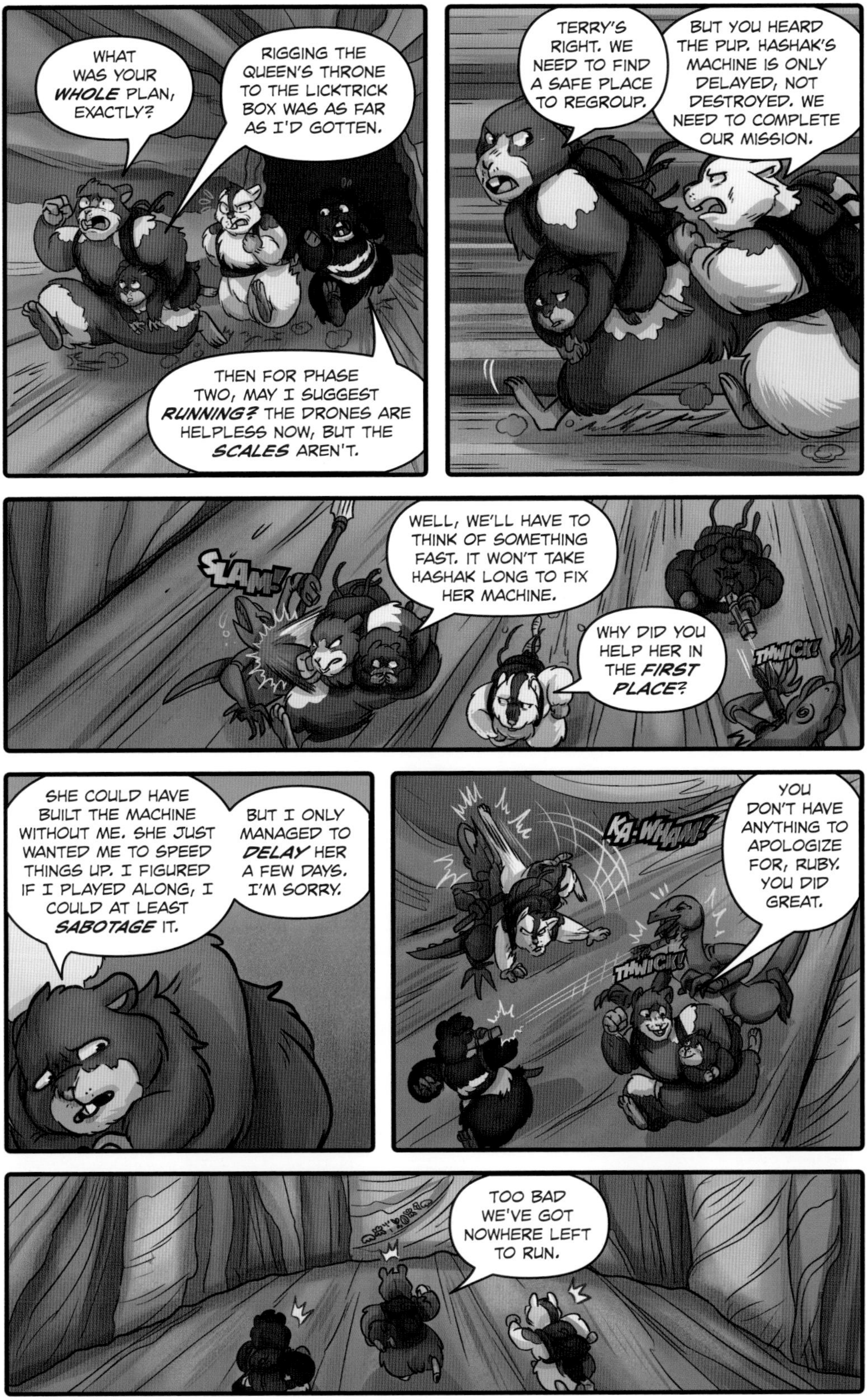

WHAT WAS YOUR *WHOLE* PLAN, EXACTLY?
RIGGING THE QUEEN'S THRONE TO THE LICKTRICK BOX WAS AS FAR AS I'D GOTTEN.
THEN FOR PHASE TWO, MAY I SUGGEST *RUNNING?* THE DRONES ARE HELPLESS NOW, BUT THE *SCALES* AREN'T.
TERRY'S RIGHT. WE NEED TO FIND A SAFE PLACE TO REGROUP.
BUT YOU HEARD THE PUP. HASHAK'S MACHINE IS ONLY DELAYED, NOT DESTROYED. WE NEED TO COMPLETE OUR MISSION.
SLAM!
WELL, WE'LL HAVE TO THINK OF SOMETHING FAST. IT WON'T TAKE HASHAK LONG TO FIX HER MACHINE.
WHY DID YOU HELP HER IN THE *FIRST PLACE?*
THWICK!
SHE COULD HAVE BUILT THE MACHINE WITHOUT ME. SHE JUST WANTED ME TO SPEED THINGS UP. I FIGURED IF I PLAYED ALONG, I COULD AT LEAST *SABOTAGE* IT.
BUT I ONLY MANAGED TO *DELAY* HER A FEW DAYS. I'M SORRY.
KA-WHAM!
YOU DON'T HAVE ANYTHING TO APOLOGIZE FOR, RUBY. YOU DID GREAT.
THWICK!
TOO BAD WE'VE GOT NOWHERE LEFT TO RUN.

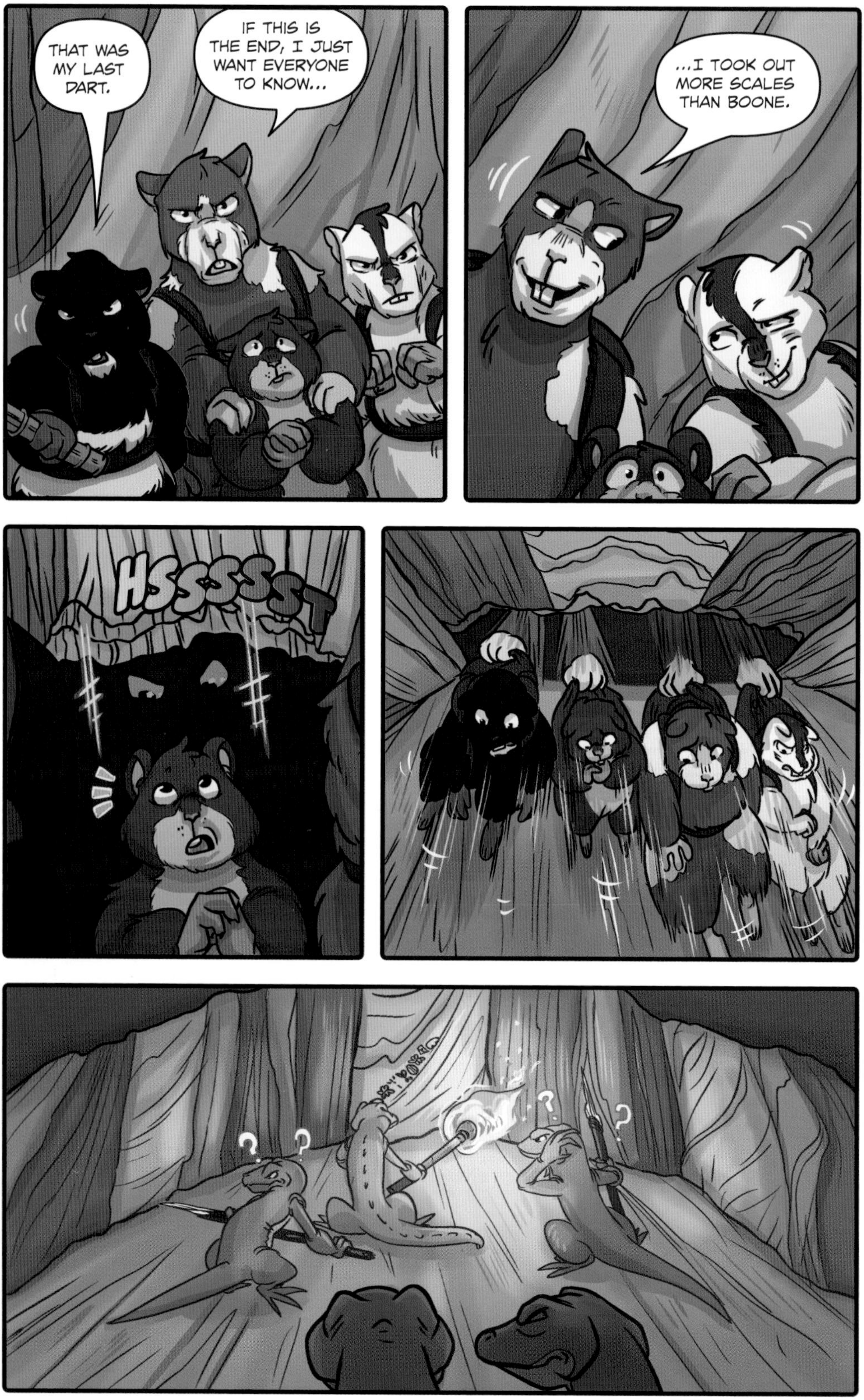
THAT WAS MY LAST DART.
IF THIS IS THE END, I JUST WANT EVERYONE TO KNOW...
...I TOOK OUT MORE SCALES THAN BOONE.
HSSSSST

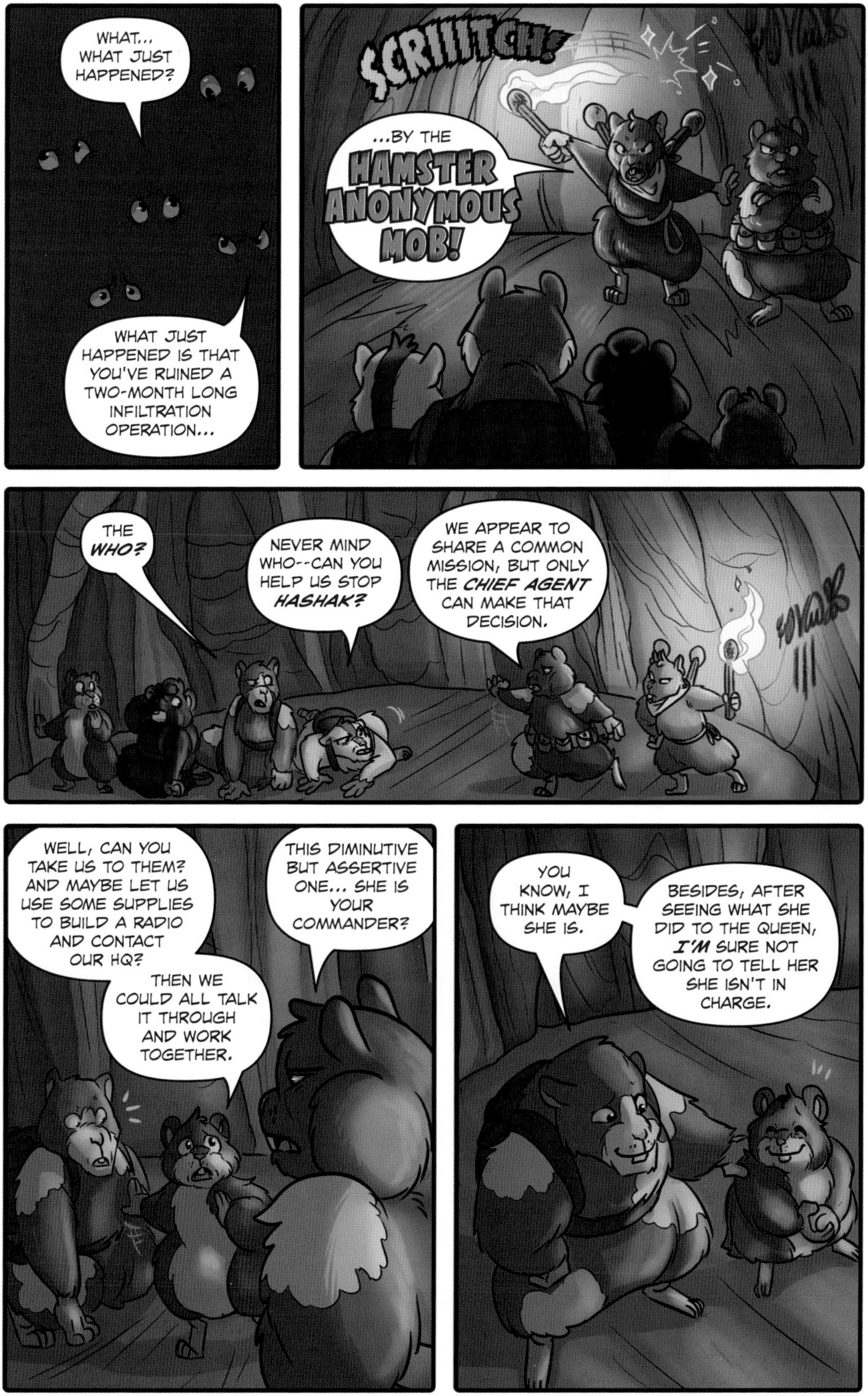
WHAT... WHAT JUST HAPPENED?
WHAT JUST HAPPENED IS THAT YOU'VE RUINED A TWO-MONTH LONG INFILTRATION OPERATION...
SCRIIIITCH!
...BY THE HAMSTER ANONYMOUS MOB!
THE *WHO?*
NEVER MIND WHO--CAN YOU HELP US STOP *HASHAK?*
WE APPEAR TO SHARE A COMMON MISSION, BUT ONLY THE *CHIEF AGENT* CAN MAKE THAT DECISION.
WELL, CAN YOU TAKE US TO THEM? AND MAYBE LET US USE SOME SUPPLIES TO BUILD A RADIO AND CONTACT OUR HQ?
THEN WE COULD ALL TALK IT THROUGH AND WORK TOGETHER.
THIS DIMINUTIVE BUT ASSERTIVE ONE... SHE IS YOUR COMMANDER?
YOU KNOW, I THINK MAYBE SHE IS.
BESIDES, AFTER SEEING WHAT SHE DID TO THE QUEEN, *I'M* SURE NOT GOING TO TELL HER SHE ISN'T IN CHARGE.

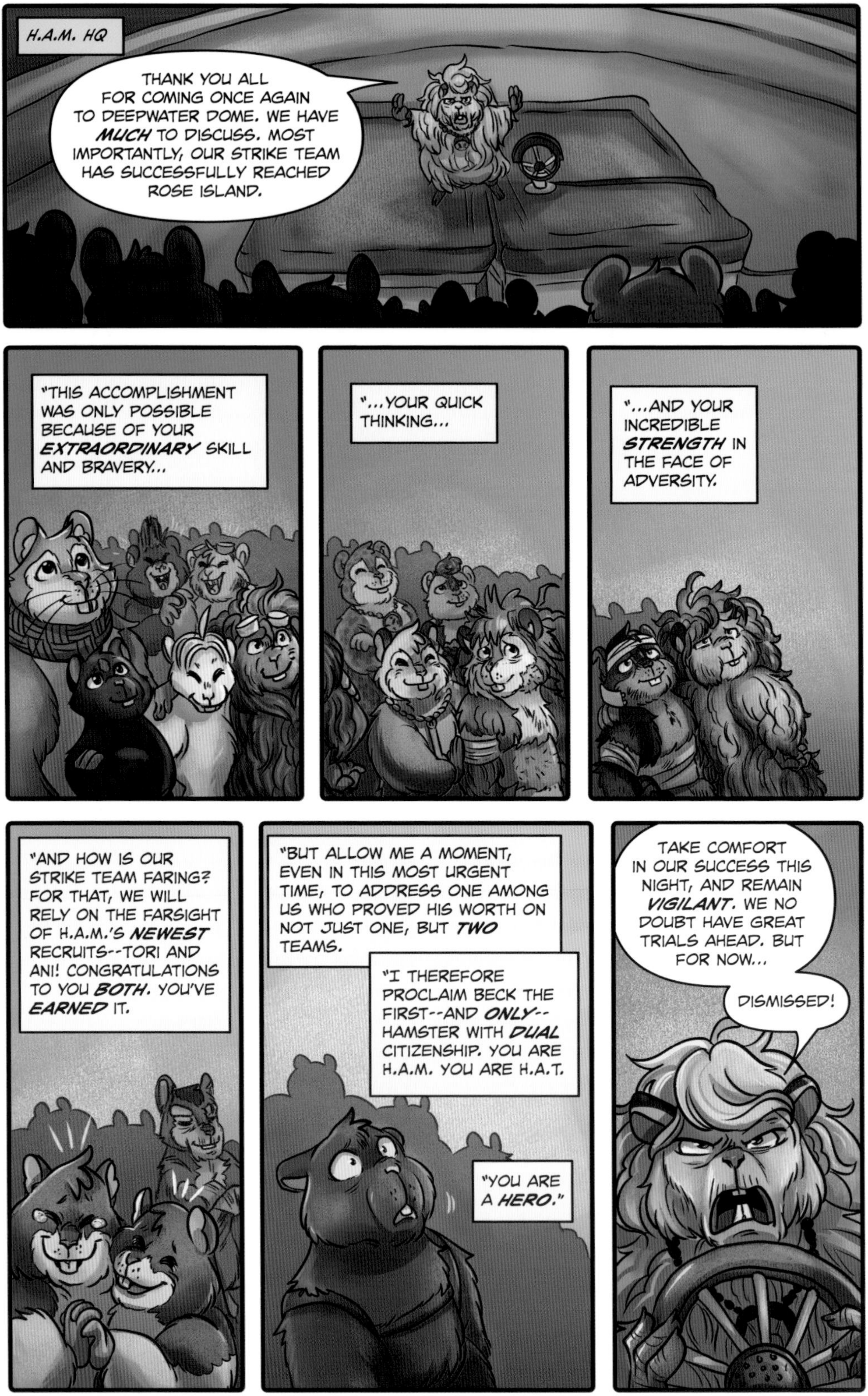
H.A.M. HQ
THANK YOU ALL FOR COMING ONCE AGAIN TO DEEPWATER DOME. WE HAVE MUCH TO DISCUSS. MOST IMPORTANTLY, OUR STRIKE TEAM HAS SUCCESSFULLY REACHED ROSE ISLAND.
"THIS ACCOMPLISHMENT WAS ONLY POSSIBLE BECAUSE OF YOUR EXTRAORDINARY SKILL AND BRAVERY...
"...YOUR QUICK THINKING...
"...AND YOUR INCREDIBLE STRENGTH IN THE FACE OF ADVERSITY.
"AND HOW IS OUR STRIKE TEAM FARING? FOR THAT, WE WILL RELY ON THE FARSIGHT OF H.A.M.'S NEWEST RECRUITS--TORI AND ANI! CONGRATULATIONS TO YOU BOTH. YOU'VE EARNED IT.
"BUT ALLOW ME A MOMENT, EVEN IN THIS MOST URGENT TIME, TO ADDRESS ONE AMONG US WHO PROVED HIS WORTH ON NOT JUST ONE, BUT TWO TEAMS.
"I THEREFORE PROCLAIM BECK THE FIRST--AND ONLY--HAMSTER WITH DUAL CITIZENSHIP. YOU ARE H.A.M. YOU ARE H.A.T.
"YOU ARE A HERO."
TAKE COMFORT IN OUR SUCCESS THIS NIGHT, AND REMAIN VIGILANT. WE NO DOUBT HAVE GREAT TRIALS AHEAD. BUT FOR NOW...
DISMISSED!

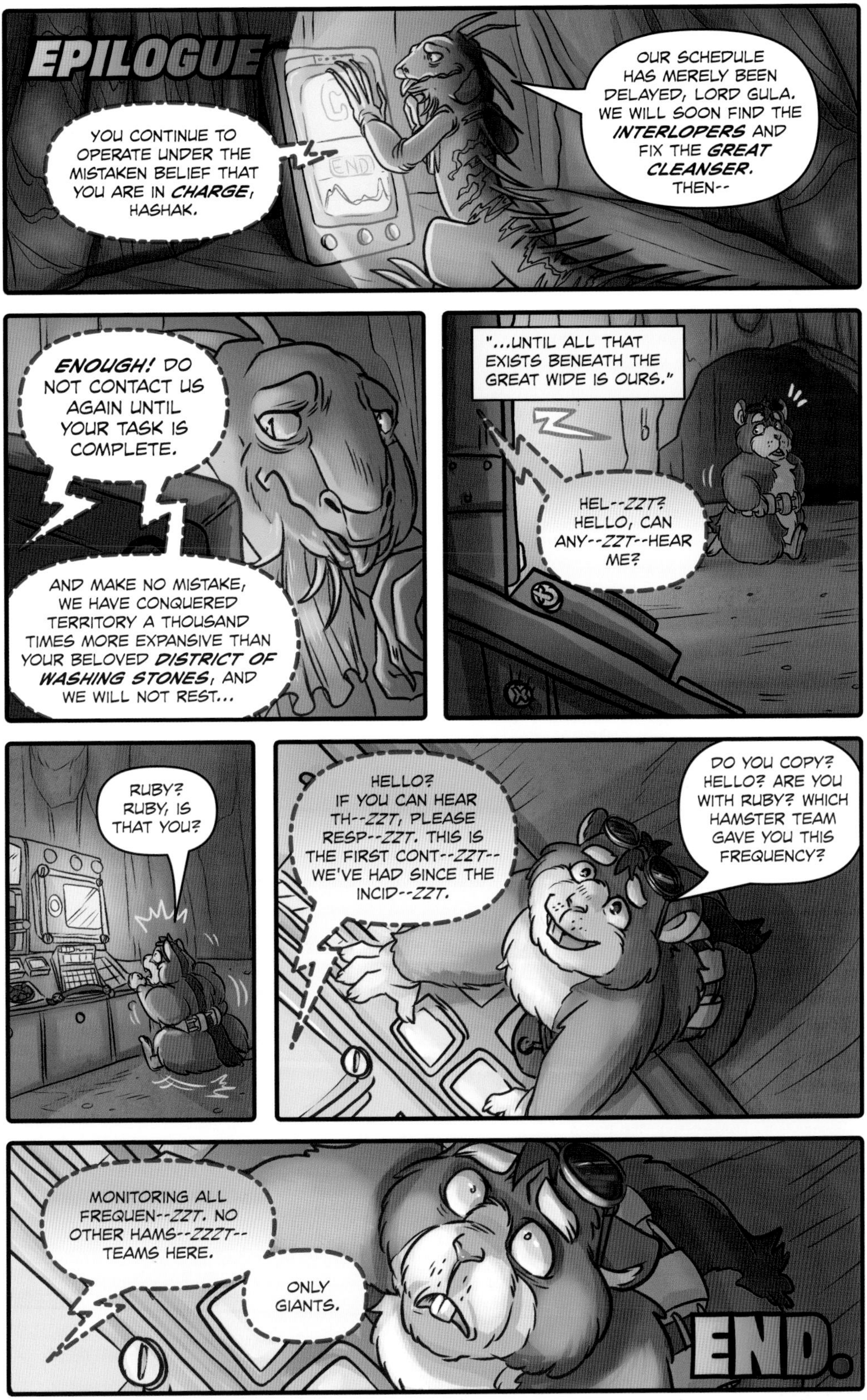
EPILOGUE
OUR SCHEDULE HAS MERELY BEEN DELAYED, LORD GULA. WE WILL SOON FIND THE *INTERLOPERS* AND FIX THE *GREAT CLEANSER.* THEN--
YOU CONTINUE TO OPERATE UNDER THE MISTAKEN BELIEF THAT YOU ARE IN *CHARGE*, HASHAK.
ENOUGH! DO NOT CONTACT US AGAIN UNTIL YOUR TASK IS COMPLETE.
AND MAKE NO MISTAKE, WE HAVE CONQUERED TERRITORY A THOUSAND TIMES MORE EXPANSIVE THAN YOUR BELOVED *DISTRICT OF WASHING STONES*, AND WE WILL NOT REST...
"...UNTIL ALL THAT EXISTS BENEATH THE GREAT WIDE IS OURS."
HEL--*ZZT*? HELLO, CAN ANY--*ZZT*--HEAR ME?
RUBY? RUBY, IS THAT YOU?
HELLO? IF YOU CAN HEAR TH--*ZZT*, PLEASE RESP--*ZZT*. THIS IS THE FIRST CONT--*ZZT*-- WE'VE HAD SINCE THE INCID--*ZZT*.
DO YOU COPY? HELLO? ARE YOU WITH RUBY? WHICH HAMSTER TEAM GAVE YOU THIS FREQUENCY?
MONITORING ALL FREQUEN--*ZZT*. NO OTHER HAMS--*ZZZT*-- TEAMS HERE.
ONLY GIANTS.
END.

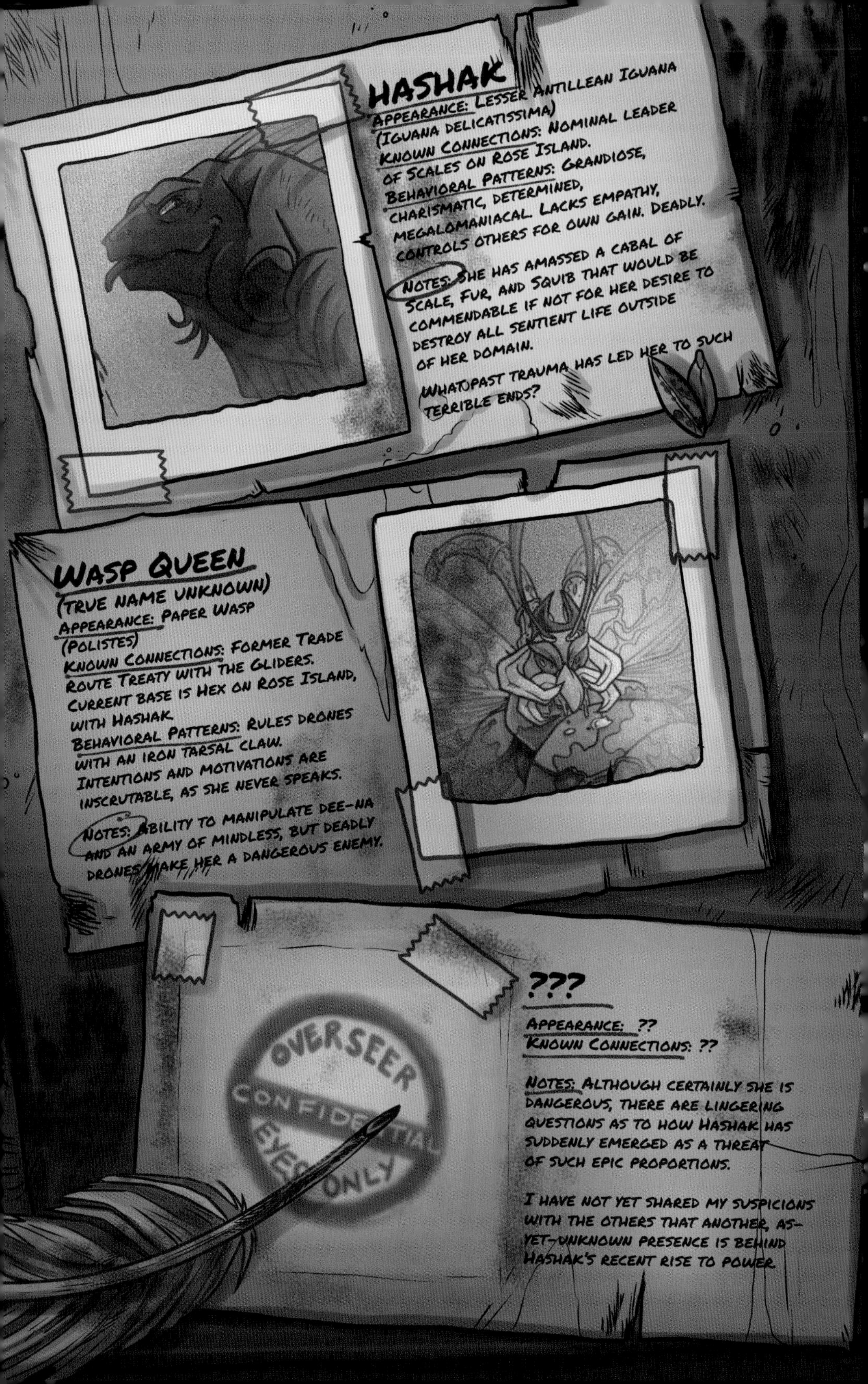

HASHAK
Appearance: Lesser Antillean Iguana (Iguana delicatissima)
Known Connections: Nominal leader of Scales on Rose Island.
Behavioral Patterns: Grandiose, charismatic, determined, megalomaniacal. Lacks empathy, controls others for own gain. Deadly.
Notes: She has amassed a cabal of Scale, Fur, and Squib that would be commendable if not for her desire to destroy all sentient life outside of her domain.
What past trauma has led her to such terrible ends?
Wasp Queen
(True name unknown)
Appearance: Paper Wasp (Polistes)
Known Connections: Former Trade Route Treaty with the Gliders. Current base is Hex on Rose Island, with Hashak.
Behavioral Patterns: Rules drones with an iron tarsal claw. Intentions and motivations are inscrutable, as she never speaks.
Notes: Ability to manipulate dee-na and an army of mindless, but deadly drones make her a dangerous enemy.
OVERSEER
CONFIDENTIAL
EYES ONLY
???
Appearance: ??
Known Connections: ??
Notes: Although certainly she is dangerous, there are lingering questions as to how Hashak has suddenly emerged as a threat of such epic proportions.
I have not yet shared my suspicions with the others that another, as-yet-unknown presence is behind Hashak's recent rise to power.

Artist Process

with Michelle Nguyen

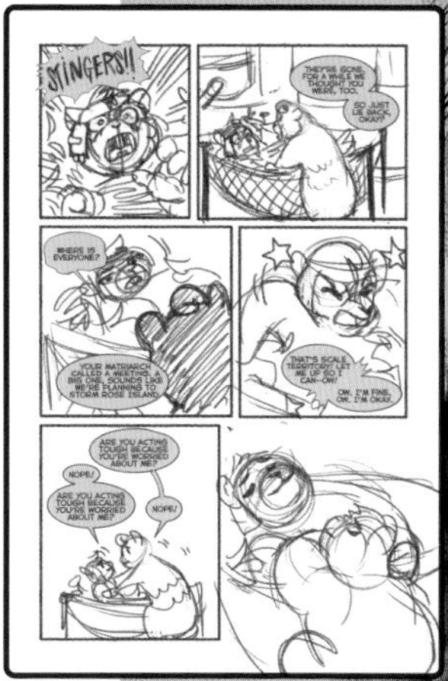
STINGERS!!
THEY'RE GONE FOR A WHILE WE THOUGHT YOU WERE, TOO.
SO JUST LIE BACK, OKAY?
WHERE IS EVERYONE?
YOUR MATRIARCH CALLED A MEETING. A BIG ONE. SOUNDS LIKE WE'RE PLANNING TO STORM ROSE ISLAND.
THAT'S SCALE TERRITORY! LET ME UP SO I CAN--OW!
OW. I'M FINE. OW. I'M OKAY.
ARE YOU ACTING TOUGH BECAUSE YOU'RE WORRIED ABOUT ME?
NOPE!
ARE YOU ACTING TOUGH BECAUSE YOU'RE WORRIED ABOUT ME?
NOPE!

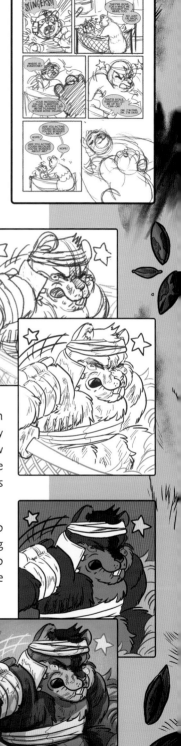

THUMBNAILS: During the first step of the art process, I read the full chapter script that Ben & Emily wrote, which will include dialogue, character actions, and reference photos or information that would help with crafting the page. After several read-throughs, I start thumbnail drawings, which are incredibly loose sketches that show the basic layout of a page, highlighting where all the characters are, and how the dialogue fits in with the images. This is generally the stage where I get the most feedback from the team, such as notes on character poses, backgrounds, and facial expressions.

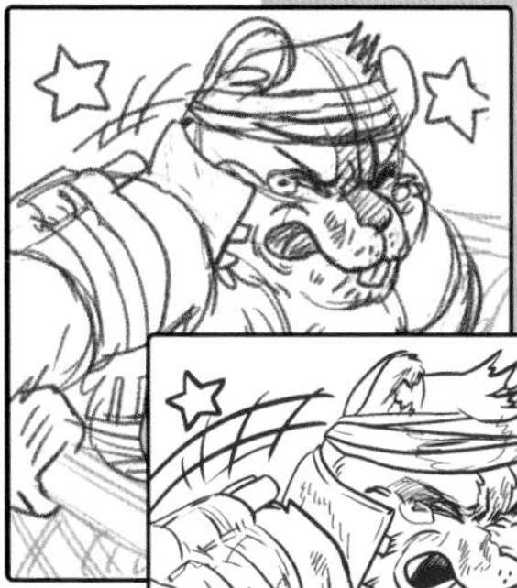

PENCILS: After all the thumbnails are completed, I move on to more defined lines which are called "pencils." Pencils are more detailed versions of thumbnails and will be pretty close to their final form. For me, it's easier to draw the background in one color and characters in another to help distinguish the important bits. The pencil stage is the most time-consuming stage of drawing for me, because I need to ensure that each illustration is as accurate as possible, making sure that all elements conform to the right perspective and all the hamsters (and other animals!) are correctly proportioned.

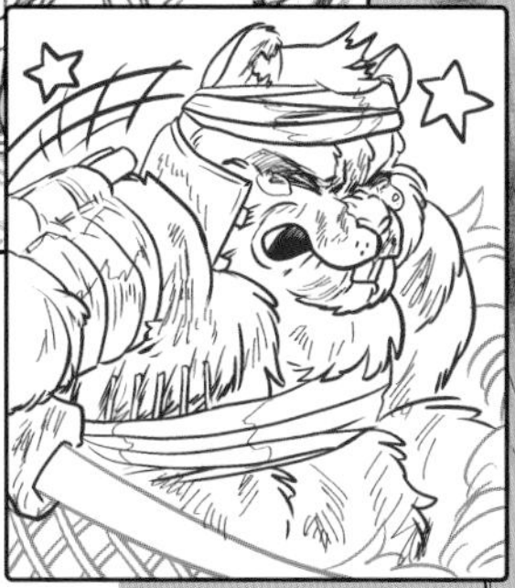

INKS: These are the final lines, which we refer to as "inks." With the foundation built through the pencil stage, inks are generally the fastest stage for me. Even though the final page may not show all black lines, I usually do everything in a uniform color with the background drawings in a dark shade of gray, then change the colors of the lines during the coloring stage.

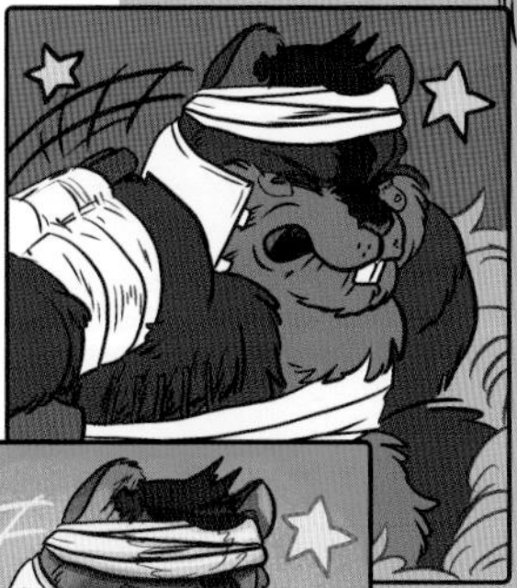

FLATS: I am very lucky to be married to an excellent illustrator who agreed to be my coloring assistant for the series! In the flatting stage, Adrian takes the final inked page and fills in basic colors to corresponding characters and backgrounds, which is often time consuming and tedious. (Thank you, Adrian!)

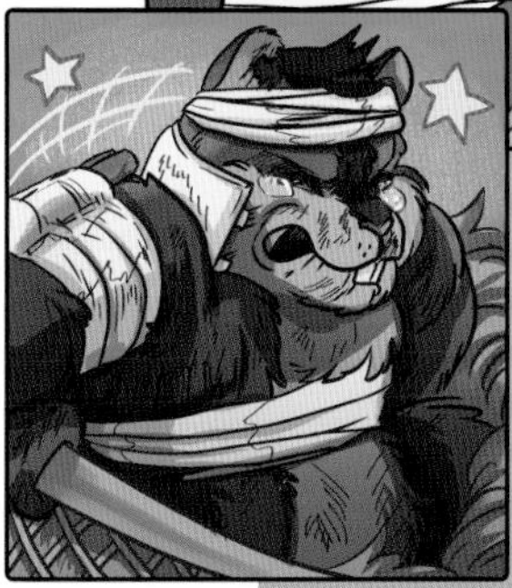

COLORS: What I call the "fun stuff"! During the last art stage, I add in effects like lighting, shadows, textures, and atmospheric lighting. This is my favorite part of drawing comics. I get to experiment with how colors help portray emotions and actions, and even how the time of day will affect certain colors. After the colors are approved by the team, my job here is done, and the page gets passed to our letterer, Thom!

Writing Process with Emily and Ben

EMILY AND BEN: Hi! We're Emily and Ben, and we wrote *The Underfoot!*

EMILY: That's right—we wrote it together, which can be challenging, especially if you don't have a psi-link with your partner. So, we thought we'd explain how the "magic" happens behind the panels.

BEN: First, we brainstorm the main plot points (story events) about our little hamsters' adventures during the book. A H.A.M.'s life is exciting—

EMILY: Well, not when they're napping.

BEN: True. But the rest of the time it's filled with adventure and mystery, so it's hard to decide which plot points to use. Sometimes we even come up with a few that we don't end up using in the book at all. But once we've chosen our favorite story events, we decide how the plot will progress in each chapter of the book. For example, H.A.P. was betrayed by the wasps in Chapter 1.

EMILY: Then Buddy and Terry narrowly escaped the wasps in Chapter 2.

BEN: The team came up with a plan to fight the wasps (and Hashak) in Chapter 3.

EMILY: And finally, Ruby defeated their Queen in Chapter 4.

BEN: Which was super gross.

EMILY: I thought it was cool! Not all plots have gross endings, though. And our job is to make sure that all of the plots resolve and intersect with each other in fun ways!

BEN: For example, Ruby's radio improvements in Chapter 1 were used to get our little friends onto Rose Island and inside of The Hex, so that they could help Ruby escape after she destroyed the Queen.

EMILY: The most important plot (stopping Hashak from building her weapon) is called the "A Plot;" and the other plots are "B Plot," "C Plot," etc.

BEN: When we have enough plots, it's time to write the script! Here's an example of a page from this book:

A Plot: Stop Hashak!

OKAY, AMELIA, YOU HAVE MY ATTENTION. WHAT DO YOU PROPOSE?
WE SEND A JOINT TEAM TO STOP HER.
BREACHING ROSE ISLAND WILL REQUIRE THE GIFTS OF ALL THREE COLONIES.
BUT EVEN WITH OUR COMBINED SKILL, IT WON'T BE EASY.
THE ISLAND IS SURROUNDED BY HARDBACKS AND HIGH WALLS. STINGERS PATROL ABOVE. NO FUR HAS EVER CROSSED ITS BORDERS AND RETURNED.

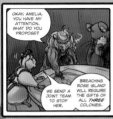

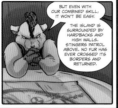

B Plot: War of the Wasps

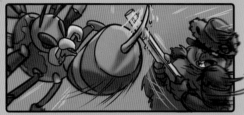

C Plot: Hamster Teams Establish Communications

WHAT AM I SUPPOSED TO SEE HERE?
...
IT IS A DISASTER, ISN'T IT?
WELL, IT'S DEFINITELY NOT A SOLUTION.

D Plot: Skirmishes of Squirrels

NEIL TOOK US TO THE MEDIATION SITE, BUT ALL WE FOUND WERE SLEEPING GLIDERS AND A HAT.
WE WERE HOPING JUNIP AND HIS DREY COULD FILL IN THE BLANKS, BUT THEY DON'T REMEMBER MUCH BEFORE FALLING ASLEEP.
I REMEMBER WE USED TO HAVE THREE GENERATIONS' WORTH OF GATHERED FARMA.

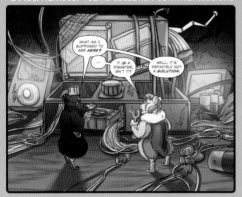

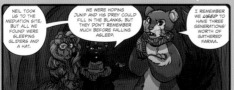

PAGE TWENTY-SIX (one panel):

Panel 1. Buddy is looking down at Terry, who is unconscious at her feet.

BUDDY:
He'd better hurry.

Panel 2. Close up of Buddy, squinting down the scope of her rifle, aimed right at the reader.

BUDDY:
'Cuz I might not know much about clouds or whirly-birds.

BUDDY (linked):
But I know **exactly** what **this** is.

Panel 3. The angle has shifted to behind Buddy. She is propped on one knee, taking aim. Terry is right beside her, unconscious. A swarm of wasps is now plainly visible. There are lots of them. There is no hope for our heroes.

BUDDY:
This is a **disaster**.

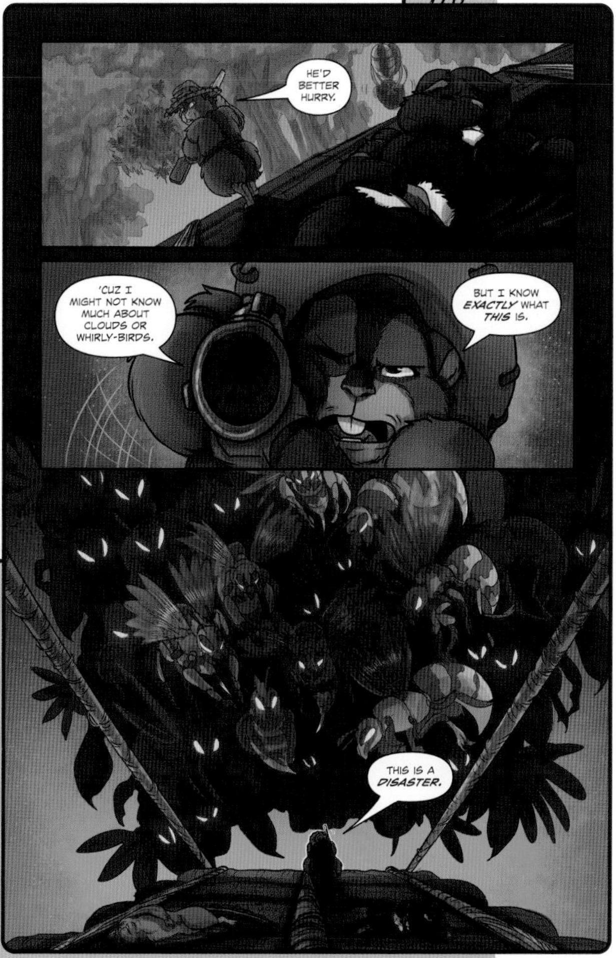

HE'D BETTER HURRY.
'CUZ I MIGHT NOT KNOW MUCH ABOUT CLOUDS OR WHIRLY-BIRDS.
BUT I KNOW *EXACTLY* WHAT *THIS* IS.
THIS IS A *DISASTER.*

Writing Process (Continued)

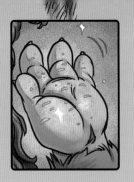

EMILY: As you can see, the script page describes what happens in each panel, including art, characters, real-world details, captions, sound effects, dialogue, actions, and emotions. We try to make sure the artist—

EMILY AND BEN: Hi, Michelle!

EMILY: —knows if there are recurring items seen later in the book (like Buddy's hat, or fairyfly scales), which will help her decide how to draw them. Sometimes we even send her pictures to reference for details.

11:04
Ben
Did the HAP just leave them sleeping?? Did they move them all away somewhere to wake up? (Assuming they could hold their breath enough to do so.) Otherwise I'm thinking Junip would be more concerned with dispatching a HAM team to save the rest of his/her(?) squirrel group than anything else.
So yeah, we need to streamline & hammer this out ASAP so Michelle can draw it.
Mar 4, 2019, 6:18 PM
Revised scripts sent
Also, what did we name the river around Rose Island (I don't have the map handy)
Thanks, just saw! I'll review shortly
Paw Tonic River I believe. I don't have the map out but we can double check, just put a note
iMessage
Emily
I have found our reptiles' place of deep worship.
iMessage

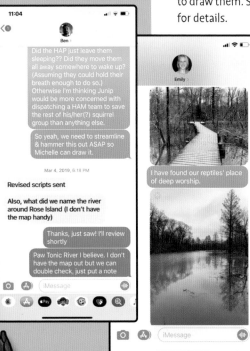

BEN: Then comes editing. We fine-tune the script, taking turns suggesting ideas and correcting mistakes until we're both happy.

EMILY: This is where having a psi-link would be helpful.

BEN: But since we don't have one, email and texting work fine, too.

EMILY: We also have the help of a professional editor, who adds an extra level of polish to really make the story shine!

EMILY AND BEN: Hi, Grace!

BEN: And after all of that, we send the script to Michelle. When she's done with the art...

EMILY: ...It goes to a letterer, who adds the balloons with the words, and also any sound effects!

EMILY AND BEN: Hi, Thom!

BEN: And then, after a final review to try to make sure everything is just perfect, it goes to you, the reader.

EMILY AND BEN: Yay! Hi, reader! We loved writing this book for you. We really hope you loved reading it!

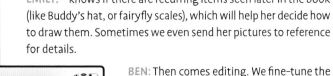

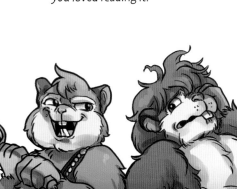

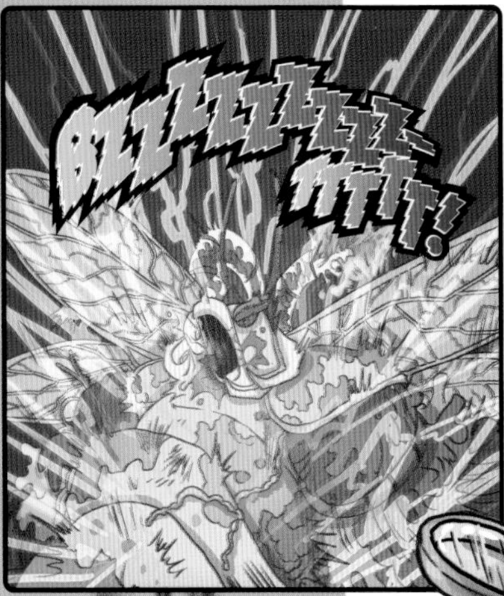